The "Real Easy" Ear Training Book

A Beginning/Intermediate Guide to Hearing the Chord Changes

Roberta Radley
Assistant Chair,
Ear Training Department,
Berklee College of Music

SHER MUSIC CO.
Petaluma Ca.
www.shermusic.com

This book is dedicated in loving memory to my late father, Robert Anthony Radley, one of my all-time biggest fans.

Published by Sher Music Company
P.O. Box 445
Petaluma CA 94953
www.shermusic.com

ISBN 1-883217-61-X

Printed in the United States of America.

Editors: Bill Brinkley, Allan Chase, Roberta Radley, Chuck Sher.

All musical examples performed and recorded by Brad Hatfield of Brad Hatfield Productions.

Cover artwork: Roberta Radley, *Untitled*, 1970. Block print.
Cover design, book design and production, music typesetting:
Wm.R.Brinkley & Associates, Inc. Watertown, MA.
www.wrbrinkleydesign.com

Contents

List of Activities

ACKNOWLEDGEMENTS

Thank you to Mr. Chuck Sher for publishing my debut book *The "Real Easy" Ear Training Book.* This has been an incredible opportunity and experience for me, a life-time dream fulfilled. I am honored to have my book included in the very good company of the Sher Music catalogue. Throughout this project, you've always offered 110% encouragement and support.

A heart-felt "thank you" to my sisters and brother, Maureen, Christina and Richard Radley, who have always been there for me no matter what. But especially to my mother, Mary Catherine Bernadette, my earliest musical mentor, who can still hit all the high notes…a loving thank you.

Thanks to all my students, both in the "live" as well as "virtual" classroom. You have taught me a tremendous amount and have been an inspirational audience. Your contributions appear in every line of this book.

Thank you to my colleague, Allan Chase, who devoted many hours to text editing as well as offering expert advise on musical and pedagogical issues. Thank you for your excellent eye.

Thanks to my dear friend, Brad Hatfield, who performed and recorded all of the musical examples you hear on the CD's. Such a talented and creative musician, he made the "real music" examples come alive with an authenticity true to the intention of the original song recordings. As an ear training book, it was imperative to me that students be engaged as motivated listeners throughout their studies. Thanks, Brad!

Having left the best for last, a huge "thank you" to my husband, Bill Brinkley, for contributing on so many levels to the making and realization of this book. From book design to putting the final touches to text editing and conceptual clarity, Bill has been there every step of the way with me and for me. An accomplished musician (one very fine guitarist!) he has offered me counsel on many musical aspects of the book. Bill's work ethic and drive to make things the best they can be is of the highest level and is one of the things I most admire about him. Behind every woman who writes a book on "hearing the changes" is a great man. Thank you, sweetheart.

Introduction

Welcome to *The "Real Easy" Ear Training Book*, where we will take the journey together to "hearing the changes." It is a challenging journey, but with a good map to follow, and plenty of gas in the tank, we'll make it.

In my student days, ear training didn't come easy, particularly when it involved hearing chords and recognizing chord progressions. Though I had been playing piano for several years, all those chords my hands were playing, and my eyes were seeing on the page, weren't registering consciously in my ear. It wasn't until I attended Berklee that this dilemma came to the foreground, and I had some catching up to do, and fast! I was in awe of my classmates who already had some experience with identifying chord patterns by ear, and that pushed me to find my own ways of doing the same. Thus, the approaches and techniques I developed as a student for "hearing the changes" have become the essence of what's in this book.

I also tribute the thousands of ear training students I've worked with over the past 30 years—they helped me understand the multiple challenges and learning styles that each student possesses. As a result, I can anticipate what your challenges and questions will be, and have developed a repertoire of varied approaches in assisting you through the maze of hearing the changes.

This book is designed for a wide and varied audience. You can work through it on your own, with a friend, a teacher, band members, or classmates. If you are a teacher, I hope you find that this book enhances your work with your students, and adds to your own fine methods of teaching ear training.

The chord patterns and musical references are not limited to any particular style of music. All contemporary genres are represented: pop, rock, Latin, fusion and jazz, etc. In addition, the audio files are not "piano-centric," and many different instrumentations are used in order to appeal and relate to a rich community of musicians.

There are only good ways to practice hearing the changes, no bad ones. The fact that you're taking these first steps towards recognizing chords and chord progressions is in itself a very good thing. In fact, the only bad thing would be to avoid trying, postponing the practice to a future "better" time. Taking the first steps now or later will still be first steps. So why delay? There's no time like the present.

Is it "cheating" to use your instrument in figuring out the changes? Absolutely not! Our goal is to hear chord progressions on our own, using only our inner hearing. Along the way we may need help: at those times, use your instrument, or a keyboard, for reference. In fact, double-checking on an instrument to confirm your answers is the smart thing to do. After all, for many of you, developing your ability to hear the changes will increase your command as a player.

I do recommend singing as a great way to internalize the sound of the chord progression. Throughout this book, you'll be frequently asked to sing, to "feed" your inner hearing, as well as to confirm out loud what your inner hearing is hearing.

A complete knowledge of music theory is not required to hear the changes, but some theoretical knowledge will be very helpful. This is an ear training book, not a theory book, but at times I will reference harmonic theory as a guide. Many of our brains are filled with harmonic theory; now it's time to put that knowledge to work in hearing the harmony.

This book incorporates popular chord patterns, step by step, slowly adding to our harmonic vocabulary list. To avoid being overloaded with too many options, we'll start with just a few harmonic choices. We'll begin by hearing the bass line in the major key, then gradually add major and minor diatonic triads to the mix, discuss the relationship of melody and harmony, continue on with seventh chords recognition, explore hearing minor key harmony, and conclude with hearing some common non-diatonic chord patterns.

Take the time you need with each lesson; you can't rush ear training, in many ways it's a life-long process. As you move on to each new chapter, don't worry if you haven't mastered the current one: mastery comes with extensive practice and experience over time. For example, Chapter One, "Hearing the Bass Line," works with bass line identification; every chapter following it does so as well. This gives you plenty of opportunity for "two steps forward, one step back" in your work.

I cannot emphasize enough how important it is to apply your harmonic ear training practice to "real music." This book references tune after tune for you to listen to and practice. Whether you're primarily an instrumentalist (vocalists included!), a composer, or both, applying this ear training practice is invaluable.

We will follow the steps recommended below for a successful experience in learning how to hear the changes.

1. Be organized, you can't hear everything at once, you need to break the listening experience down into a few steps, building the answers as you go. Repeat CD exercises and examples as often as needed to increase your accuracy and understanding.
2. Hearing the bass line is the first step: most likely this is where the roots of the chords are presented.
3. The next step is to consider the likely chord choices the bass line suggests. This is a great way to apply your knowledge of harmonic theory, limiting the chord choices to two, maybe three, likely possibilities.
4. Within this limited world of likely choices, listen for whether you hear the chords as being inside the key (diatonic) or outside the key (non-diatonic). This step breaks things down into those two general categories.
5. Check whether you hear a major or minor third interval from the root to the third of each chord; this alone can often provide you the answer. I refer to this as using the "vertical" approach—listening up from the bass note of the chord.
6. In addition to step five, I recommend listening for the particular note in the key that defines the chord sound. For example, hearing Ti (scale degree 7 of the key) indicates you're most likely hearing the third of the V triad. I call this using the "horizontal" approach. For many of you, this will be a new approach, and will require some getting used to, but it will be very helpful, particularly when the chord progression is moving quickly. We will apply the horizontal and vertical approaches to "hearing the changes" in order to double the opportunity for successful results.
7. Repetition is key. Becoming familiar with popular chord patterns prepares you for when you encounter them in a variety of tunes.

8. Yes, building a repertoire is essential. Learning to recognize popular chord patterns through real music gives credence to the practice routines. Why memorize the sound of I, VI–, IV, V, I? Because this chord pattern exists in thousands of songs we play and listen to every day! Why not learn a tune and practice the exercise at the same time?
9. Practical application is most important; consequently, we will explore many real world song selections for practice, and application of the practice. Real music made a believer out of me, and I hope it will make a believer out of you.
10. Put these popular chord patterns into your music making. How are you able to recognize these chord progressions, if you don't "live them?" Again, it is essential to "take it to the streets" and out of the classroom, to really understand the concepts presented in this book.

Next is a brief description of each section featured in the book, our "road map" to follow.

CD Icons  

Two CDs accompany this book. The numbered CD icons indicate that there is an audio file for your listening. Some of these audio files demonstrate a lesson concept, and many of them represent an Activity dictation assignment. If the CD track contains several examples, you will hear my voice direct you from one example to the next. CD 1 has audio for chapters 1–9 (tracks 1–81), CD 2 has audio for chapters 10–12 (tracks 1–32).

Remember, this is an ear training book, so take every opportunity to listen. If a picture is worth a thousand words, certainly listening is everything when it comes to understanding an ear training concept.

Activities and Answer Keys

The Activities are at the heart of the matter. This is where you will work out with hearing the changes using a variety of practice routines. At times you will be asked to sing, to play, to compose, to analyze, but the main intent of practice is to recognize the chords and chord progressions by ear. There is a ton of dictation work here to keep you busy.

All answers are readily available in the Answer Key Appendix for your review. This gives immediate feedback on your work, which is particularly helpful if you're using the book solo, and at your own pace. If at times the work is overwhelming, simply listening to the chord progression while viewing the answer key can be very helpful.

Bonus

In the Bonus sections, I often encourage you to take the practice to the next level, incorporating the practice into your daily listening and music making activities. This is another way to "make it real," and another opportunity for you to own the idea in a deeper way.

Tips

Here I offer you additional strategies for hearing the changes. I hope you will find these "tricks of the trade" helpful. Many of these tips have been contributed by students over the years.

Notes

This section clarifies definitions or provides additional information about the topic at hand.

Stump the Band

These are opportunities to quiz your friends and classmates in a fun way. Playing the teacher is a great opportunity to test your own knowledge of the material.

Hooking Up With *The Real Easy Book*

Sher Music has a marvelous series of books aimed at helping young players learn the jazz repertoire and the skills needed to perform in a small jazz band ensemble setting. Along with providing classic jazz repertoire, each book includes suggested chord voicings for piano and guitar, written bass lines, and basic drum groove patterns. I will reference the first volume in this series throughout this book for additional practice with and application of hearing the changes, an essential skill for a successful and rewarding experience playing jazz.

Rewind

Each chapter will conclude with a "Rewind" activity to practice a concept covered in previous lessons. This "two steps forward, one step back" approach is essential as we build upon and develop our ability to hear the changes. Remember, mastery develops over time and with repeated practice.

For Your Consideration

This is an opportunity for you to share questions, insights and strategies with teachers, classmates or friends. It's not what you do, but how you do it, that can often make the difference in getting the most out of your practice time and studies.

Making It Your Own

Applying the lesson concepts to your own listening world and music making will make a significant difference. "Making It Your Own" is an opportunity for you to personalize the learning experience, "owning" the concepts in a much deeper way.

Discography

Throughout the book, I will reference repertoire for applied practice of hearing the changes. Every song title featured or referenced in this book is listed in the Discography (p. 149). Exercises are one thing, but hearing and being able to identify the changes in the "real thing" is the ultimate challenge (and rewarding) experience. I encourage you to listen to as many of these recordings as possible as you practice hearing the changes. Adding these songs to your audio collection is a worthwhile investment.

Now that you've studied the road map on how the book works, and are fueled up for the long journey, let's get started. As a musician, learning to trust your ear is a very satisfying, confidence-building experience. It's incredibly hard work, but undeniably worth it! Don't miss out on taking this trip of a lifetime…start your engines!

1 Hearing the Bass Line

Introduction

Learning to hear chord progressions can be very challenging. With so much sound happening simultaneously, making harmonic sense out of all those notes, as they fly from one chord to the next is not so easy! "Patience is truly a virtue" when it comes to "hearing the changes." Organization and patience are required as you increase your ability to answer questions, step by step, about the harmonies you hear. We will take these steps together, chapter by chapter, and I guarantee you that by the end of the book, you will be well on your way to successfully recognizing chords and chord progressions by ear.

So what is the first step to take?

Listening first for the bass line is a good place to start. In most cases, that's where we'll hear the chord roots which introduce each chord within the progression. Other chord tones may follow in the bass, clearly outlining the chord sound, but recognizing the root of the chord is the best way to get us on track to hearing the changes.

How do we place these chord roots in a harmonic context?

Throughout this book, we will use the scale degrees, described as both numbers and solfege syllables, to determine what functions the bass notes we hear represent within the scale. Using these translation tools of numbers (scale degrees 1, 2, 3, etc.) and/or solfege (Do, Re, Mi, etc.), we will interpret bass lines as tonal melodic phrases rather than as a series of unrelated intervals. We'll start our work of hearing bass line patterns in the major key. For now, limiting our choices to only seven pitches, we will see recurring patterns; familiarity with these bass patterns will benefit us greatly as we begin our work of "hearing the changes." Now, let's first get familiar with our scale degree numbers and soflege translating tools.

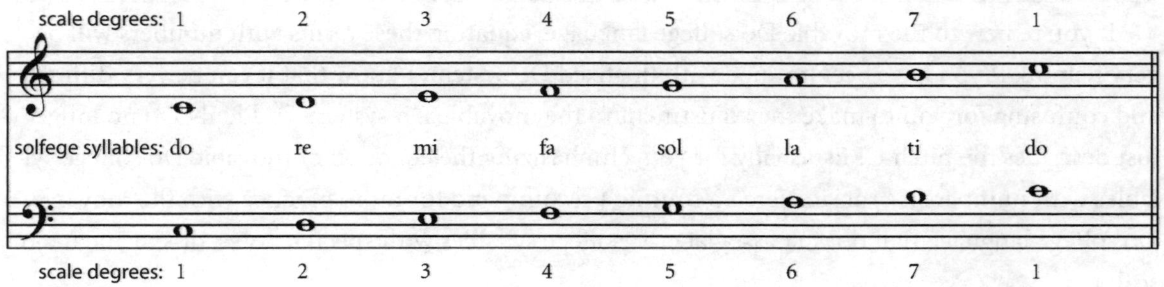

Learning the Solfege Language

Before we begin identifying the notes in a bass line, let's become familiar with the numbers and "movable Do" solfege systems.

Many people refer to the seven pitches of the major scale simply by numbers, which makes perfect and logical sense. We will too, but we'll also use solfege syllables. Why? Solfege is the musical language used to identify the names of the notes. The biggest advantage of the solfege syllables over numbers is that they are only one syllable long, making them very easy to speak or sing. The solfege syllables within the major scale are: Do, Re, Mi, Fa, Sol, La, Ti, Do.

There are two variations of the solfege language. In many countries, the "fixed Do" solfege language is used. In a fixed Do system, the note C is always called Do, the note D is always called Re, etc., regardless of the key the music is in. The names of the notes are always referred to by solfege, never by letter names. This fixed Do system is particularly useful for developing an absolute recognition of the pitch, but does not describe the function, the "why" of the notes.

Throughout this book, we will use the "movable Do" solfege language. The movable Do solfege language is very useful for developing relative pitch, understanding the "why," i.e., the function, of the notes within the key. The movable Do solfege syllables equate exactly with numbers:

Do is the first note of the scale, or scale degree 1.

Re is the second note of the scale, or scale degree 2.

Mi is the third note of the scale, or scale degree 3, and so on to Ti (see previous chart, p.1).

The solfege names and numbers are interchangeable when using the movable Do solfege language. These solfege syllables are called "diatonic" because they refer to only those notes that are in the major scale. We will be working within the major key only for the next several chapters.

Activity One *Singing the Major Scale with Numbers and Solfege Syllables*

Listen to CD1, track 1, while reading the example below. Then try singing along, using both numbers and solfege syllables.

Note The pronunciation of the solfege vowels are: a (ah); e (ay); i (ee); and o (oh). Here's a phrase that might whet your appetite for a solfege meal: do (as in *do*nut); re (as in *rai*sin); mi (as in *me*at); fa (as in *fa*va bean); sol (as in filet of *sole*); la (as in *la*tte); and ti (as in *tea*). I often think of the "Do–Re–Mi" song from the "Sound of Music" as another fun way to remember the sound of solfege.

If you're new to the movable Do solfege language, equating these terms with numbers will be very helpful. If you have been trained with the fixed Do system, I know that it can be very difficult and confusing for you to make the adjustment to the movable Do system. Suddenly Do no longer just describes the pitch C! Especially for you, emphasizing the equation of movable Do solfege syllables with numbers is crucial. Here's a routine I recommend for more practice with the movable Do solfege language that doesn't associate the solfege syllables with specific notes, or specific major scales.

Using the "Sol-fa" System

The "Sol-fa" system is a generic way of hearing how each solfege syllable relates back to Do. In this first chapter, we are using the C major scale for demonstration, but we could use any major scale when working with Sol-fa. It's the best way to get away from thinking actual pitches, and instead, to focus on the function of each scale note as it relates back to the tonic, Do.

You don't need an instrument to practice Sol-fa. You can establish any pitch as your Do and go from there. A good warm-up routine is to sing every solfege syllable as it relates directly back to Do. Sing "do re, do mi, do fa..." etc., and then descend from Do, "do ti, do la, do sol..." etc. through the scale. There are so many patterns you can explore, or you can create random scale passages, coming back often to Do to confirm that you haven't wandered off the path into another key. Though you don't need an instrument to practice Sol-fa, it might be helpful to use one at the beginning, double-checking the accuracy of your pitches.

Activity Two *Practice with Sol-fa*

Here are several short Sol-fa patterns to practice singing. The "/" marks are where to take a breath.

1. do re ti do / fa mi do re do / sol la sol do / ti re do
2. do mi re do / sol re ti do / fa mi sol do / ti sol re do
3. do ti la do re do / sol la fa sol do / mi do sol fa ti do
4. do sol ti do / la sol ti do / fa mi re ti do / ti sol do
5. do fa sol do / fa la sol ti do / sol ti re fa mi do

Stump the Band Create some of your own Sol-fa patterns and see if a classmate can sing them correctly. Have your classmate read your Sol-fa patterns, or better yet, play your examples and see if your partner can sing them back with the correct solfege syllables. Then reverse roles.

Another fun way to challenge your classmates' Sol-fa skills, and yours as well, is to figure out the solfege translation to familiar melodies. Give them the solfege syllables to sing or play, can they identify the title of the song? Give them the title of the song, can they determine the solfege syllables? Of course, you've got to have done your homework first and know the correct answer!

Bonus One of my former students told me about a solfege game he likes to play when tied up in a traffic jam. He translates the numbers on the license plates into solfege syllables; now there's a random approach to practicing Sol-fa, and a great use of time when stuck in traffic!

Hearing the Diatonic Bass Line as a Melody

Now that you're warmed up from the Sol-fa practice, let's apply it to hearing the bass line as one diatonic melodic phrase, rather than as a series of unrelated intervals, using numbers and solfege syllables as our translating tools. This will make it easier to remember the line, and, after some practice, you will begin noticing how often certain bass line patterns repeat in the chord progressions of songs.

Tip I often use the analogy of hearing bass line pitches as a series of unrelated intervals to the children's game of "connect-the-dot" pictures, where only upon completing all the connections do you then discover what the picture is. Using solfege when hearing a bass line will begin to predict early on what the musical "connect-the-dot" picture might be.

Activity Three *Singing Bass Lines Using Numbers and Solfege*

Below are several short bass line examples to get familiar with. Here are some steps to take.

1. Play each example on your instrument, listening along and translating the notes into numbers, and then into solfege syllables.
2. Play the example once again, singing along using numbers, then solfege syllables.
3. The next step is to only sing the bass line using numbers, then solfege. Let's see if you can begin to internalize the sound of these bass lines, translating with our new movable Do solfege language. Singing is a great way to feed your "inner hearing," which will help you become more independent and confident when playing and recognizing bass lines.

TIP When singing the bass line (whether reading or listening), sing in whichever octave most comfortably fits your vocal range: there's no need to match these low bass notes exactly (unless you're a "basso profundo!").

Bonus Get creative! Using the blank staves below, try making up your own bass line patterns, and again, remember to translate these lines into numbers and solfege. The more you "speak" the language of solfege, it will be a great way to translate and recognize bass line patterns.

Make sure you're hearing the lines as you write, keep it simple. Using stepwise motion rather than leaps is a good way to start. Exchange with another classmate, can you read and sing each other's lines, and of course, using numbers and solfege!

Activity Four *Singing Root Motion of the Chord Progression from Lead Sheets*

A good "hands-on" activity is to read through the chord changes on a lead sheet, singing the chord roots in numbers and solfege. You can do this exercise in a variety of ways.

1. Sing through the root motion unaccompanied. At the beginning, you might want to support your singing by also playing the bass notes, to make sure you're singing the correct pitches.
2. Play the chords as you sing the root motion. This provides a harmonic context for the bass notes, and gives a fuller picture of how the bass notes and chords relate. When the chords are diatonic, they can help you hear the root motion easily. Don't be surprised if a few non-diatonic chords throw you off track. They may make the diatonic bass notes sound non-diatonic at those moments.
3. Listen to a recording of the song as you read and sing through the root motion of the chord changes. This is the ultimate and most beneficial, and enjoyable, workout.

This "listen and look" exposure practice is a great way to begin recognizing how often bass line patterns repeat themselves. Start with songs where the chord roots are diatonic, even if all the chords may not be. It is so important to take our practice routines to the world of "real music." It made a believer out of me!

Here are a few song selections to try, but you'll need to do this routine with lots of tunes to make a believer out of you!

"Daniel" Elton John

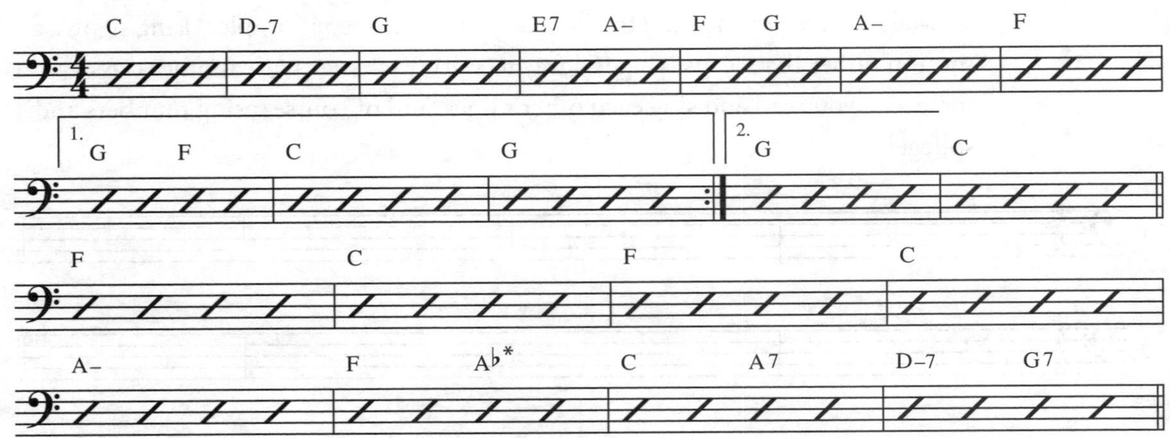

* non-diatonic "le" (pronounced "lay")

"Little Wing" Jimi Hendrix

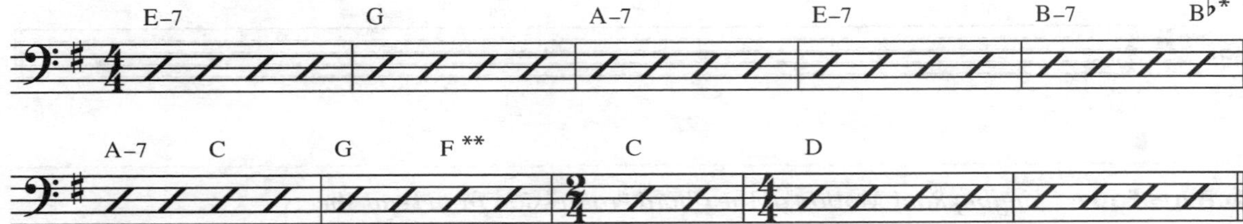

* non-diatonic "me" (pronounced "may")
** non-diatonic "te" (pronounced "tay")

"I Will" The Beatles

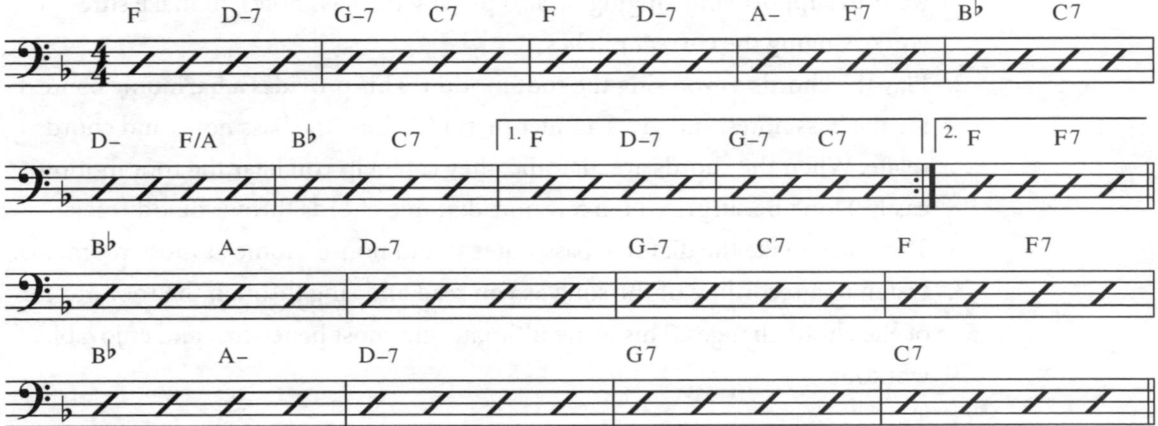

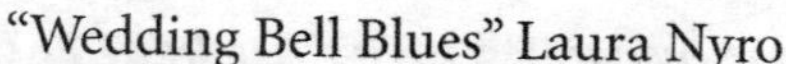

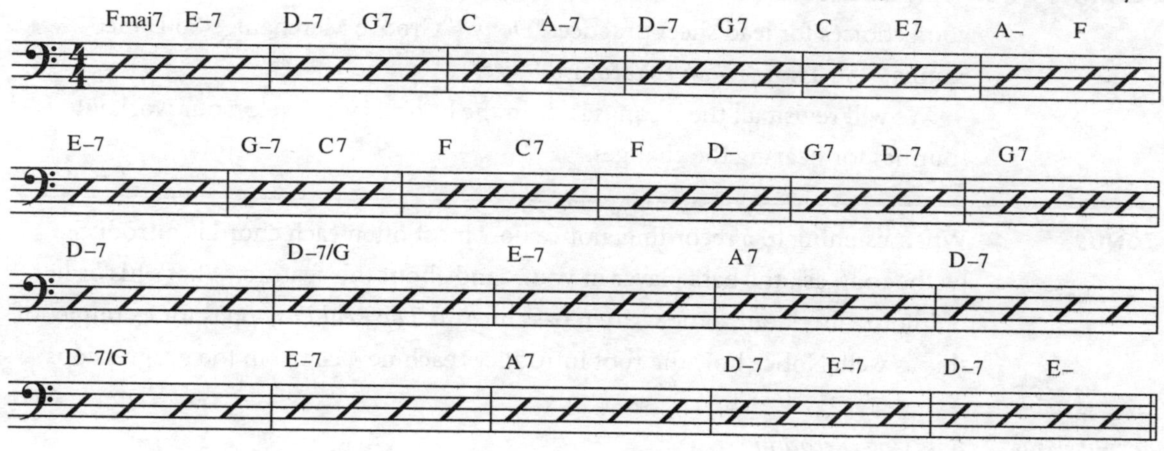

"Fly Me to the Moon" Bart Howard

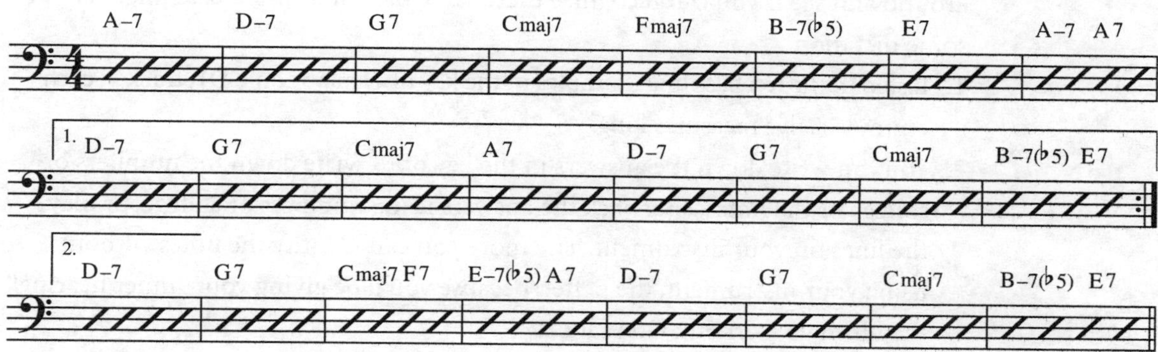

"Don't Know Why" Norah Jones & Ray Turk

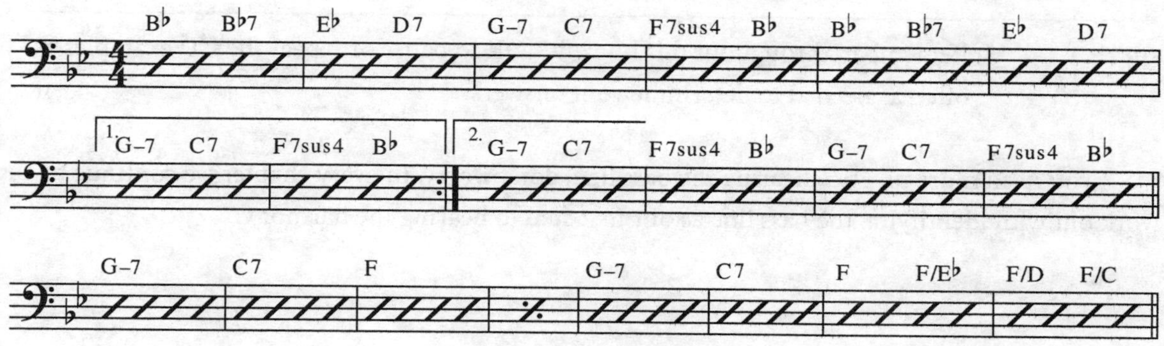

"New York State of Mind" Billy Joel

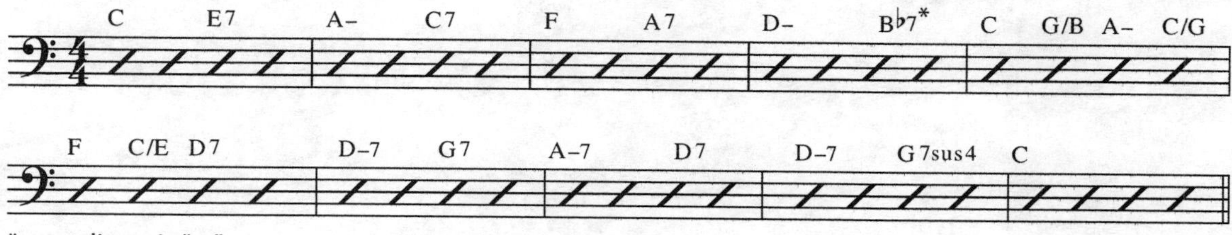

* non-diatonic "te"

HOOKING UP WITH *THE REAL EASY BOOK* The following tunes from *The Real Easy Book* are also good choices for lead sheet practice: "Doxy," "Groove Merchant," "So Danco Samba," "St. Thomas" and "Yardbird Suite."

We will revisit all these songs later in the book as we develop our workout routines for hearing the changes.

BONUS When listening to a recording, notice how most often each chord is introduced by the root; ask the bass player in your band about this feature. What's his or her opinion? Check out some written bass lines in *The Real Easy Book* for examples of this as well. Notice how the root introduces each new chord in the progressions.

ACTIVITY FIVE *Bass Line Dictation*

You've just spent time reading, playing and singing through some diatonic bass lines. I call this the exposure, "listen and look" routine. Now it's time to flip things around and see if you can recognize these same bass lines when listening. Let's do some dictation.

1. Listen to the ten bass line examples in the key of C major on CD1, track 2; each example is five measures long.
2. You can write down the answers in the key of C, write down the numbers or solfege of the notes, sing back the answers using numbers or solfege, or play the lines on your instrument. The more you can identify the notes without using your instrument, the better, because you'll be giving your "inner hearing" the ultimate workout. Good luck!
3. Now check with the answer key (Appendix: p.119, Activity Five, CD1, track 2) to see how you did.

TIP Remember, throughout this book, it's OK to pause or repeat the CD examples as often as needed to determine your answers.

If you need more practice hearing the bass line, don't worry. In every chapter we continue to work out with identifying the bass line as our first step to hearing the harmony.

Activity Six *Rewind... Know Your Major Scales*

It's important to refresh your memory of a few major scales in addition to C major. Practice writing out, playing and singing through the following major scales. This is another great way to practice the movable Do solfege system. More on that in Chapter Two when we discuss the benefits of transposition. You'll also find a thorough knowledge of major scales very helpful when we build chords. Stay tuned!

Write out the indicated scales in bass clef, given our featured work with bass lines this chapter.

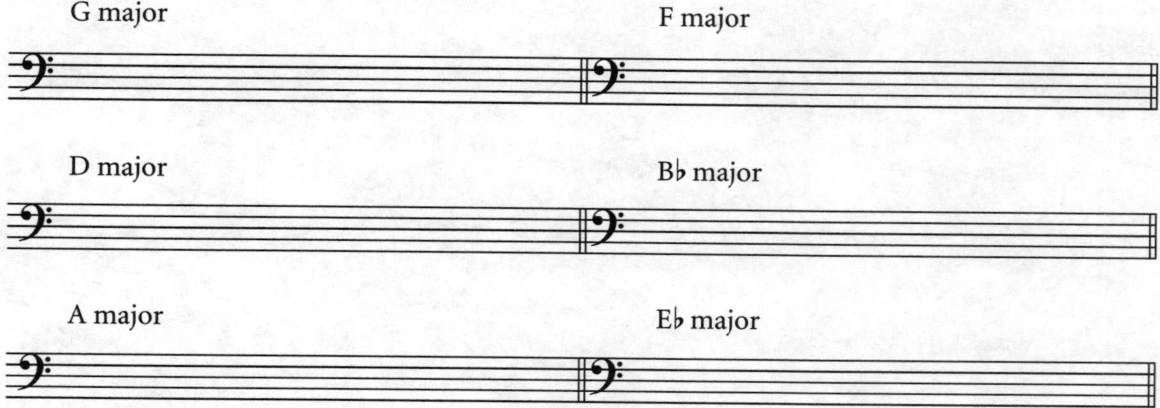

For Your Consideration Discuss with your classmates the value of singing to internalize the sound of the bass line. How is it different from playing?

Making It Your Own Get lots of practice identifying bass lines to songs you're familiar with, reading through lead sheets as well as transcribing some of your favorites from CD's.

2 Hearing Major Triads

Introduction

In this chapter, we'll study the sound of the major triad, and focus in on hearing the diatonic I, IV and V major triads found in the major scale. The blues will be spotlighted as an excellent demonstration of I, IV, V in action, along with several other songs that feature additional I, IV, V chord patterns. We'll continue our workout with identifying diatonic bass lines, the harmony's foundation. We'll add the topic of transposing to the mix, which is a very practical way to begin recognizing recurring bass line and chord patterns. The ability to transpose will also increase your fluency to play and read in a variety of keys, a "must" for the complete musician. We've got lots to do, so let's get started!

Hearing the Major Triad Sound

The major triad has a root (1), a major 3rd above the root (hence the name "major" triad), and a perfect 5th above the root (or, a minor third interval above the 3rd). When listening to any chord, the third is the most important chord tone to identify, because it determines the basic quality of the chord. When chords are changing quickly in the progression, we often don't have enough time to hear all the chord tones (1, 3 and 5). For major triads, recognizing the major third interval between the root and the 3rd is most important.

Within the major scale, the relationship between Do, Mi and Sol is a major triad.

Often, this approach to identifying the major triad in relation to a scale (or key) is easier than a purely intervallic approach. Sing through the C major scale above, using our new solfege syllables, then sing "do, mi, sol" for the I major triad.

Note The chord tones (the first, second and third notes of the triad) are labeled: 1, 3 and 5 to show their intervallic relationship to the root of the chord, or their relationship to Do in the major scale.

Activity One *Building Other Major Triads*

Refer back to the six major scales you wrote out in Chapter One's "Rewind" section (Activity Six, p. 9), noticing how Do (1), Mi (3) and Sol (5) of these scales also form major triads. Using the staves below, rewrite these major scales, and then build their corresponding I major triads. As I mentioned in Chapter One, knowing your major scales thoroughly will greatly help your knowledge of building and identifying chords.

When labeling these major triads with a chord symbol, simply writing the letter name of the chord root is sufficient.

Activity Two *Practice Playing and Singing Major Triads*

1. Play a major triad on your instrument or a keyboard and sing along using numbers (1, 3, 5) or solfege (Do, Mi, Sol). You can play the chord as a "block," meaning all notes at once, or you can arpeggiate the chord tones in sequence (1, 3, 5) as you sing. Pay particular attention to the major third interval between the root and third of the chord.
2. Play only the root of the chord on your instrument and sing up the triad arpeggio, again, using numbers and solfege. Then play the entire chord to check your work.
3. Remember, it's important to sing with the numbers and solfege translators, which helps to reinforce the "meaning" of the notes. Only singing "la, la, la" won't do as good a job.

Bonus When you're away from your instrument, you can still practice your ear training exercises by singing. For example, sing "do, re, mi, fa, sol," then simply "do, mi, sol," to work out with the major triad sound. This only takes a few minutes, and is a great way to pass the time while waiting in line, or stuck in that same traffic jam you were in last chapter. Plus, the more you practice away from your instrument, the more confident you become relying on your inner hearing to do the job.

Activity Three *Identify the Major Triads*

Listen to the ten chord examples on CD1, track 5, and determine if you're hearing a major triad or not. Double-check your answers by singing the interval from the root to third of the chord, is it a major third? Does it sound like Do to Mi in the major scale?

Check with the answer key (Appendix: p.120, Activity Three, CD1, track 5) to see how you did. The ones that were not major triads are minor triads. There'll be more about minor triads in the next chapter.

Hearing the I, IV and V Major Triads

There are three diatonic major triads built on Do (1), Fa (4), and Sol (5) of the major scale. (Remember that "diatonic" means staying exclusively within the scale for our choice of notes.) Whereas we identify individual notes with Arabic numbers: 1, 4 and 5, we will identify these triads with Roman numerals: I, IV and V.

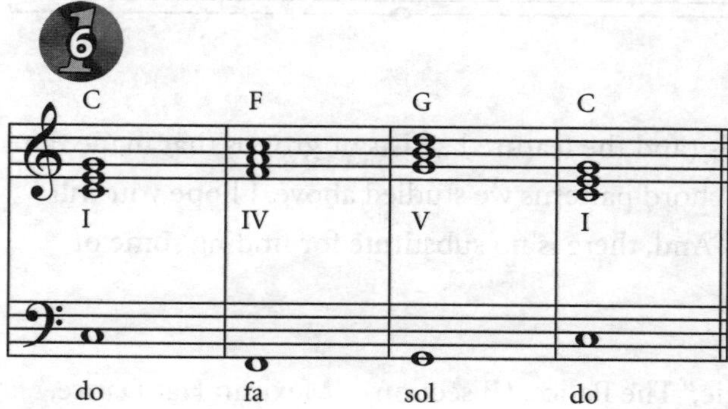

Play the I, IV and V chords in the key of C on your instrument or a keyboard, or listen to the example above on CD1, track 6. Listen to how each of these chords has the same major sound quality because of the major third interval between the root and third of each chord. Later in this chapter, we will explore these three diatonic major triads, I, IV and V, in other major keys as well.

Now it's time to put it all together, listening to progressions that only include the I, IV and V major triads and becoming comfortable with recognizing them.

Before you try doing dictation of chord progressions, it's important to spend time exposing yourself to them with the "listen and look" routine. Making this direct connection of the chord sounds with their names, using numbers and solfege is key. Remember, "la, la, la" won't get you too far when it comes to finding the right chord on your instrument, or when you have to write down the chords.

Activity Four *Practice Singing Along with I, IV, V Progressions*

Listen to the following I, IV, V progressions on CD1, track 7. The first step is to listen to the root motion outlined in the bass line, distinguishing Do (1), Fa (4) or Sol (5). Then listen to the quality of the major third interval between the root and third of each triad and try singing along. This is the best way to confirm that the triad is major. Remember to practice with both numbers and solfege for the complete workout!

The following list includes several song titles (and the featured artists or groups that made the songs popular) that demonstrate the same five chord patterns we studied above. I hope you will check out some of these songs to "make it real." And, there is no substitute for finding some of your own examples as well. Enjoy!

Pattern 1 "Every Little Thing She Does is Magic," The Police, (B section); "Mexican Hat Dance," traditional; "No Buts and No Maybes," Professor Longhair; "Under the Boardwalk," The Drifters, (A section); "Blue Bayou," Linda Ronstadt, (A section); "When I'm Sixty Four," The Beatles, (A section).

Pattern 2 "Imagine," John Lennon; "My Girl," The Temptations; "In the Midnight Hour," Wilson Pickett; "Blue Sky," The Allman Brothers, (guitar solo); "Just Like You," Keb' Mo', (A section); "Start Me Up," The Rolling Stones; "Respect," Aretha Franklin, (B section).

Pattern 3 "La Bamba," Los Lobos (original by Richie Valens); "When the Saints Go Marching In," Louis Armstrong; "Mandeville," Bill Frisell; "Stir It Up," Bob Marley; "Old Time Rock and Roll," Bob Seger; "Here Comes the Sun," The Beatles.

Pattern 4 "Bad Moon Rising," Creedence Clearwater Revival; "Respect," Aretha Franklin, (A section); "Just Like You," Keb' Mo', (B section); "Come Away with Me," Norah Jones, (B section), "Blue Sky," The Allman Brothers; "Nowhere Man," The Beatles.

Pattern 5 "You are My Sunshine," Norman Blake; "Lean on Me," Bill Withers; "Brown Eyed Girl," Van Morrison; "Teach Your Children Well," Crosby, Stills & Nash; "The Lion Sleeps Tonight," traditional, "Me and Bobby McGee," Janis Joplin; "Back in the High Life," Steve Winwood; typical turn-around changes in last two measures of a 12 bar blues.

Bonus The following four songs are excellent examples of combining some of the above chord patterns under one roof. You can make a lot of great music out of three simple chords! Speaking of making music, play through these songs with classmates or band members, paying particular attention to the featured chord patterns. Practice singing through the root motion as well as the root/3rd relationship of each chord. Singing along with the actual song recordings would be ideal.

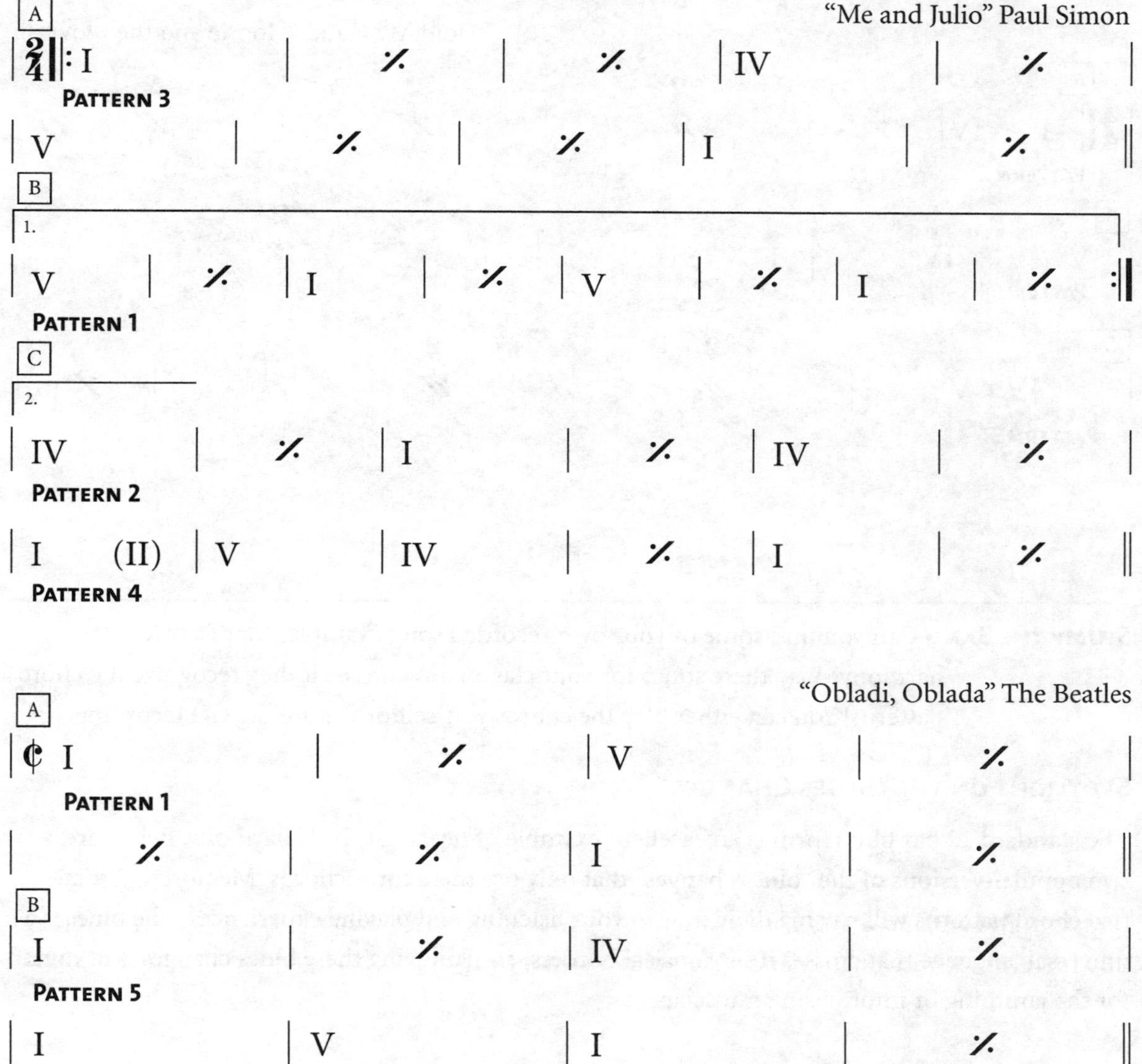

"Have You Ever Seen the Rain?" Creedence Clearwater Revival

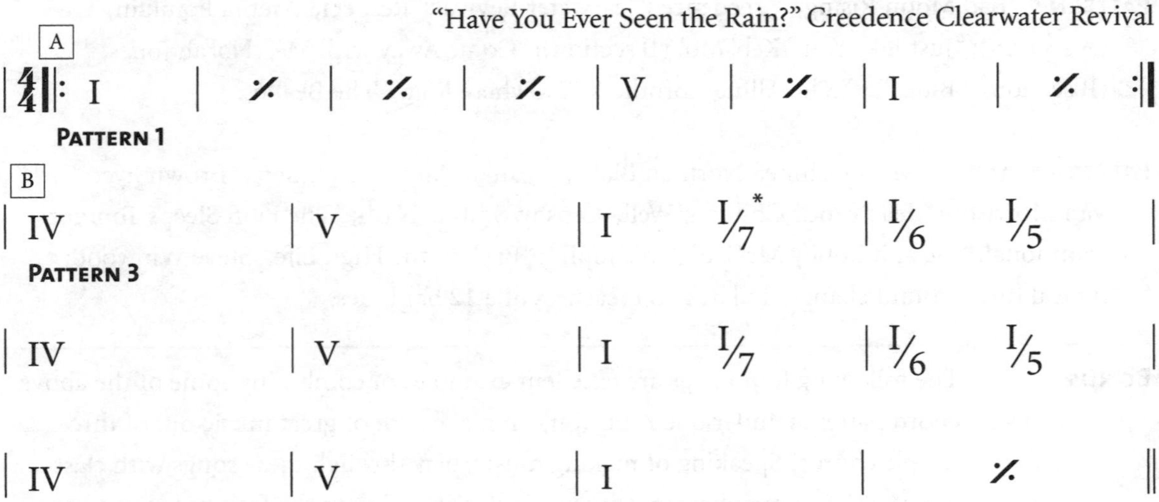

[A]

| 4/4 ||: I | ⁒ | ⁒ | ⁒ | V | ⁒ | I | ⁒ :||

PATTERN 1

[B]

| IV | V | I $I/_{7}$* | $I/_{6}$ $I/_{5}$ |

PATTERN 3

| IV | V | I $I/_{7}$ | $I/_{6}$ $I/_{5}$ |

| IV | V | I | ⁒ ||

* chord inversion, play the 7th as bass note rather than root

"Hold My Hand" Hootie and the Blowfish

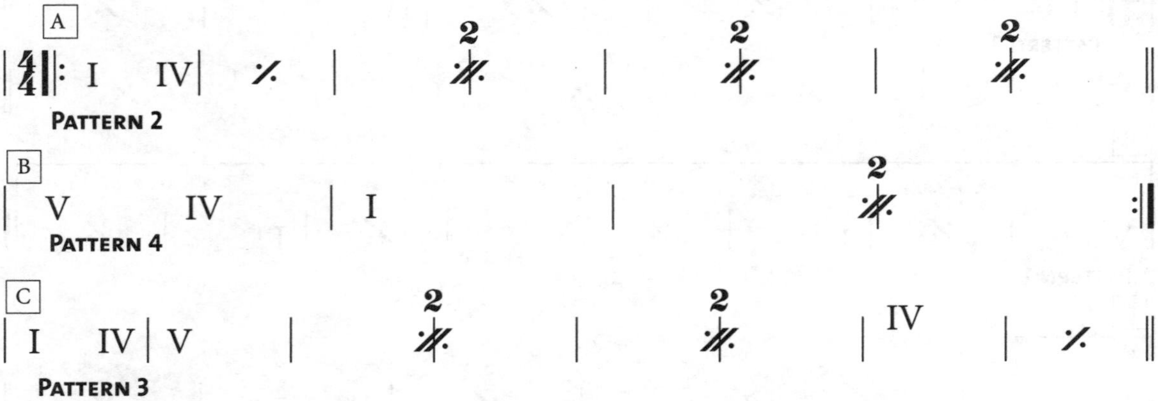

[A]

| 4/4 ||: I IV | ⁒ | 2 ⁒ | | 2 ⁒ | | 2 ⁒ | ||

PATTERN 2

[B]

| V IV | I | | 2 ⁒ | :||

PATTERN 4

[C]

| I IV | V | 2 ⁒ | | 2 ⁒ | | IV | ⁒ ||

PATTERN 3

STUMP THE BAND Can you find some of your own recorded song examples that feature I, IV, V harmony? Play these songs for your classmates and see if they recognize the chord patterns! You can either play the chords yourself or feature the CD recording.

SPOTLIGHT ON THE "BLUES CHANGES"

The standard 12 bar blues form is an excellent example of hearing I, IV, V harmony. Below are two popular versions of the "blues changes" that only use these three chords. Memorizing these two chord patterns will pay big dividends in your listening and playing experiences. The blues is a universal language that crosses most musical borders, and knowing these blues changes is a "must" for the jamming or improvising musician.

4/4 I	(IV)	I	⁒
IV	⁒	I	⁒
V	(IV)	I (IV)	I (V)

Hooking Up with *The Real Easy Book* You will find many blues tunes in *The Real Easy Book* that demonstrate these same blues changes. Check them out!

Tip When you're playing in the band and get lost in the song form, listening for these harmonic markers, the I, IV or V chords, can help get you back on track, especially if this is during a solo section where the melody is not being played for reference. For example, within the standard 12 bar blues form, the I chord opens up the first four bar phrase, the IV chord marks the second four bar phrase, and the V chord marks the final four bar phrase.

Also, notice in the four songs we worked with earlier how placement of the I, IV and V chords played a significant role in marking the different sections of the song form.

In the dictation exercises that follow, let's see how well your hard work with the "listen and look" routine has prepared you for quickly and comfortably recognizing the following I, IV, V chord progressions. Lots of repetition, hearing the same chord progressions over and over is required to attain mastery level, but their identification gets easier with practice. Let's give it a try!

Activity Five *Recognizing I, IV, V Progressions*

1. Listen to the following ten progressions in the key of C major on CD1, track 9; each example is three or four measures long. Only the I, IV and V chords will be used.
2. First, listen to the bass line which outlines the root motion of the chords. Not all examples will start with the I chord.
3. Because we're only using these three chords for now, step 2 will already give you the answer, but it is important to pay attention to the entire chord sound. Down the road, we'll add more and more chords to the mix—spending time now really listening to the major quality of the chord sound will pay off.
4. Check your results with the answer key (Appendix: p.120, Activity Five, CD1, track 9).
5. Now play these progressions on your instrument or keyboard for some additional "hands-on" practice.

Let's talk about how we can use our number and solfege translators to easily play these progressions in different keys.

Transposing

Using numbers or the movable Do solfege system will help make the task of transposing an easy one. For example, if we want to change the bass line below from the key of C to the key of F, using either numbers or solfege will do the job.

Listen to CD1, track 10. If we've transposed correctly, both bass lines will have the exact same sound pattern and contour.

Similarly, we can apply the same approach for transposing the chords. Often singers will perform a song in a different key from the original. If you are accompanying a singer, the ability to transpose the chord progression quickly and correctly will come in handy. And better yet, if you are that singer, having the chord chart already written out in your key will make the band members very happy! They won't have to transpose on the spot, thus avoiding potential mistakes and assuring a better performance all around. Listen to the example below.

Using numbers and solfege is the most efficient and practical way to transpose. You can get optimum value from the transposing process if you bring your ears along for the ride. Listening and even singing along as you write or play in the new key will assure making fewer mistakes. There are several benefits to knowing how to transpose. Playing bass lines and chord progressions in different keys helps to emphasize the similar sound patterns that result. And, playing in a variety of keys will make you a more well-rounded, fluent instrumentalist as well.

Activity Six *Transposing Bass Lines and Chord Progressions*

1. Write out these two bass lines (exs. 1, 2) and two chord progressions (exs. 3, 4) in the keys of F, B♭, E♭, G, D and A.
2. Now, play these bass lines and progressions in the different keys on your instrument or keyboard.
3. If you first translate each example into numbers or solfege, then memorize these translations, you'll find transposing the example to be very easy! We will discuss in greater detail the benefits of memorizing bass line and chord patterns in the next chapter.
4. If done correctly, each transposed example should maintain the same sound pattern as the original. Make sure you play back all your answers to double-check. If you are using a music notation program such as Finale®, take advantage of the playback feature to check your work.
5. Transposing is one of the best ways to really get the sound of the musical pattern engrained in your inner hearing.
6. Refer to the answer key (Appendix: p. 120, Activity Six) to check your results.

Bonus Transpose the blues or other songs featured in this chapter into some new keys. Be practical. If you're a singer, choose the key that best suits your vocal range. If you play guitar, you might find transposing to sharp keys more "instrumentally friendly." If you play saxophone, you might prefer the flat keys. Have a discussion with your classmates or band members about the advantages and disadvantages of playing in certain keys, and why.

Activity Seven *Rewind... More Work with Bass Lines*

1. Identify the bass lines in the following five examples on CD1, track 12; each example is five measures long. This time, don't write down the actual pitches, write only the numbers or solfege identification of the notes. Then check the answer key (Appendix: p. 122, Activity Seven, CD1, track 12) for your results.
2. Next, memorize each line by its numbers or solfege translation. Then, play each line in three different keys, your choice.
3. If possible, don't write out the lines in the new keys and read. Rather, see if you can play the lines directly on your instrument from your memorized number/solfege translation. This will push you to trust your memory, and your ears, as you anticipate what the line will sound like before you play it. Hearing the line as you play gives you stronger command over the notes in the various keys, assuring a flawless performance.

For Your Consideration Discuss with your classmates how transposition benefits recognition of bass lines and chord patterns.

Making It Your Own Can you think of some popular songs that only use I, IV and V harmonies? There are thousands out there. In this chapter, we examined the standard 12 bar blues harmonies, and explored some other common I, IV, V chord patterns. Traditional folk and children's songs are another great source for hearing these simple chord changes. Can you add to the song list with some of your favorites? Share them with you classmates and watch that song list grow!

3 Hearing Minor Triads

Introduction

In this chapter we will add minor triads to our list of chord possibilities and incorporate them into diatonic chord progressions in the major key as the II–, III– and VI– triads.

Our first step in hearing the changes continues with recognizing the diatonic bass notes, which in most cases represent the root motion of the chord progression. We will now take the second step, identifying whether we hear a major or minor third interval up from the root to the third of each chord. I refer to this as the "bottom-up" or "vertical" approach to identifying the overall chord quality as major or minor. Using the vertical approach will be our main focus of work in this chapter.

In addition, we'll work in some of the new keys you practiced in Chapter Two. Being fluent with these bass line and chord patterns in a variety of keys will make you a more well-rounded and versatile musician.

We will also spend time discussing the benefits of memorizing music and how this plays a significant role in our ability to confidently recognize, internalize, and perform the chord changes to tune after tune. Let's begin.

Hearing the Minor Triad Sound

In this chapter we introduce the minor triad, which has a root (1), a minor 3rd above the root (hence the name "minor" triad), and a perfect 5th above the root (or, a major third interval above the 3rd). For minor triads, recognizing the minor third interval between the root and the ♭3rd is most important.

Lowering the third of a major triad one half step gives us a minor triad. The solfege syllable for a minor third is "Me" (pronounced "may"). So, the solfege for a minor triad becomes "Do, Me, Sol" as opposed to the major triad "Do, Mi, Sol." There'll be more about minor key solfege in Chapter Eleven.

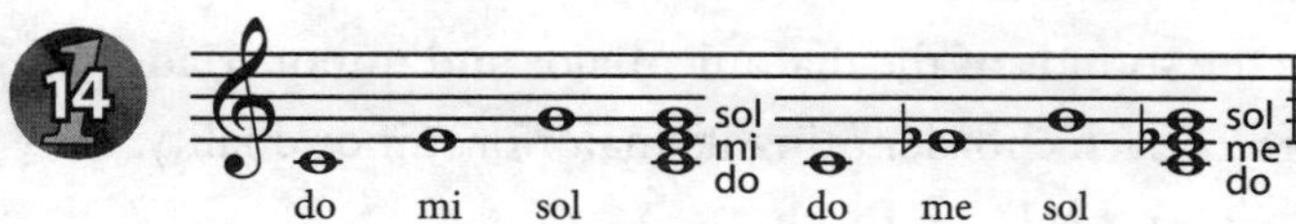

Activity One *Building Minor Triads*

Using the blank staff below, write out the following major and minor triads.

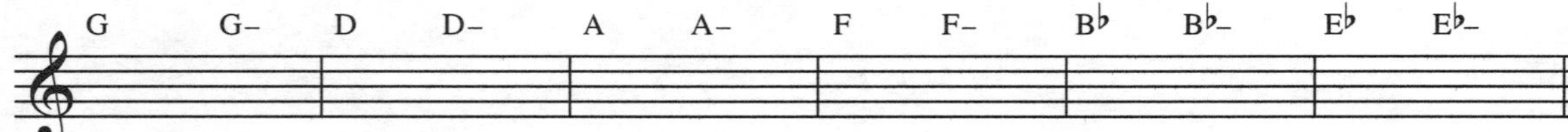

Note There are a few ways to notate minor triads in the chord symbol. Throughout this book we will use the dash (–) to indicate minor, i.e., C–. Other possibilities are: Cm, Cmi and Cmin.

Activity Two *Practice Playing and Singing Minor Triads*

1. Play a minor triad on your instrument or keyboard and sing along using numbers (1, ♭3, 5) or solfege (Do, Me, Sol). Pay particular attention to the minor third interval between the root and third of the chord.
2. Play a major triad and change it to a minor triad by lowering the third a half step. Listen to the difference. Do the opposite, starting with a minor triad, raise the third by a half step to make a major triad.
3. Practice singing major and minor triad arpeggios, both while playing the chords as well as *a capella* ("a capella" means sung without instrumental accompaniment).

Spend time comparing the sounds of major and minor triads to learn about each one's own distinctive sound. Remember, it's the third of the triad that makes the difference.

Activity Three *Identify the Major and Minor Triads*

Identify the following ten triads on CD1, track 15, as major or minor. Check your results with the answer key (Appendix: p. 123, Activity Three, CD1, track 15).

Stump the Band Try testing a classmate on hearing major and minor triads. Play several major or minor triads (block style or arpeggiated) and see if your partner can figure out which ones are which. Then reverse roles!

Hearing the II–, III– and VI– Triads

There are three diatonic minor triads built on Re (2), Mi (3) and La (6) of the major scale. As we learned in the last chapter, we will identify these minor triads with Roman numerals as well. Listen to CD1, track 16 to hear the II–, III– and VI– chords. Play these three minor triads on your instrument or keyboard, noticing how they all have in common the minor third interval between the root and third of the chord. Don't just play in the key of C, practice your transposing skills and play in other keys as well. Next, compare the sounds of the diatonic major and minor triads within the key. Sing up from the root to the third of each chord, noting its major or minor quality. Let's get some practice with this "bottom-up" or "vertical" approach.

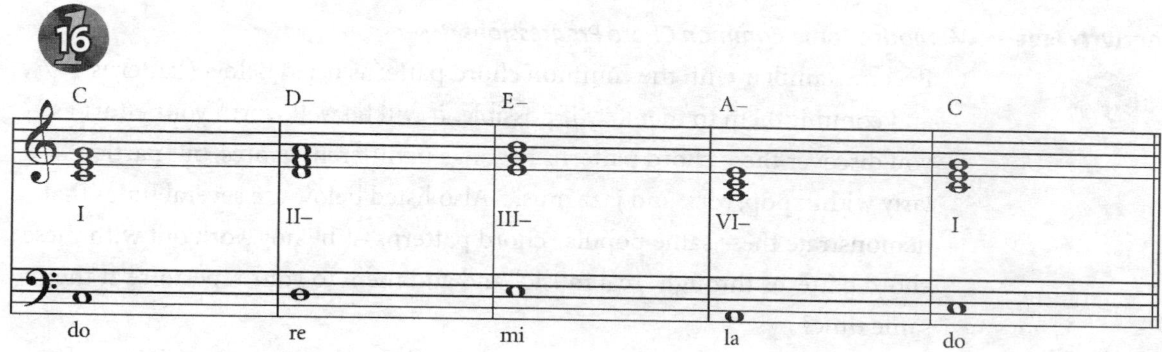

Note We will remain consistent in using all upper case Roman numerals for labeling the diatonic chords: I, II–, III–, IV, V and VI–. A more traditional system uses lower case Roman numerals to designate the minor triads: I, ii, iii, IV, V and vi. You are welcome to use either system, and it is good to be aware of both.

Activity Four *Practicing the Vertical Approach*

1. Listen to CD1, track 17 and sing along with each chord's root and third, recognizing the major or minor third quality. Remember to use numbers and solfege to fully understand the placement of each chord within the key. We'll work in the key of G for this example, but try this exercise in other keys as well.
2. First use numbers, singing: "1/major third; 2/minor third," etc.
3. Then use solfege, singing: "do/mi, major third; re/fa, minor third," etc.
4. Take the time now to memorize the quality of these six diatonic triads. Don't just visualize the chords, know their sound quality as well.

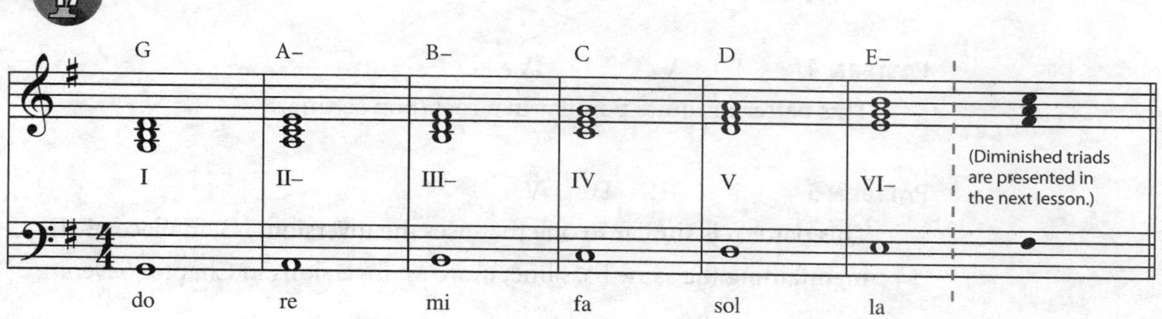

Bonus Play each diatonic triad as it relates directly back to the I chord: I, II–, I; I, III–, I; I, IV, I; I, V, I; and I, VI–, I. You'll notice that within these mini patterns there are varying degrees of "motion." For example, when the I chord moves to the III– or VI– chords, there is a subtle degree of movement, with two out of the three notes staying the same. When the I chord moves to either the II–, IV or V chords, there is a more pronounced sense of movement, with fewer notes in common. We will explore the theory behind these differences in the next chapter.

Activity Five *Memorize Some Common Chord Progressions*

1. Become familiar with the common chord patterns listed below (Patterns 1–7), and commit them to memory if possible. It will be well worth your effort as you discover these chord patterns in songs in different genres, but particularly within pop, rock and jazz music. Also listed below are several tunes that demonstrate these same popular chord patterns. Why not work out with these chord patterns through "real music" and add them to your repertoire at the same time?
2. Spend some time every day listening to these chord patterns on CD1, track 18. Exposure to these progressions is essential before you try determining the answers yourself. Follow the same routine as with Activity Four. The first step once again is to focus in on the root motion of each progression, singing along with solfege and/or numbers. Then, sing up from the root to the third of each chord, determining its major or minor quality. Remember, singing helps to internalize the sound.

Pattern 1 I VI– IV V I

Probably the most popular chord pattern of them all!

Pattern 2 I VI– II– V I

Notice how similar this pattern is to Pattern 1; these are often interchangeable patterns.

Pattern 3 III– VI– II– V I

This pattern is a common substitute for Pattern 2, particularly in jazz.

Pattern 4 I V VI– IV I

This pattern is quite popular in a rock/pop setting.

Pattern 5 I III– IV V I

This pattern is similar to one that uses the inversion, I/3, in place of III–, maintaining the same bass line; more on inversions in Chapter Seven.

Pattern 6 I II– III– IV III– II– I

This pattern describes the common stepwise connection between chords, both ascending and descending.

Pattern 7 I IV III– VI– II– V I

This pattern incorporates all six diatonic triads we've covered thus far; at times we'll see a variation that includes some non-diatonic harmony above this diatonic bass line.

Here is a list of tunes, and the artists or groups that made them famous, that correspond to the above chord patterns.

Pattern 1 "Stand by Me," Ben E. King; "Duke of Earl," Gene Chandler; "Every Breath You Take," The Police; "Don't Play That Song," Aretha Franklin; "Octopus's Garden," The Beatles; "All I Have to Do is Dream," The Everly Brothers.

Pattern 2 "Why Do Fools Fall in Love," Frankie Lymon and the Teenagers; "This Boy," The Beatles; "I Got Rhythm," any number of jazz artists; "You Send Me," Sam Cooke; "We're In This Love Together," Al Jarreau; "Beyond the Sea," Bobby Darin.

Pattern 3 Refer to Pattern 2 listings.

Pattern 4 "With or Without You," U2; "No One," Alicia Keys; "Shower the People," James Taylor; "Tattoo," Jordan Sparks; "Hurts So Good," John Cougar; "Let It Be," The Beatles; "Don't Stop Believing," Journey.

Pattern 5 "And When I Die," Blood, Sweat & Tears; "Beauty and the Beast," Walt Disney film score; "Crying," Roy Orbison; "Everytime You Go Away," Paul Young; "I Won't Last a Day Without You," The Carpenters.

(In Chapter Seven we'll listen to several examples of I, I/3, IV, V for comparison.)

Pattern 6 "Here, There, and Everywhere," The Beatles; "Surrey with the Fringe on Top," Miles Davis; "Heat Wave," Martha and the Vandellas; "Wake Me Up Before You Go-Go," Wham!; "Saving All My Love for You," Whitney Houston; "I'm Old Fashioned," John Coltrane; "I Can't Help Myself," The Four Tops; "Lately," Stevie Wonder.

Pattern 7 "Surrey with the Fringe on Top," Miles Davis; "There Is No Greater Love," McCoy Tyner; "Let There Be Love," Natalie Cole: "On the Trail," Wynton Kelly; "You Are the Sunshine of My Life," Stevie Wonder.

Experiment with different patterns, listening to all the many, many possibilities of progressions you can create. Continue to work out with the vertical approach, singing up from the root to the third of each chord, identifying the chord as major or minor.

Now that you've spent some time becoming familiar with the above progressions, let's see if you can put it all together with the next activity.

Activity Six *Sing Along with the Diatonic Bass Line and Chord Progression*

1. Listen to the following chord progression in the key of F, on CD1, track 19.
2. First, sing the bass line, using both numbers and solfege syllables.
3. Next, sing up from the root to the third of each chord, noticing its major or minor quality. For example, with the first chord, sing "1 / 3, major third," or "do / mi, major third."

Remember, every time you practice hearing a chord progression, you're also practicing hearing the bass line. In the next chapter, we'll put these progressions to the dictation test! So take as much time as you need to get comfortable with these diatonic progressions before moving on.

Bonus In Chapter One, you sang the root motion to the following songs: "Daniel," "Little Wing," "Fly Me to the Moon," "I Will," "Wedding Bell Blues," "Don't Know Why," and "New York State of Mind." Let's revisit them, adding the workout of singing the root to third of each chord. You know the routine by now; don't forget to use numbers and solfege!

There will be some non-diatonic chords throughout these songs for an extra challenge. Take the time you need, and use your instrument if necessary to help you through these "out-of-key" passages. All the work you've done thus far with hearing major and minor triads will pay off. Then when you're ready, try singing along with the "real thing."

Hooking Up with *The Real Easy Book* Return to the same songs in *The Real Easy Book* we looked at in Chapter One when working with the root motion, ("Doxy," "Groove Merchant," "So Danco Samba," "St. Thomas," and "Yardbird Suite") and now add the vertical approach practice of hearing the root/third relationship.

You'll notice that these jazz selections involve several non-diatonic chords, as well as seventh chord harmony. For now, focus on triads only; we will work out with seventh chords in great detail in Chapters Nine and Ten.

In the final chapter of this book, we will investigate some popular non-diatonic chord patterns. These jazz selections will serve as "table setters" for now. When you encounter the non-diatonic chords, take a moment to compare them to the sound of their diatonic partners. For example, in the tune, "Doxy," the second chord is G, a VI major triad: compare it to G–, the diatonic VI– triad. Back to back comparison will reinforce each chord's distinctive quality.

Activity Seven *Rewind... Transposing*

Transpose the chord progression of Activity Six into three different keys of your choice. If you memorize the pattern first, using numbers or solfege syllables as your guide, it won't be difficult at all. Bring your ears along for the ride; don't just think the names of the notes, sing along as you write. And, if you're away from your instrument, or without pencil and paper, "imagine" you're in the key of B♭, for example, and sing out the letter names of the chords. Then try another key with the same method.

We've seen the practical benefits of first memorizing the bass line or chord patterns, using numbers or solfege, when transposing. Let's take a moment to consider some of the other rewards of memorizing the music.

The Benefits of Memorizing

Here are a few of my top reasons for memorizing tunes. They will also help you make great strides with your ear training studies in hearing the changes.

1. Make it a routine to memorize one tune per week. Choose songs that fit with your current studies of hearing the changes. In this way, as you're developing your inner hearing for recognizing chord patterns, you're building a repertoire along the way. One tune a week, that's 52 tunes in a year—enough for a four-hour gig!
2. You will begin to see frequent repetition of chord patterns, tune after tune, making the memorization process quicker and quicker.
3. Knowing lots of tunes from memory makes you more "marketable" on the bandstand. You won't always need to have the written music in front of you in order to perform.
4. If you've memorized the changes, you can devote more creative attention to interpreting the tune, particularly when improvising.
5. Having the tune memorized makes it easier to transpose and play it in other keys. This is especially helpful if you are an accompanist.
6. When you learn a tune by ear, rather than from reading, you've "earned" it and have it almost memorized as a result.

For your consideration What techniques do you use when memorizing music? What do you think some of the benefits are? Share your ideas with classmates.

Making it you own Start memorizing the chord progression to familiar songs, and reap the benefits!

4 Using the Vertical Approach for Dictation

Introduction

In this chapter, we will put our knowledge of popular diatonic chord progressions to the dictation test. I hope you spent some time in Chapter Three reviewing these chord patterns, by listening, playing, and singing through the examples in order to internalize the sound. Spending time hearing these same chord patterns in "real music" examples proves invaluable to the learning process, and gives practical, as well as enjoyable application to our ear training studies.

We'll study the sound of a diminished triad, completing our diatonic palette of triads, and include it in the dictation exercises that follow.

What will be our strategy when doing dictation? Once again, we start by listening to the bass line, the root motion of the chords, and then use the vertical approach from there, listening up from the root to the third of each triad. If we follow these two steps, we should be successful.

At the end of the chapter we will discuss the theory behind these seven diatonic triads, grouping them into three functional categories: tonic, dominant and subdominant. Having an understanding of how each chord functions within the key will reveal why certain chord patterns have a good sense of balance between tension and rest within a musical phrase. Developing our ability to hear the changes requires a joint effort between the brain and the ears. I think you're ready, so let's begin!

Hearing the Diminished Triad Sound

The diminished triad has a symmetrical construction of minor third intervals from the root (1) to the ♭3rd, and from the ♭3rd to the ♭5th. The relationship of the root to the ♭5th is a diminished fifth interval (hence the name "diminished" triad).

The diminished triad is not as common as the major and minor triads, and appears only once in the major key as VII°.

Note We will use a small "o" to indicate diminished: Co. Another option is Cdim.

With major and minor triads, it is sufficient to recognize only the relationship between the root and third. However, in diminished triads, the diminished fifth also needs to be addressed, because that's the interval which distinguishes this triad from a minor triad.

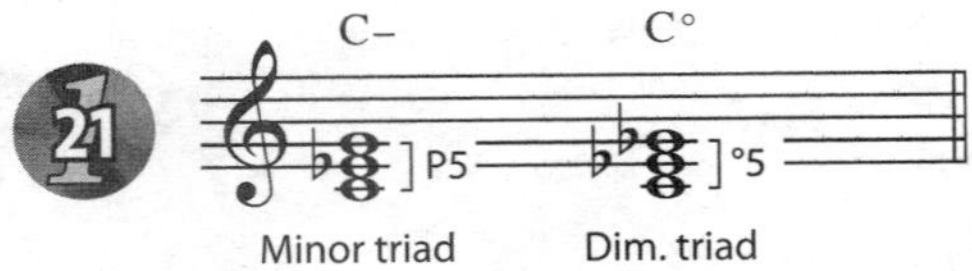

Spend time playing minor and diminished triads on your instrument or keyboard, comparing their sounds. Pay particular attention to the fifths of each chord. The solfege syllable for ♭5 is "Se,"(pronounced "say"). Practice singing "do, me, sol" for the minor triad, then "do, me, sol, se" to adjust to the diminished triad, and then "do, me, se" for the resulting diminished triad.

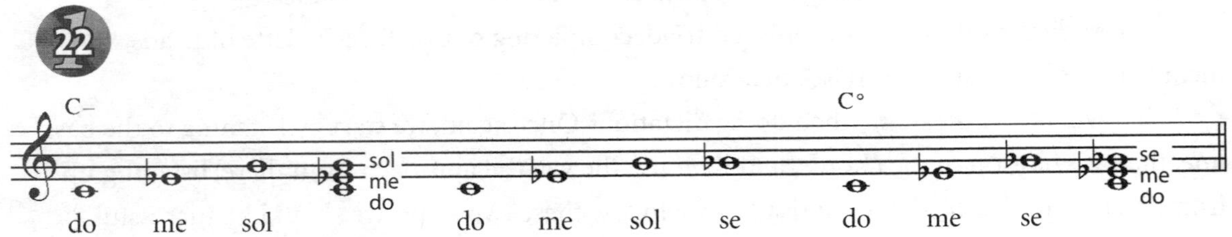

Theory reminder: using the blank staff below, write out the indicated minor and diminished triads. Sing their arpeggios as you write the triads.

Activity One *Identify the Minor and Diminished Triads*

Identify the following ten triads on CD1, track 23 as minor or diminished. Check with the answer key (Appendix: p. 123, Activity One, CD1, track 23) to see how you did.

Hearing the Augmented Triad Sound

And what about the augmented triad? Like the diminished triad, the augmented triad has a symmetrical construction, but this time using major third intervals between the root (1) and 3rd, and 3rd and ♯5th of the triad. The relationship of the root to the ♯5th of the triad is an augmented fifth interval (hence the name "augmented" triad).

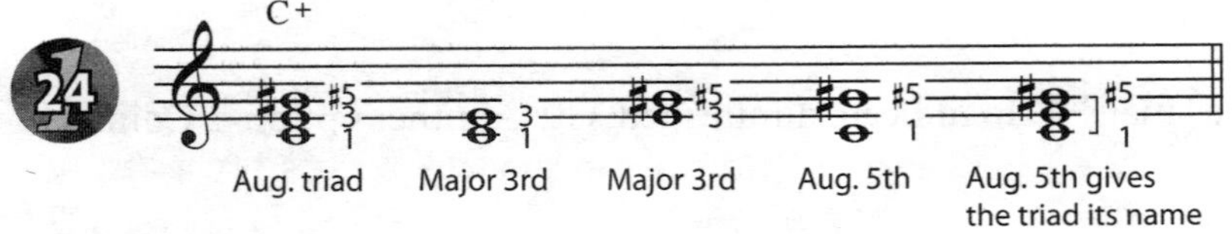

Note We use "+" to indicate augmented: C+. Another option is Caug.

It's the fifths that make the difference when comparing major and augmented triads.

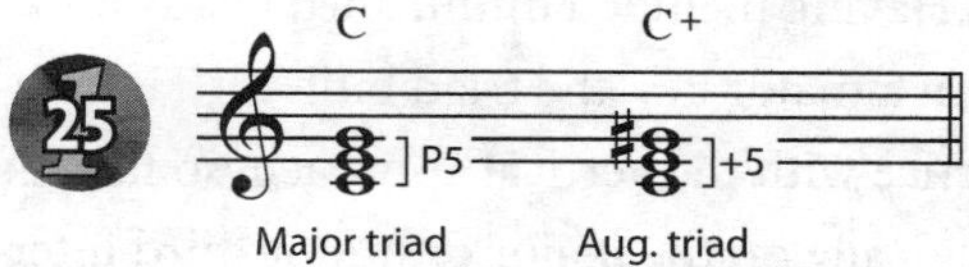

Again, spend time playing major and augmented triads on your instrument or keyboard, comparing the two back to back, paying particular attention to the fifths of each chord. The solfege syllable for ♯5 is "Si,"(pronounced "see"). Practice singing "do, mi, sol" for the major triad, then "do, mi, sol, si" to adjust to the augmented triad, and then "do, mi, si" for the resulting augmented triad.

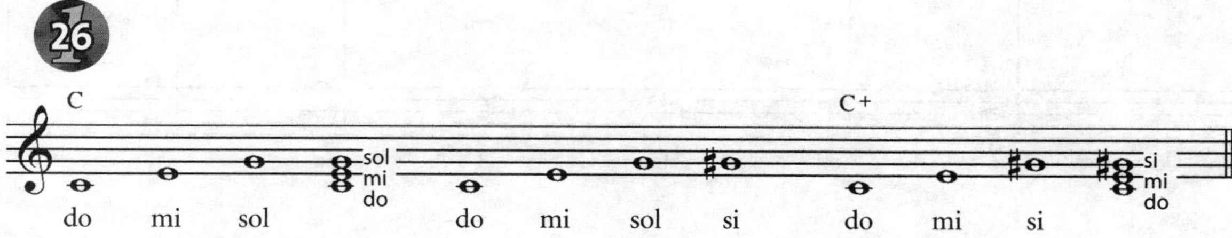

Theory reminder: using the blank staff below, write out the following major and augmented triads. Sing their arpeggios as you write the triads.

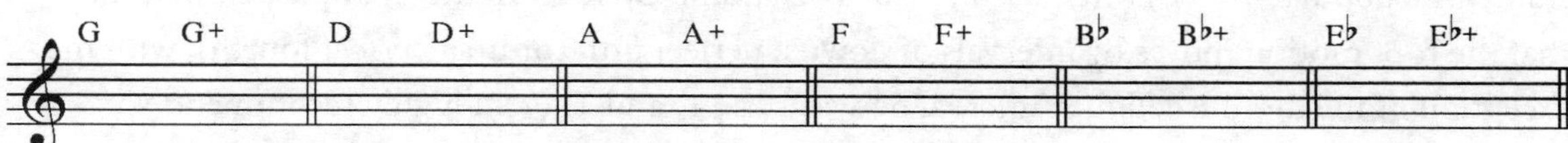

The augmented triad is not a diatonic chord in the major key. However, sometimes it's used as a development of the V chord sound, a V+ chord, when we begin to introduce some non-diatonic chords into the mix. One song that comes to mind is the introduction to Stevie Wonder's, "You Are the Sunshine of My Life."

Activity Two *Identify the Major and Augmented Triads*

Identify the following ten triads on CD1, track 27 as major or augmented. Check with the answer key (Appendix: p. 123, ActivityTwo, CD1, track 27) to see how you did.

Activity Three *Identifying All Four Triad Types*

Identify the following 20 triads on CD1, track 28 as major, minor, diminished or augmented. Refer to the answer key (Appendix: p.123, Activity Three, CD1, track 28) to check your results.

Stump the Band Among classmates, have a contest of who can sing all four triad types accurately, using solfege syllables or numbers. Play a random note on your instrument as the starting pitch for singing up a root position triad. To make it more challenging, start with the fifth of the chord, singing down the triad.

Hearing the VII° Triad

Listen to CD1, track 29 to hear all seven diatonic triads. Having included diminished triads into the mix, our palette of diatonic triads is now complete. In a major key, the triad built on Ti (7) is a diminished triad, VII°. You can never get too much practice with the vertical approach, so take the time to sing along with each of these chords. Focus specifically on the major or minor third interval between the root and third of each triad, and in the case of VII°, the diminished fifth interval between the root and fifth.

29

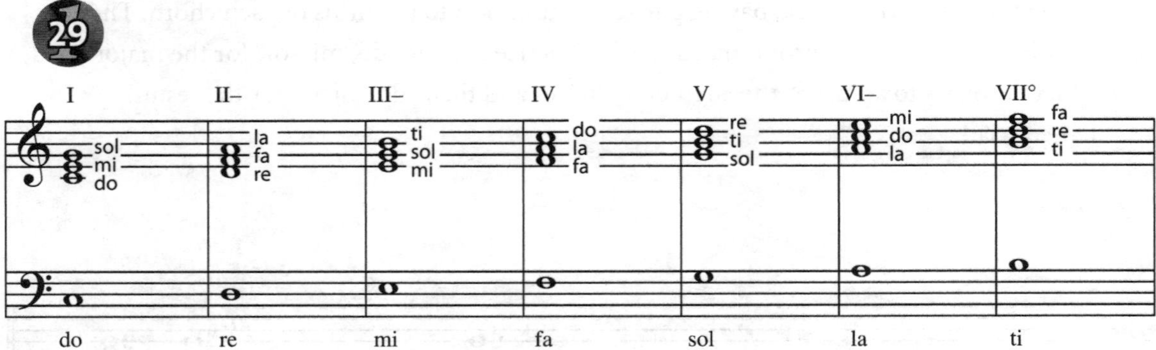

The Diatonic Cycle 5 Pattern

Very few songs simply rely upon moving up the scale by stepwise motion for their chord progressions. One popular pattern often used is called "Diatonic Cycle 5." In the example below, notice that the root motion moves by intervals of down a perfect fifth (or up a perfect fourth), with the exception of the diminished fifth interval between Fa (4) and Ti (7). I highly recommend you memorize this chord pattern. You can start the cycle at any point or practice smaller portions of it, such as the III– ,VI–, II–, V, I pattern we memorized in the last chapter. In the upcoming dictation exercises, you'll find several examples of this diatonic cycle 5 pattern in action. Get a jump start now with practicing this pattern, it will not only help you do the dictation exercises in this book, but prepare you to recognize this popular chord pattern in hundreds of songs in a variety of musical genres.

Activity Four *Practice the Diatonic Cycle 5 Pattern*

1. Listen to the diatonic cycle 5 pattern on CD1, track 30. Sing along with the root motion, using numbers and solfege.
2. Listen again, this time singing up from the root to the third of each chord, noting the major or minor quality. When listening to the VII° triad, also pay attention to the diminished fifth interval between the root and fifth of the chord.
3. Try playing this cycle 5 pattern on your instrument or keyboard, starting at different points in the progression, and in different keys. If you've memorized this pattern using numbers or solfege, it will make transposing very easy. The more you play the chord patterns in a variety of keys, the better you'll recognize and internalize the sound of the pattern.

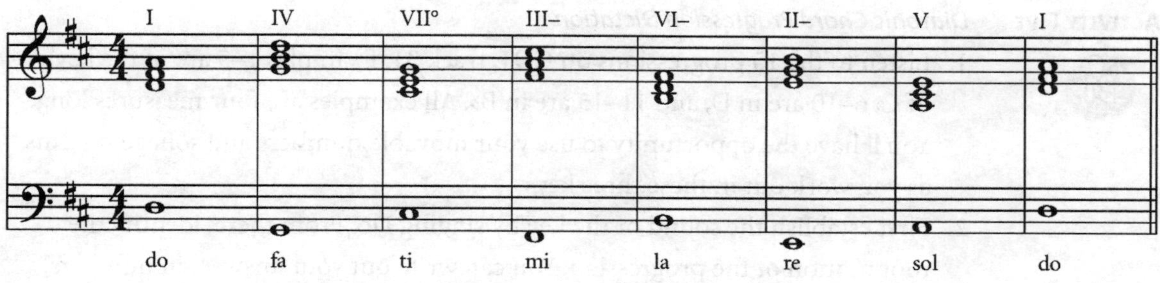

Tip Bass lines that move by stepwise motion are the easiest to identify; lines that involve large leaps are harder to recognize. That's why the Diatonic Cycle 5 pattern is a good one to memorize right from the get-go. Here's a tip to remember when double-checking your work with this pattern: every other bass note will be a step apart.

Bonus Here are a few songs that demonstrate the diatonic cycle 5 pattern. "Autumn Leaves," and "Alice in Wonderland" start the cycle with the II– chord. "You Never Give Me Your Money," "Fly Me to the Moon," and "I Will Survive," start the cycle with the VI– chord.

You'll notice that there is one non-diatonic chord featured in all these songs, the III major chord in place of the diatonic III– chord. We will learn more about this non-diatonic chord in Chapter Twelve. Taking the time to listen to these song selections will plant the sound of the Cycle 5 Pattern more deeply in your inner hearing, as well as add five more tunes to your repertoire. Enjoy!

Now it's time to put all this to the dictation test. Good luck!

ACTIVITY FIVE *Diatonic Chord Progression Dictation*

1. Listen to the 15 progressions on CD1, track 31. Examples 1–5 are in the key of C, 6–10 are in D, and 11–15 are in B♭. All examples are four measures long. You'll have the opportunity to use your movable numbers and solfege systems as you work out in these three keys.
2. First establish the sound of the key by singing Do. From there, identify the root motion of the progression. You can write out your answers in numbers, solfege, letter names of the notes, or write the notes in the bass clef. Ideally, you want to be able to use any and all of these identification tools.
3. Even though step 2 alone can give you the answer for the chords, it's important to take the time and listen up each chord structure, focusing on the major or minor quality of the third of each chord. Being thorough now will pay off big time in the long run, so no short cuts.
4. Some people find it helpful to first memorize the sound of the bass line before writing anything down. Others will want to write the answers immediately, as each chord is played. I recommend trying both methods.
5. Let your "inner hearing" and singing be your guide at first. I don't recommend you play along with the progressions as a first step. Give your inner hearing the chance to work independently, and then you can play your answers to double-check if you were correct. If you follow these steps, you will train your ear and develop self-confidence along the way. And, having confidence in doing this work is half the battle.
6. Check your answers with the key (Appendix: p. 123, Activity Five, CD1, track 31).

TIP I recommend you give your dictation work the "24-hour rule" before checking in with the answer key. Let your work sit for a day, and then review it on the next day. It's amazing how a fresh second listen can bring about improved results.

How did you do? Did you recognize some of the chord patterns you studied in Chapter Three and the diatonic cycle 5 pattern of this lesson? See if you can find examples of these chord patterns in real life music examples. That's a great way to give credence as to why we're studying these particular diatonic progressions. And, if you learn these songs, you're also practicing in an enjoyable, musical way.

BONUS Listen to CD1, track 32, and determine the changes to our mystery tune. Use the template provided on the next page. After identifying the chord progression, do you recognize this song? Check with the answer key to solve the mystery! (Appendix: p. 124, Bonus, CD1, track 32).

As you're starting to realize, harmonic dictation involves as much brain power as ear power when figuring out the changes. Being organized, taking things step by step when listening, sometimes predicting what you think the bass line will suggest for chords, are all examples of the brain power at work, helping the ears decipher and decode what they're hearing. Let's take a minute to go behind the story, and see what makes certain popular chord patterns "tick."

Some Theory Basics of Diatonic Harmony

Now that we've set the table by recognizing some common diatonic chord patterns, let's take a moment to talk about how each chord functions within the key, and why certain chord patterns establish a well-balanced diet of tension and rest within the chord phrase.

The seven diatonic triads are broken into three categories:

Tonic chords are the most stable chords within the key: I, III– and VI–.

Dominant chords (V and VII°) are the most unstable chords within the key.

Subdominant chords (IV and II–) lie somewhere in between, not as unstable as the dominant functioning chords, but still requiring a sense of resolution.

Notice that within each diatonic category there are two common tones shared within like-functioning chords, which makes their sound similar. The tonic group (I, III–, VI–) all share Mi (the 3rd of the primary I chord); the dominant group (V, VII°) shares Ti (the 3rd of the primary V chord); and the subdominant group (IV, II–) have La in common (the 3rd of the primary IV chord). Our intention is not to get too deep into theoretical explanation, but to have a general understanding of how diatonic chords relate to one another in the key.

Let's take a look at the following chord progression and examine how each chord falls into one of these three categories. This is the same progression we used in Activity Six, Chapter Three. This time, listen to the progression with a "broad strokes" approach: rather than hearing the particulars of each chord, listen for the overall sense of motion throughout the phrase as it travels through the tonic, subdominant and dominant areas.

I	IV	|	III–	VI–	|	II–	V	|	I	|
T	SD	|	T	T	|	SD	D	|	T	|

II–	III–	|	IV	V	|	I	VI–	|	I	IV	|	I	‖
SD	T	|	SD	D	|	T	T	|	T	SD	|	T	‖

Bonus Apply the chord function (T, SD, D) approach of analysis to the chord progression of songs you know. For example, notice how patterns such as I, VI–, IV, V, I; I, VI–, II–, V, I; I, III–, IV, V, I; and III–,VI–, II–,V, I all have exactly the same T, T, SD, D, T scheme in common. As you examine the changes to tune after tune, you will begin to notice how frequently chord patterns repeat themselves, following an underlying sense of balance of tension and resolve throughout the progression. Noting these recurring patterns will make memorizing songs a faster and more efficient process.

Activity Six *Create a Chord Progression*

Fill in the following scheme with chords that function in the indicated tonic, subdominant and dominant categories. Consider the resulting root motion that connects the chords as well as the mixture of chord colors when making your choices. There is no one right answer to this activity. Explore some different solutions and share with your classmates.

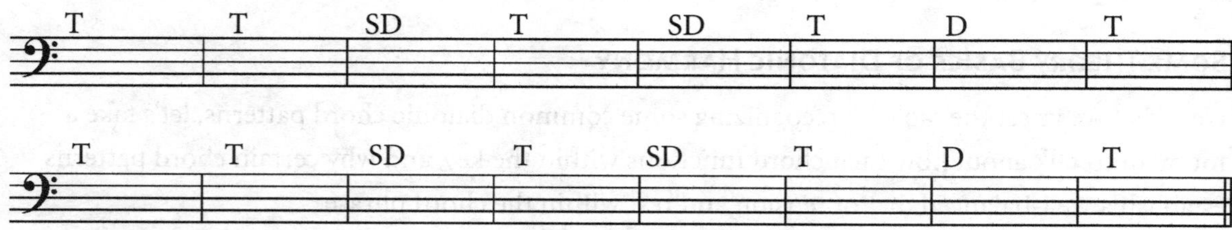

Activity Seven *Rewind... Memorizing the Chord Progression*

Memorize the chord progression to a song this week. Keep the song choice simple, one that contains mostly diatonic triads if possible. You can learn the song from a lead sheet, or for the ultimate workout, try figuring out the changes by ear from a recording. And yes, it's OK to get help from your instrument if you need to: transcribing can be challenging. Do you see any familiar chord patterns in your song? Now, play the song in three different keys to test your transposing skills. Did memorizing the song first make transposing easier? Are you playing the chord changes with greater ease and confidence because you've got them memorized?

Stump the Band Teach your classmates the changes to the song you just memorized by ear in Activity Seven, then switch roles. Teaching a song by ear rather than passing out the song leadsheet is also a good activity for teachers or bandleaders.

For your consideration Discuss with your classmates how knowing harmonic theory can be helpful in figuring out the chord changes.

Making it your own Try transcribing the chord progression to familiar songs, applying the vertical approach when determining chord quality as major or minor.

5 Introducing the Horizontal Approach

Introduction

Up to this point, we have taken a "bottom-up," or vertical approach to hearing the chord progression, focusing on hearing the relationship of the root to the third of each chord. In this chapter, we will explore taking a melodic, or "horizontal" approach to hearing and expressing the chords. This will be especially practical if you are a singer or play a melodic instrument such as trumpet, saxophone, or flute. Many a melody is an embellished chord arpeggio; and often a piano or guitar accompaniment, as well as the bass line, are expressed through arpeggios.

We'll practice listening and singing through chord arpeggios, and begin to work with voice-leading through the chord progression. Voice-leading the chords is often the basis for developing background vocal or horn lines; it is also the way most pianists and guitarists will perform the chord accompaniment, creating a smooth transition from one chord to the next.

Adding the "horizontal" approach to our bag of listening tools will make us twice as strong when identifying chord progressions.

Singing Root Position Arpeggios

Let's begin with the popular I, VI–, IV, V, I pattern. Sing the following root position arpeggios, using solfege syllables. For example, sing "do, mi, sol, mi, do; la, do, mi, do, la," etc. We will only use solfege syllables rather than numbers. In this way, we're focusing in on how the chord tones sound in relationship to the key, not the individual chord root. More on that later; for now, let's practice singing arpeggios. First sing the arpeggios along with CD1, track 33, then on your own.

Activity One *Sing Root Position Arpeggios with the Cycle 5 Progression*

1. Remember to sing both up and then down through each chord in order to link easily from one chord root to the next. Don't forget to sing with solfege syllables; only using "la, la, la" won't tell the story.
2. Try singing the arpeggios with, and then without the accompaniment on CD1, track 34. Take your time when singing through the arpeggios, this is not a race. In fact, practicing slowly allows you to be "present" every note along the way, rather than being on "automatic pilot."

(Activity One cont'd)

3. After you have internalized the sound of the arpeggio patterns, play them in different keys on your instrument. Remember, using solfege will make transposing these patterns a breeze!

34

Tip At first, you might write out the arpeggio patterns in these new keys before playing them directly onto your instrument. Write out this cycle 5 pattern in three other keys of your choice. For starters, pick keys that are "user friendly" for your vocal range, or for your instrument. When writing out the notes, "sing" along with your inner hearing voice, letting the solfege syllables lead you on.

Bonus Analyze the notes in the following bass line. First, circle the chord tones and label their function according to each individual chord, using numbers. Second, label these chord tones with solfege syllables, identifying their function within the key. Not every bass note is a chord tone; leave these non-chord tones unlabeled for now. I've done the first two measures for you as a guide. Then check with the answer key to see how you did. (Appendix: p. 125, Bonus).

HOOKING UP WITH *THE REAL EASY BOOK* For additional practice, check out some of the written bass lines featured in *The Real Easy Book*. You'll see that the chord tones have already been labeled with numbers as they relate to each individual chord. Now label these chord tones with solfege syllables, relating them to the overall key center. Notice how often the bass line is a developed series of chord arpeggios, starting with the root of each chord as the "anchor." Not every bass note is a chord tone, but the majority are.

SINGING MELODIC ARPEGGIOS

We'll use the same I, VI–, IV, V, I pattern, but this time in the key of F. Sing up one chord, then down the next, creating a more melodic shape. Notice the stepwise links from one chord to the next. This makes the line easier to sing. First sing the arpeggios along with CD1, track 35, then on your own.

Many times, a melodic phrase is an arpeggio, plain and simple. Let's look at a few examples from the following songs.

We'll explore the relationship of melody and harmony in greater detail in Chapter Eight.

Activity Two *Sing Melodic Arpeggios with the Cycle 5 Progression*

Sing the following melodic arpeggio pattern to the familiar cycle 5 progression, this time in the key of F. Notice how smooth the transition is throughout the example, connecting each chord by stepwise motion.

Bonus Get creative in making up your own melodic arpeggio patterns; it's not always a matter of up one chord, down the next. Using arpeggios is a wonderful way to open up the chord sound for accompaniments, or for developing an improvisational line. Give it a try and experiment with your own lines.

Here is something I came up with, this time in the key of D. The first example is the "skeleton" sketch I started with. The second example is a slightly embellished version, spiced up with some rhythmic energy and a few additional approach notes. Let's see what you can come up with. Use the blank staves on the next page to write your sketch and developed version.

My "skeleton" version:

My "embellished" version:

Your "skeleton" version:

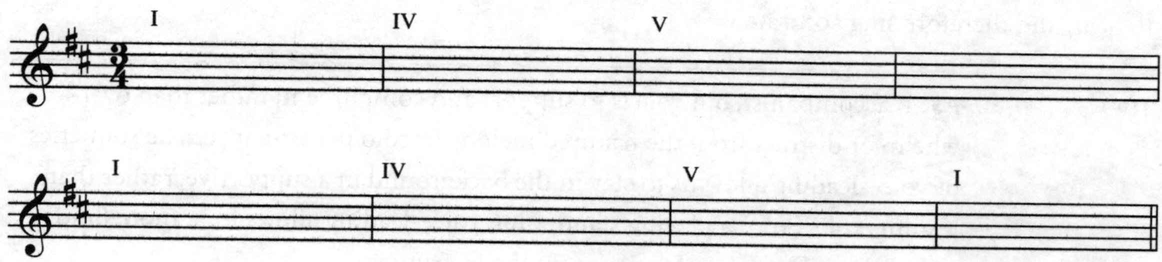

Your "embellished" version:

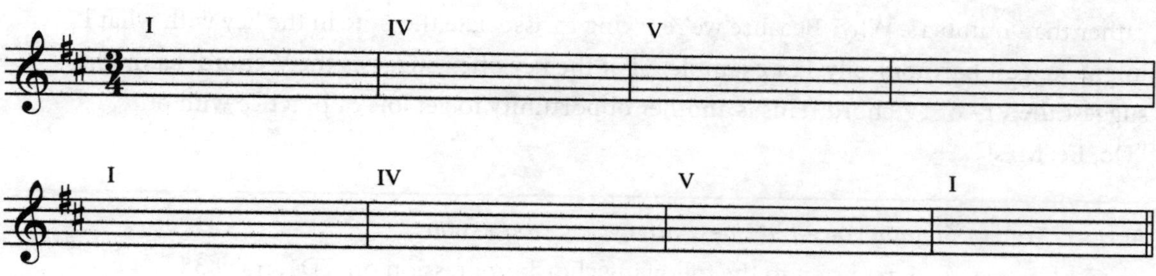

Stump the Band Exchange your written examples with another classmate. Can your partner play or sing back your lines? Did he or she offer any constructive feedback about what you wrote?

Voice-Leading through a Chord Progression

Another melodic, or horizontal approach to hearing the chord progression is called "voice-leading." With voice-leading, we listen to the way individual chord tones move from one chord to the next. Notice in the example below (once again, I, VI–, IV, V, I) the smooth connection from chord to chord. There are many instances of either common tones or stepwise motion linking the chords. These voice-led lines are often easier to sing because you don't have to sing leaps.

Knowing how to voice-lead chord progressions has many practical advantages. It is often the basis for developing simple background vocal or horn lines. It is also the way most pianists and guitarists will perform the chord accompaniment, creating a smooth transition from one chord to the next.

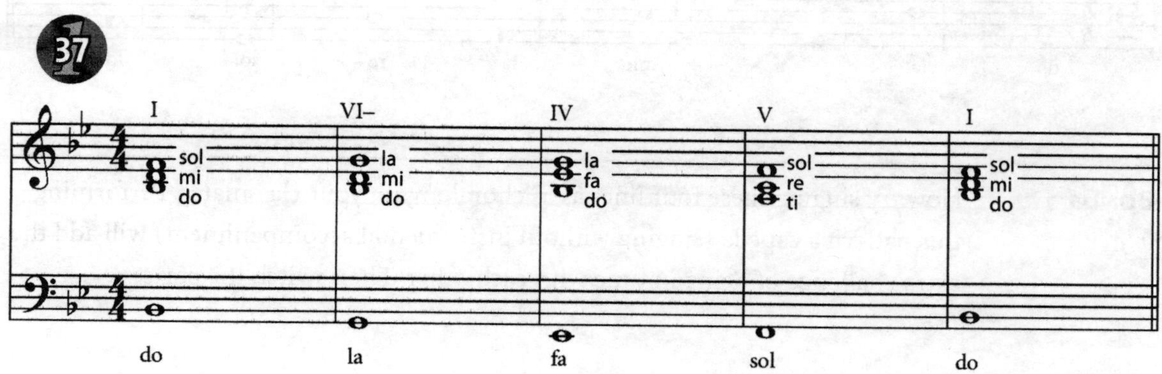

Experience it for yourself. Sing along with each voice-led line (CD1, track 37), noticing how easy it is to go from one chord tone to the next. Common tone or stepwise motion is much easier to hear, and therefore sing accurately.

Tip As an accompanist, our role is to support and compliment, rather than overwhelm or distract from the featured melody or solo performance. The subtleties of voice-leading allow us to stay in the background in a supportive, rather than leading, role. From a playing standpoint, voice-leading allows for a more fluid, rather than choppy, performance on the instrument.

Similar to our work with arpeggios, voice-leading uses the key as a point of reference, rather than the individual root of each chord. Therefore, we'll sing all the voice-led lines using solfege rather than numbers. Why? Because we're trying to associate the note in the key with what it might suggest harmonically. For example, Ti of the key often suggests the V chord. La might suggest the VI– or IV chord. This is another opportunity to get lots of practice with our "Do, Re, Mi's!"

Activity Three *Singing Voice-Led Lines with Cycle 5 Progression*

1. First listen to the following chord progression on CD1, track 38.
2. Next, sing the root motion along with the recording, using solfege syllables. This will solidly anchor each chord in relation to the sound of the overall key.
3. Then, sing each voice-led line across the progression, again using solfege. You'll notice that compared to singing the root motion, these lines are easier to sing because of the their common tones and stepwise motion. For example, sing "sol, la, fa, sol, la, la, sol, sol" for the top line.
4. It is very important to sing each voice-led line along with the recording in order to reap the full benefit of hearing how each line fits in with the overall harmonic context.

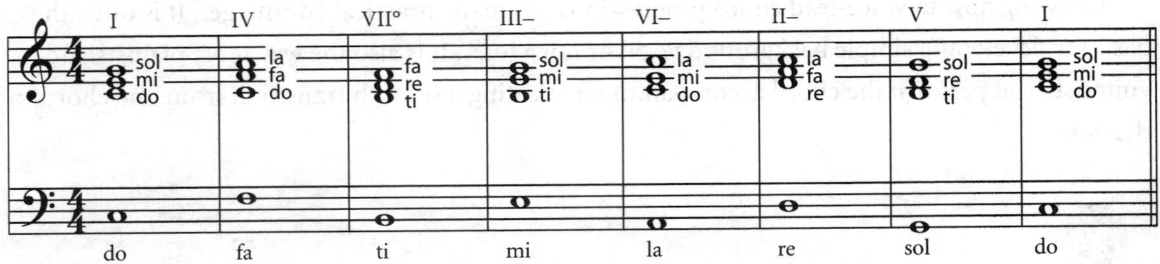

Bonus Now try singing these four lines as a "chorale" with your classmates. Performing this pattern a capella (singing without instrumental accompaniment) will add the extra challenge of being in tune with each other. Then switch the parts.

Extra Bonus Now take the challenge one step further and sing this voice-led pattern along with a recording of one of the cycle 5 tunes we've worked with thus far. Try singing along with the Beatles on "You Never Give Me Your Money," or with Frank Sinatra on "Fly Me to the Moon." You will need to make one small adjustment in the pattern, changing III– (Sol) to III (Si). Remember that both of these songs start the cycle 5 pattern with the VI– chord. Enjoy!

With practice, you'll begin to associate certain notes in the key with what they might suggest harmonically, but this will take some time. In this chapter, we're "setting the table," getting used to identifying the chord tones with solfege. In the next chapter, we'll begin to use this technique for dictation purposes.

Activity Four *Write Out the Root and Voice-Led Lines*

Try your hand at it now: write out the root motion and voice-led lines to the following chord progression in the keys of C, D and B♭. This progression is a combination of two patterns you memorized earlier from Chapter Three. Remember, let solfege be your guide in creating the lines and transposing them into the different keys. Check your results with the answer key (Appendix: p. 125, Activity Four).

Tip Can you see how these voice-led lines have the potential to be the beginnings of simple background vocal or horn lines in an arrangement? Adding some rhythmic spice is often all you need to create some tasteful background accompaniment. Remember to not overdo it; "Less is more" is a good rule of thumb. When listening to song arrangements, check out the background harmony lines: they are often voice-leading in action!

ACTIVITY FIVE *More Practice with Voice-Leading*

Using the same examples from Activity Four, sing through all the lines using solfege to internalize the sound of the progression. Hearing all the lines together provides the greatest benefit, so try the following suggestions for more practice.

1. Play the progression on a keyboard, noticing how voice-leading makes it easy to play.
2. Record yourself singing or playing each line, overdubbing the parts.
3. Sing all four lines as a "chorale" with your classmates.
4. You can also sing these voice-led lines as melodic arpeggios, singing up one chord structure, then down the next.

BONUS Choose your own song and create voice-led lines for background vocal harmony parts. Perform your arrangement with classmates or band members. Guaranteed, the singers will love you because you've given them parts they can easily read, hear and thus give you a solid performance. Everyone's happy!

Here is an example of something I came up with as background vocal parts to Paul Simon's "Me and Julio." For now, I've chosen solfege for the lyrics. Try singing these lines along with the recording for some fun.

A

2/4 (repeat begins)

I			IV	
sol mi do	⁒	⁒	la fa do	⁒
Root motion DO			FA	

V			I	
sol re ti	⁒	⁒	sol mi do	⁒
SOL			DO	

B

1.

V		I		V		I	
sol re ti	⁒	sol mi do	⁒	sol re ti	⁒	sol mi do	⁒ (repeat ends)
SOL		DO		SOL		DO	

C

2.

IV		I		IV		I II
la fa do	⁒	sol mi do	⁒	la fa do	⁒	sol mi do ( )
FA		DO		FA		DO RE

V	IV		I		
sol re ti	la fa do	⁒	sol mi do	⁒	etc.
SOL	FA		DO		

Extra Bonus Often, background vocal parts are made up on the spot, "by ear." There are no written charts to refer to. Try your ear at this with the simple I, IV, V, I pattern we studied in Chapter Two. If your line starts on Sol, where will it lead? And how about the Mi or the Do line? Don't write the lines down, do this by ear. Then treat yourself to singing these lines along with recordings of "La Bamba," "Old Time Rock and Roll," or "Stir It Up." You'll be jammin'!

In the next chapter, we'll put the vertical and horizontal approaches together for a complete workout with hearing the changes and lots of dictation work. In combination, these two approaches can work wonders!

Activity Six *Rewind... Using the Vertical Approach*

Figure out the chords to the following progression (another mystery tune!) using the vertical approach. First determine the root motion, then determine the quality of the interval between the root and third of each chord: is it major or minor? Use the template below to fill in your answers. Here's a clue: there are two places where there's a non-diatonic chord, and it's the same chord. Upon completing your work, do you recognize the name of this song by its chord progression? Check with the answer key for the correct solution, and the name of this classic Beatles song, (Appendix: p. 126, Activity Six, CD1, track 39).

For additional practice, analyze the resulting chord progression two ways: first label the Roman numerals, and then determine if the chord's function is tonic, subdominant or dominant. Do you recognize some recurring patterns here?

For Your Consideration Discuss with classmates some of the benefits of using solfege syllables rather than numbers when describing and recognizing chord tones.

Making It Your Own Practice singing the various arpeggio patterns and voice-led lines through the chord progressions to familiar songs. The more tunes you practice with, the easier the solfege will begin to roll off your tongue.

6 Using the Horizontal Approach for Dictation

Introduction

In the last chapter, we began our exploration of using a horizontal approach to hear the chord progression. We sang through diatonic chord arpeggios, and sang through chord progressions using the voice-leading technique. In both cases, we sang using solfege syllables rather than numbers, getting used to hearing the chord tones as members of the key. In this chapter we will take the horizontal approach to the next level, using it for dictation. We'll find that in some situations, particularly when the chords are moving quickly, using the horizontal approach is more successful than the vertical approach when trying to identify the chord progression.

Similar to the vertical approach, we'll focus in on the third of each chord as the "guide tone," the note that best describes the chord quality as major or minor, but we will describe each guide tone as it relates to the sound of the overall key, using solfege syllables. With practice, we'll begin to memorize and associate these guide tones with specific diatonic chords, giving us another strategy for determining the changes.

A new chord structure, the Vsus4, will also be introduced in this chapter. Let's give those "Do, Re, Mi's" another workout!

Hearing the Individual Notes of the Chord

Let's spend some time listening to each individual line in the following voice-led progression, and then see what chords result. Try to hear the notes of each line as solfege syllables rather than as a series of intervals, much like we did when working with bass lines in Chapter One. Sing along with each individual line on the recording, or join with classmates to sing all three.

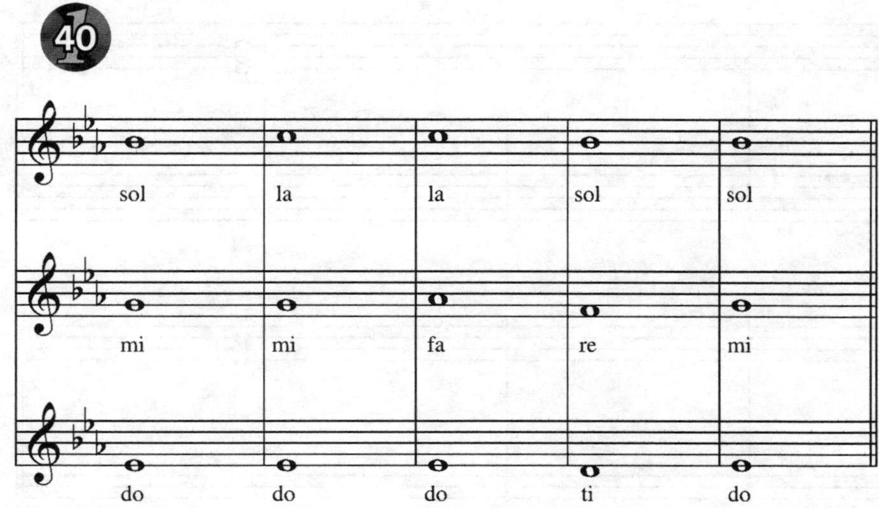

Now figure out what chords those three lines make up. That's right, it's the familiar I, VI–, IV, V, I pattern we've studied earlier, but this time we've heard all the details of each line, and every note, along the way.

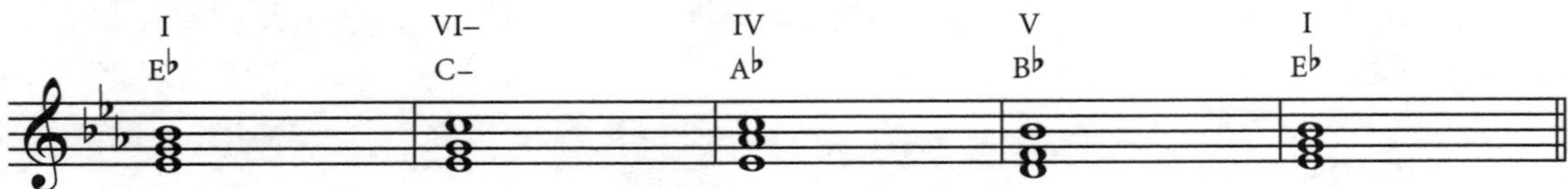

Activity One *Transcribe the Voice-Led Chord Lines*

1. Listen to the following three examples on CD1, track 41 and transcribe each line. Use the templates provided below to fill in your answers. Establishing Do and the overall sound of the key in your ear as the first step will enable you to hear each line as a tonal phrase.
2. Now determine what those three lines mean harmonically. What are the chords being outlined? Fill that answer in with both chord symbols and Roman numerals.
3. Also create the root motion line for each of these examples, giving these chord tone lines a solid foundation below.
4. Check with the answer key (Appendix: p. 126, Activity One, CD1, track 41) to see how you did.

Why take this detailed, horizontal approach at times? Because sometimes you'll want to know exactly what's being played. At times, your band will need to "cover" the song exactly by audience request; check out these vocal background lines to Bob Marley's "Stir It Up."

"Stir It Up" Bob Marley

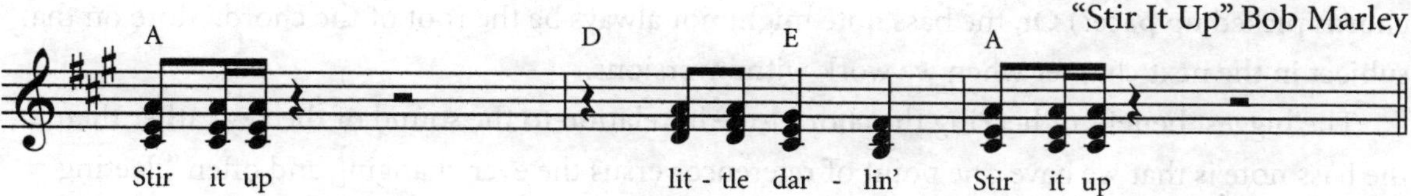

And sometimes, using the horizontal approach might be easier than using the vertical approach when figuring out the chord progression. Let's see how.

Hearing the Third of the Triad as the "Guide Tone"

In earlier chapters, using the vertical approach, we listened up from the root to the third of the triad, and determined if this relationship was major or minor. We will refer to the third of a triad as the "guide tone," the note that best describes the chord color as major or minor. Now, using solfege syllables, let's give a closer listen to this guide tone, the third of the chord, in relation to the sound of the key. For example, the third of the I major triad is Mi of the key; the third of the II– triad is Fa of the key, etc. It will be helpful to make a chart of these guide tones. We'll do so by grouping the chords into two categories: those with major thirds, and those with minor thirds.

The Guide Tone Chart

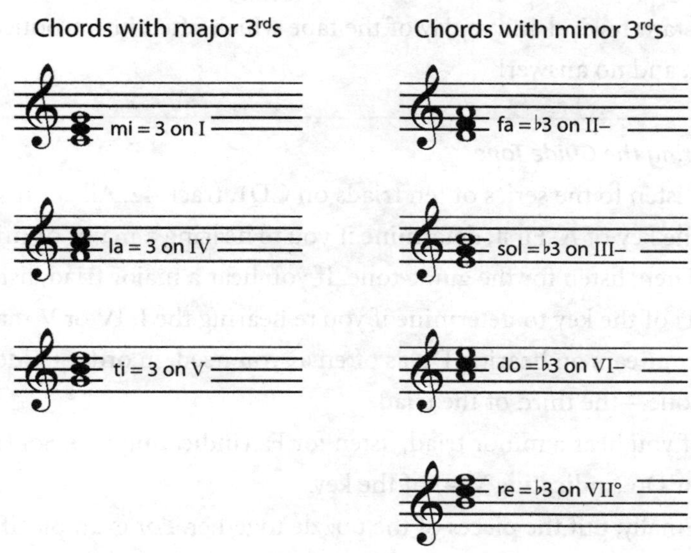

Why do we need to take this extra step of knowing how the chord tones sound in relation to the key rather than each individual bass note? Because sometimes the chords are moving by too fast in the progression to hear up from the root to the third of the chord. (Remember how frantic and rushed you felt trying to sing up from the root to the third of the chords in "Daniel" when the chords picked up pace?) Or, the bass note might not always be the root of the chord. More on that subject in the next chapter when we work with inversions.

The biggest benefit of hearing the chord tone in relation to the sound of the key rather than the bass note is that we have one point of reference versus the ever changing and often "fleeting" individual bass notes in the progression. We are "grounded" in the sound of the overall key, and have time to prepare with questions like: "I know I hear a major triad, but I'm not sure if it's the IV or V chord." Preparing ahead with the question, "Is La or Ti there?" will most likely give you the answer. Let's try this with a few examples.

Tip

One of the biggest benefits of using the horizontal approach is the opportunity to think ahead in preparing questions (educated guesses) about upcoming chords in the progression.

For example, in the key of C, let's say in the fourth measure of the song, you're not sure if you're hearing an E– or E chord. Prepare ahead of time to hear either G (Sol) or G♯ (Si). Plant the sound of one of these notes in your ear, with a 50/50 chance that you've picked the right one initially. But if not, it's the other choice by default. When that fourth measure comes along, you're ready for it with a prepared question, and therefore, will likely receive the answer.

This is another example of how much thinking is involved in figuring out the changes, it's not simply a pure listening experience. And, it beats the alternative of constant rewind and replay of the tape which often just produces more frustration, and no answer!

Activity Two *Hearing the Guide Tone*

1. Listen to the series of ten triads on CD1, track 42. All chords will be diatonic in the key of A. First, determine if you're hearing a major or minor triad.
2. Then, listen for the guide tone. If you hear a major triad, listen for Mi, La or Ti of the key to determine if you're hearing the I, IV or V major triad. Refresh your ears on hearing Do as often as you need, in order to identify the guide tone—the third of the triad.
3. If you hear a minor triad, listen for Fa (indicating II–), Sol (indicating III–) or Do (indicating VI–) of the key.
4. Finally, put the pieces of the puzzle together. For example, if you heard a major triad, and Ti of the key, then the answer is the V triad. Or, if you heard a minor triad, and Do of the key, the answer is the VI– triad. At first, this is a lot to remember, so have the Guide Tone Chart (p. 49) in front of you for reference.
5. Refer to the answer key (Appendix: p. 127, Activity Two, CD1, track 42) to check your results.

Stump the Band Now let's try the opposite. This time play the guide tone, the third of the triad. Have your partner identify the note in solfege, and tell you what the resulting chord is. For example, in the key of G, if you play an F♯, your partner would identify the guide tone as Ti, and tell you it's the V chord. Don't forget to first play the scale to establish the tonality. Another variation on this game is to play the guide tone, having your partner play back the correct corresponding chord. Keep the Guide Tone Chart handy for reference.

By far, the biggest challenge with using the horizontal approach is the translation work involved — converting solfege syllables (how we hear the chord tone in respect to the sound of the overall key) to numbers (identifying what that chord tone is in respect to the individual chord). With practice, this conversion process will get easier and faster.

Activity Three *Progression Dictation Using the Horizontal Approach*

1. Listen to the following five chord progressions in the key of A on CD1, track 43; each example is four measures long. The progressions will be voice-led, therefore, the bottom line will not represent the root motion but will be a voice-led line along with the other two lines. This is an opportunity to put the horizontal approach to the test.
2. One approach is to transcribe all three individual lines, as you did in Activity One, and then determine the resulting chords. If you take this route, I suggest you transcribe the outside (top and bottom) lines first, reserving the more challenging middle line for last.
3. Or, you can take the steps we used in Activity Two to figure out the chords, first determining if you're hearing a major or minor triad, then listening for the corresponding guide tone.
4. If you use one approach in doing the assignment, double-check your work with the other approach, for the full experience.
5. Check the answer key (Appendix: p. 127, Activity Three, CD1, track 43) to see how you did.

Bonus Determine the changes to the following progression, tracking all three individual lines. Use the blank template provided below. These are the changes to Bernstein's "One Hand, One Heart" from "West Side Story." Hint: there is one non-diatonic note in measure 7. Check the answer key (Appendix: p.128, Bonus, CD1, track 44) for the results. And, if possible, sing these lines along with the original recording.

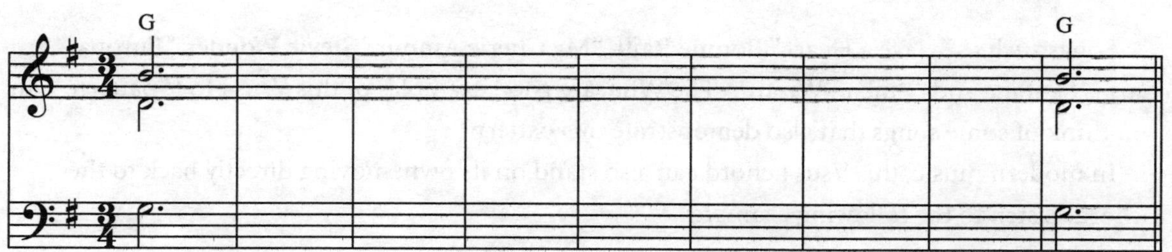

Again, it's tempting to only use the vertical approach because it's a simpler process. But there will be times when it won't work. The horizontal approach is definitely more complicated, involving more steps, but it will usually do the trick when we've exhausted our attempts with the "bottom-up" approach. Having two ways to get the answer is better than being limited to only one approach.

In the next chapter we will work with inversions, when the bass note is not the root of the chord. This will be another opportunity for us to combine our vertical and horizontal approaches to hearing the chord progression. But before we move on, let's introduce the Vsus4 triad into the mix of chord possibilities.

The Vsus4 Triad

The "sus4" chord is a unique structure: instead of a traditional major third, it has a perfect fourth interval "suspended" above the root of the chord in place of the third. It is a variation of the V triad sound, and is an excellent example of how harmony moves melodically, or horizontally through the chord progression.

45

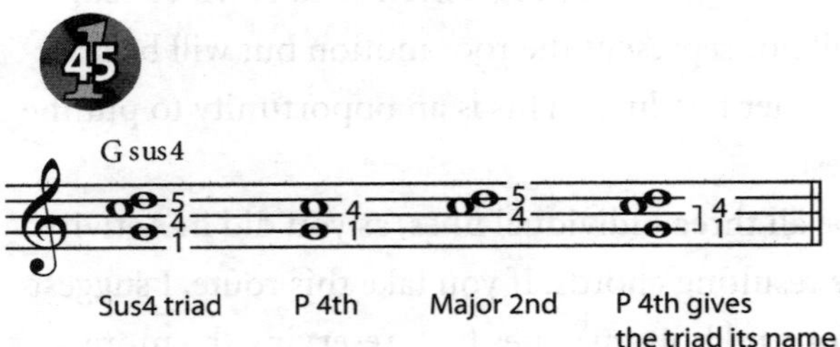

Traditionally, this suspended fourth (Do of the key) above the root of the V chord would resolve to the third (Ti of the key), before the V chord resolved back to the I chord. This pattern remains quite popular in contemporary music as well. Listen to the progression below:

46

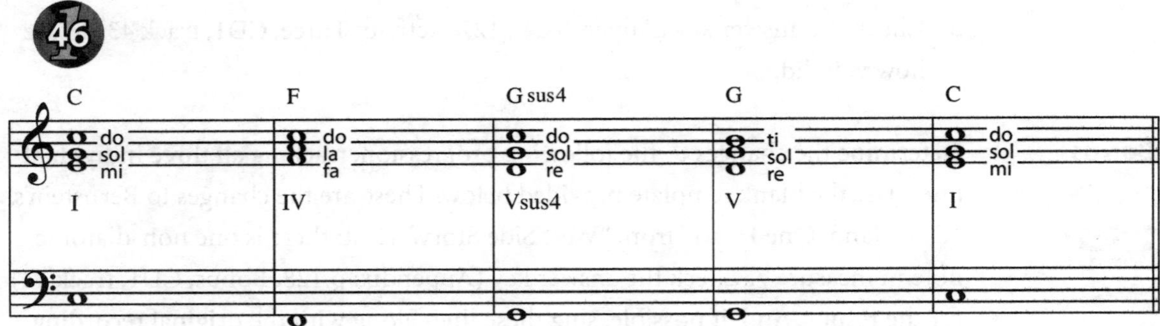

Songs such as "Have a Heart," Bonnie Raitt, "My Cherie Amour," Stevie Wonder, "Europa," Carlos Santana and "Pinball Wizard," The Who, are good examples of this Vsus4 to V pattern. Can you think of some songs that also demonstrate this pattern?

In modern music, this Vsus4 chord can also stand on its own, moving directly back to the I chord. Listen to the following example:

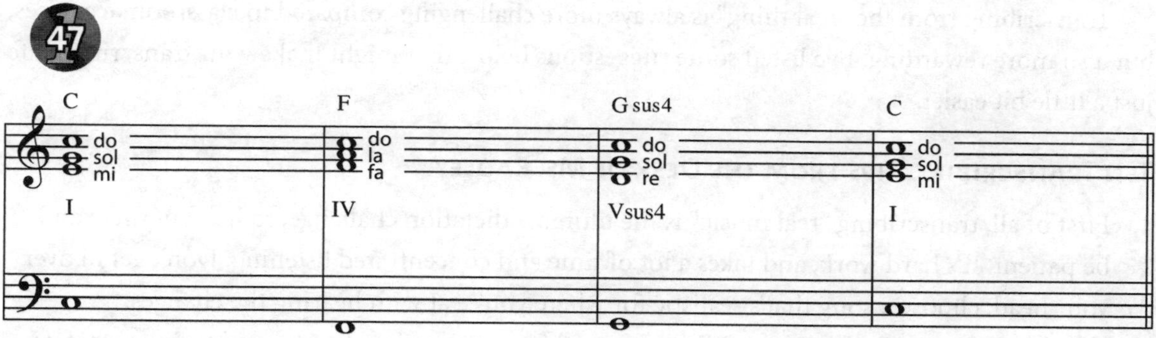

"Passion Dance," McCoy Tyner, "Groovin'," Young Rascals, "Don't Know Why," Norah Jones and "You Don't Have to Be a Star," Marilyn McCoo & Billy Davis Jr., demonstrate the Vsus4 sound as a stand-alone. See if you can find your own examples of this pattern.

Because the Vsus4 chord has no third, the "sus4" is the guide tone. Listen to the two voiceled progressions (above, CD1, tracks 46, 47) once again, paying particular attention to the line that contains the "sus4" guide tone. Sing these two patterns with your classmates, "chorale" style. Switch parts for the full workout.

Did you notice that Do of the key is the "sus4" guide tone? This is another good opportunity to use the horizontal approach in order to distinguish the Vsus4 from the V chord. If you hear Do of the key, it's the Vsus4, if you hear Ti, it's the more standard V chord. Let's practice hearing the difference.

Activity Four *Hearing the Vsus4 Chord*

Transcribe the five progressions on CD1, track 48 that demonstrate the Vsus4 sound. They are in the key of B♭, five measures per example. Then check with the answer key (Appendix: p. 128, Activity Four, CD1, track 48) for the results.

Bonus

Transcribe the changes to Carlos Santana's "Europa," using the template provided below. This selection features the Vsus4 sound. You can either listen to CD1, track 49 for the changes (only triads), or take the challenge of transcribing from the "real thing," (includes seventh chord harmony). Then check in with the answer key to see how you did (Appendix: p. 128, Bonus, CD1, track 49).

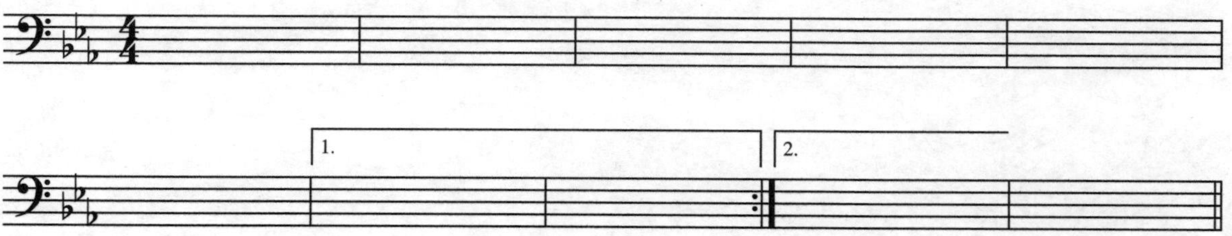

Transcribing from the "real thing" is always more challenging compared to classroom exercises, but also more rewarding. I've listed some suggestions below that might make your transcribing life just a little bit easier.

Ten Transcribing Tips from the Desk of Ms. Radley

1. First of all, transcribing "real music" is the ultimate dictation challenge, so hang in there and be patient. It's hard work, and takes a lot of time and concentrated listening. Don't get in over your head, choose a song that's realistic for where you're at with hearing the changes.
2. "Live" with the recording for a while before picking up pencil and paper and trying to notate. You want to have a solid sense of the song memorized in your mind's ear before doing the translation work. I often refer to my mind's memory of the song rather than the live listening of the song, and do my notation work in the silent cracks, "playing back the tape in my memory" for reference. If you've taken this step, then you can recall the chord phrase at a slower, more manageable pace as you begin the translation process.
3. It's OK to use your instrument if you need to, especially when checking your work. Play the chords back, or play along with the recording, to see if there's a perfect match.
4. Using notation software such as Finale® has the wonderful built-in feature of playback, use it!
5. Use the pause button frequently, listening back to short phrases rather than overloading with too much information.
6. Take breaks, returning to the work with a pair of fresh ears and concentration. It's amazing what new things you'll hear on the second, third, fourth rounds… it's an ever-evolving process.
7. Invest in software that allows you to loop, slow down the music without changing the pitch, isolate and pan tracks etc. Ah, the wonders of modern technology, and very reasonably priced I might add!
8. Be organized in your approach to listening. Don't go for everything at once. Take the logical steps we've been practicing here: listening for the bass line first, and then using a combination of the vertical and horizontal approaches to determine chord quality.
9. Use your theoretical knowledge to limit the likely choices. In more cases than not, predictable patterns will occur in the chord progression.
10. "Patience is a virtue." The more transcribing you do, the faster and easier it will become. The resulting rewards are invaluable. Transcribing is a great way to get deeply inside the music and really understand its inner workings. Hang in there, it's totally worth it!

Activity Five *Rewind... Voice-Leading*

Voice-lead the changes to "Golden Slumbers," our mystery tune from the last chapter. Use the template given below to fill in your answers, then check with the answer key (Appendix: p. 129, Activity Five, CD1, track 49) to see how you did. Upon completion, sing the voice-led progression with classmates, "chorale" style. Be the fifth Beatle!

* voicing has been inverted here

For Your Consideration Discuss with your classmates the challenges and the benefits of transcribing the chord changes from the "real thing." What approaches do you find helpful when transcribing?

Making It Your Own Try identifying the chord progression to familiar songs using both the vertical and horizontal approaches. The combination effect is great.

7 Hearing Inversions of the I, IV and V Triads

Introduction

In this chapter we will work with inversions, when the bass note is not the root of the chord, when the chord is not in "root position." Inversions are trickier to hear, and we'll not be able to use our "bottom-up" approach as easily. This is where our work in the last two chapters of using the horizontal approach, listening for how chord tones sounds in relation to the key will come in handy. Let's continue our workout with hearing chord tones as solfege members of the key. We'll focus on hearing inversions of the I, IV and V major triads in this chapter.

Inversions

Let's begin with a couple of definitions. A triad is in "first inversion" when the third of the chord is the bottom note of the voicing. "Second inversion" has the fifth of the chord as the bottom note. As we saw in the last two chapters, when we voice-lead chord progressions, not all the chords will be in root position—several of them will result in inversions.

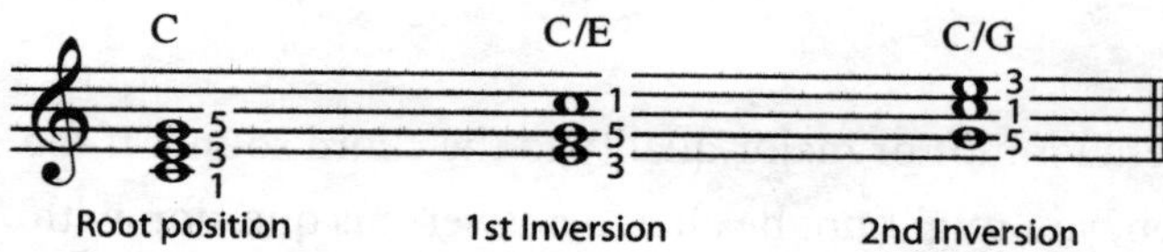

Tip When a triad is inverted, you can easily find the root: it will always be the top note of the interval of a fourth in the chord voicing.

Sometimes the bass line to a chord progression uses inversions to create stepwise connections from one chord to the next. Or in some cases, the bass note remains the same, called a "pedal tone," as the chords are changing above. Using inversions gives the bass line more opportunity for variations, rather than always stating the root of the chord.

As listeners, we can no longer assume the bass note is always the root of the chord, therefore our role as "chord detectives" becomes more challenging. Let's investigate the I, IV and V triads separately, determining a strategy for recognizing them when disguised as inversions. Ready, Dr. Watson?

Hearing the 1st and 2nd Inversions of the I Chord

Let's start with the 1st inversion of the I chord. How will we know if we're hearing root position III– or the first inversion of the I chord, I/3? Both have Mi as the bass note, and there are two common tones between them: Mi and Sol of the key.

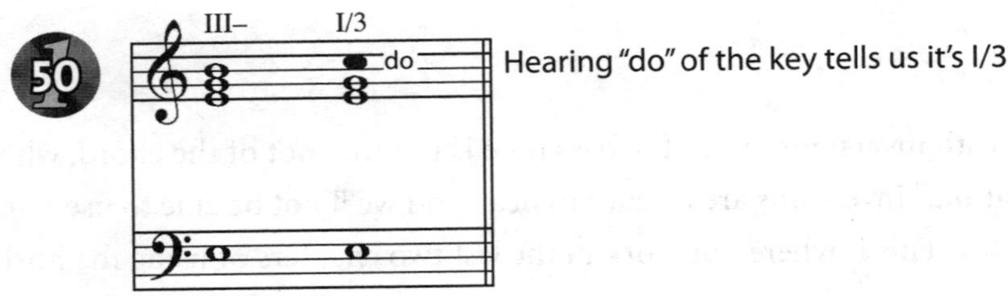

Note We will continue to label the chord structure with an upper case Roman numeral, but will use an Arabic number to indicate the specific inversion of the chord. This number will correspond to the root of the individual chord, not the overall key. In traditional harmony the I/3 chord is notated I^6_3, or abbreviated as I^6. This notation describes how the upper notes relate intervallically back to the bottom note of the voicing (a 6th and a 3rd). It's a good idea to be familiar with both notational systems in order to communicate in both worlds.

---

51 First determine if you hear an overall minor or major quality to the chord sound. If the chords are moving quickly in the progression, you might not be able to answer this question with confidence. This is where using the horizontal approach can help. If you hear Do of the key, then you're hearing the inversion, I/3. Do would clash with the sound of the III– chord. Check it out on CD1, track 51!

Many songs ("Still the One," Shania Twain; "Lady in Red," Chris deBurgh; "So Much Mine," The Story; and "Mercy, Mercy, Mercy," Joe Zawinul, just to name a few) use the following popular progression,

I | I/3 | IV | V or Vsus4,

in lieu of the root position pattern mentioned back in Chapter Three,

I | III– | IV | V.

Now let's work on hearing the 2nd inversion of the I chord and compare it with hearing the root position V chord. This is a bit more challenging because both chords are major triads. Again, using the horizontal approach will be necessary. If you hear Do of the key, it's the second inversion of the I chord, I/5; if you hear Ti, it's the V chord. Also, does the chord sound stable (tonic) or unstable (dominant) in the key? If stable, then it's probably I/5; the V chord is unstable in the key and usually wants to resolve back home to the I chord. Again, referring to your theoretical knowledge of how chords function within the key can be helpful with hearing such details.

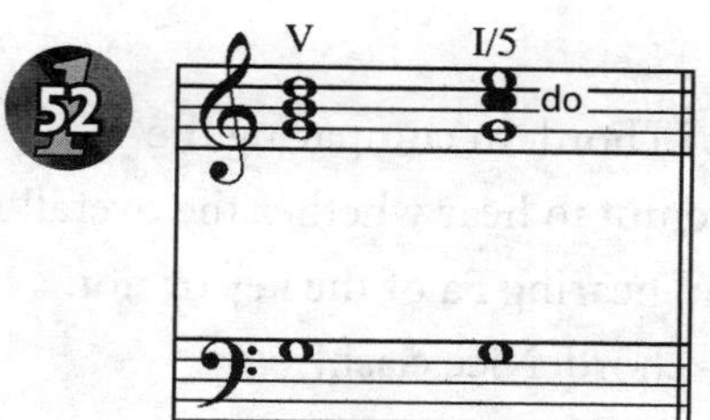

Note In the traditional world, I/5 is indicated as I^6_4 (once again, showing the intervals of a 6th and 4th from the upper notes to the bottom note of the voicing).

And if that isn't enough detail to keep straight, comparing the differences between the sounds of Vsus4 and I/5 is even more subtle because both chords contain Do of the key. In this case, harmonic context will play an important role. Does the chord sound stable or unstable? If stable, then it's the I/5 choice.

Before we work out with some full-length chord progressions, let's isolate the following choices. Are you hearing the root position III– or V chords, or inversions of the I chord?

Activity One *Hearing Inversions of the I Chord*

1. Listen to the ten examples in the key of F on CD1, track 53 and determine if you're hearing inversions of the I chord or their root position partners. You have four choices: I/3, III–, I/5 or V.
2. Remember to first establish the sound of the key in your ear before answering.
3. This is a great opportunity for you to keep practicing with solfege!
4. Check your results with the answer key (Appendix: p. 129, Activity One, CD1, track 53).

Here is a sample progression that uses inversions of the I chord; notice the stepwise connection in the bass line. To maximize the practice benefits, substitute the diatonic root position chords for the inversions (substituting III– for I/3; the V chord for I/5). Comparing the two versions back to back will really pronounce the subtle differences.

I | II– | I/3 | IV | I/5 | V | I

Inversions give us the opportunity to put the horizontal approach to good use, getting lots of practice with the translation process, converting solfege in the key to what that means on the individual chord. Next, let's explore inversions of the IV chord.

Hearing the 1st and 2nd Inversions of the IV Chord

We'll take the same approach here as we used for inversions of the I chord. In comparing the 1st inversion of the IV chord, IV/3, with root position VI–, first attempt to hear whether the overall chord sound is major or minor. As a second step to success, are you hearing Fa of the key or not? If you hear Fa, it's IV/3, if not, it's VI–. Try singing Fa over the VI– chord. Nice clash!

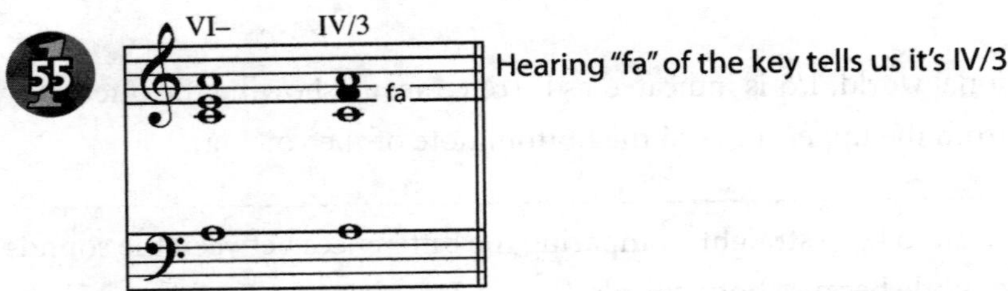

The 2nd inversion of the IV chord, IV/5, is quite common. You'll often hear it at the end of a chord phrase, just before resolving to the I chord (I, IV/5, I). This is called a "plagal cadence." We'll hear more of this pattern in the Bonus section coming up later in the chapter.

Comparing IV/5 with the root position I chord, both chords are major triads. But in this case, they have a different "feel" in the key. The I chord is stable (tonic), a point of rest in the key, where the IV chord is unstable (subdominant), wanting to move on towards a point of resolution. Using the horizontal approach, if you hear Fa of the key, it's IV/5, if not, it's the I chord. Put Fa to the test, does it clash or not with the chord sound?

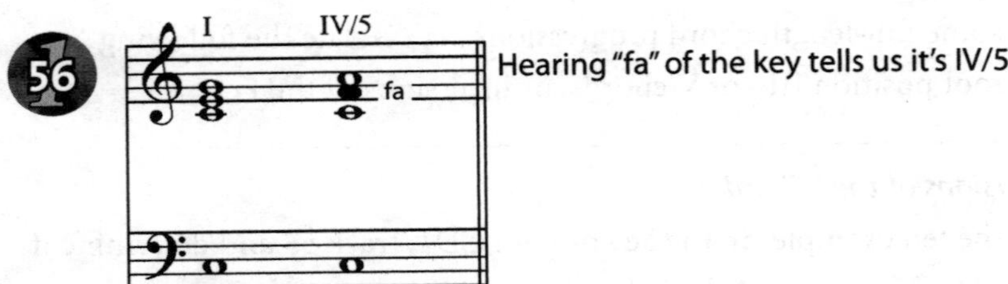

In the next activity, we'll work on hearing the differences between inversions of the subdominant IV chord, and the tonic functioning I and VI– chords.

Activity Two *Hearing Inversions of the IV Chord*

1. Listen to the following ten examples in the key of F on CD1, track 57. Determine whether you're hearing IV/3, VI–, IV/5 or the I chord.
2. Use a similar approach as in Activity One to determine the answers.
3. Check your answers with the key (Appendix: p. 129, Activity Two, CD1, track 57).

Here is a sample progression using inversions of the IV chord. Once again, notice the stepwise activity that results in the bass line, and the temporary tonic pedal tone at the end of the phrase.

I | III–/5 | IV/3 | V | I | IV/5 | I

Finally, let's give a listen to the inversions of the V chord.

Hearing the 1st and 2nd Inversions of the V Chord

Once again, let's compare the inversions of V/3 and V/5 to their root position counterparts. The big difference between hearing V/3 and root position VII° is the chord quality: one is a major triad, the other is a diminished triad. Also, listen for Sol of the key on the V/3. What's tricky is that both of these chords have a dominant function in the key, and in most cases both want to resolve back to the I chord.

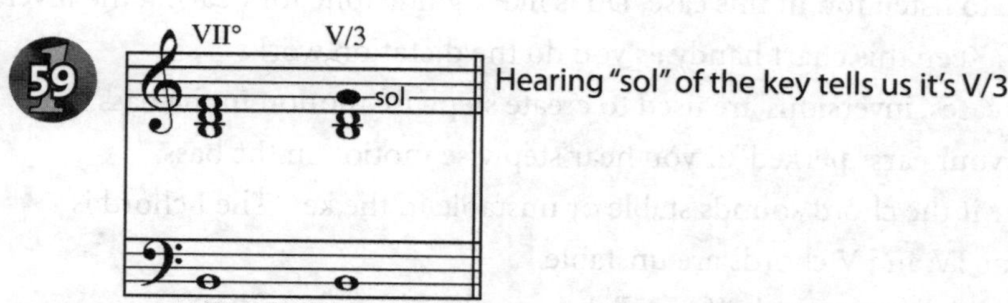

What note distinguishes V/5 from root position II– ? That's right, it's Ti of the key for the V/5. Also, listen to the overall chord quality: one is a major triad, the other is minor.

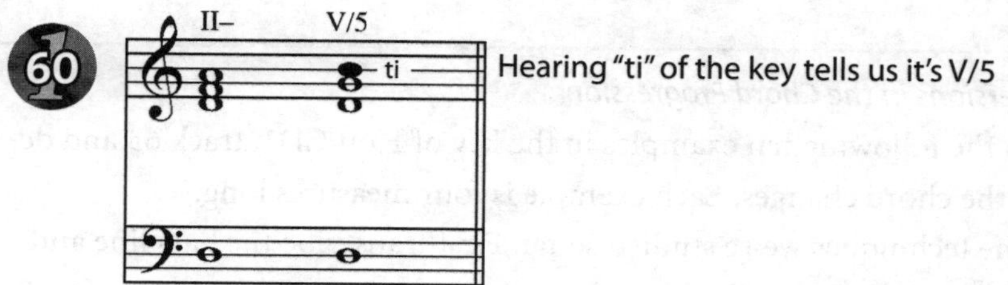

In the next activity we'll practice hearing the inversions of the V chord.

Activity Three *Hearing Inversions of the V Chord*

1. Listen to the following ten examples in the key of F on CD1, track 61. Your choices are now V/3, VII°, V/5 or II–.
2. Remember you have two ways to listen: one is hearing the overall chord quality; the other is hearing the specific note in the key that distinguishes one chord from the other.
3. Refer to the answer key (Appendix: p. 129, Activity Three, CD1, track 61) to see how you did.

In the following example, notice inversions of all three triads (I, IV and V), that result from the descending scale bass line. To get the most out of this practice, replace some of these inversions with their diatonic root position partners; it will give a slightly new twist to the harmonic movement. For example, by replacing the IV/3 with VI–, you'll change a subdominant function to a tonic function. How does this effect the overall forward motion of the chord progression?

I | V/3 | IV/3 | I/5 | IV | I/3 | V/5 | I | IV/5 | I

TIP Before we do a major workout with hearing inverted chords as part of the progression, here are a few suggestions and clues to consider.

1. There's a lot to keep straight and remember here! Make a chart of the inversions of the I, IV and V chords, and what features to remember when comparing them to their root position partners. For example, when comparing I/3 and III–, one sound is major, the other minor, and Do of the key is the distinctive note to listen for. In this case, Do is like a guide tone for hearing the inversion, I/3. Keep this chart handy as you do the dictation work.
2. In most cases, inversions are used to create stepwise motion in the bass line. So have your ears "perked" if you hear stepwise motion in the bass.
3. Consider if the chord sounds stable or unstable in the key. The I chord is stable; the IV and V chords are unstable.
4. If the chord sounds a little "funny," then maybe it's an inversion.

So let's try our hands, or rather, our ears, at some dictation work with progressions involving inversions. Good luck!

ACTIVITY FOUR *Hearing Inversions in the Chord Progression*

1. Listen to the following ten examples in the key of F on CD1, track 63 and determine the chord changes. Each example is four measures long.
2. Use all the techniques we've studied so far. First transcribe the bass line and then apply both the vertical and horizontal approaches when listening for the chord qualities.
3. If you've used the vertical approach in getting your answers, double-check using the horizontal approach.
4. It's often helpful to do some, rather than all of the examples, in one sitting. In this way your attention stays fresh each time you visit the progressions. Even double-checking your work on the next day sometimes reveals a new insight you didn't hear on the first round. In fact, pay particular attention to the second example, there's an inversion of the II– triad. Can you find it?
5. Check in with the answer key (Appendix: p. 129, Activity Four, CD1, track 63) for the results.

If you had some difficulty with this activity, use the answer key as a helpful guide for the "trouble spots."

STUMP THE BAND As you know, there's a lot of brainwork involved in determining whether you've heard an inversion or not. Quiz your classmates about the many features and clues involved with hearing inversions. Here are some samples questions to ask: What kind of bass line pattern is typical with inversions? What note of the key distinguishes a VI– from a IV/3? What's a plagal cadence? How do you hear the difference between a VII° and V/3, and what do they have in common? Exercise those brain cells!

Bonus

Let's "take it to the streets" and transcribe the changes to the following tunes. Each song excerpt features lots of inversions of the I, IV and V chords. Notice in most cases, the typical stepwise connection from one chord to the next using inversions. You'll get a wonderful workout as a result, and get to see these inversion patterns in action.

On the template below, answer using Roman numerals only, in order to focus in on the chord patterns that are featured. I recommend you first transcribe from the excerpts recorded on CD1, track 64 (a good "table setter") then listen to the "real thing." Check the answer key (Appendix: p. 130, Bonus, CD1, track 64).

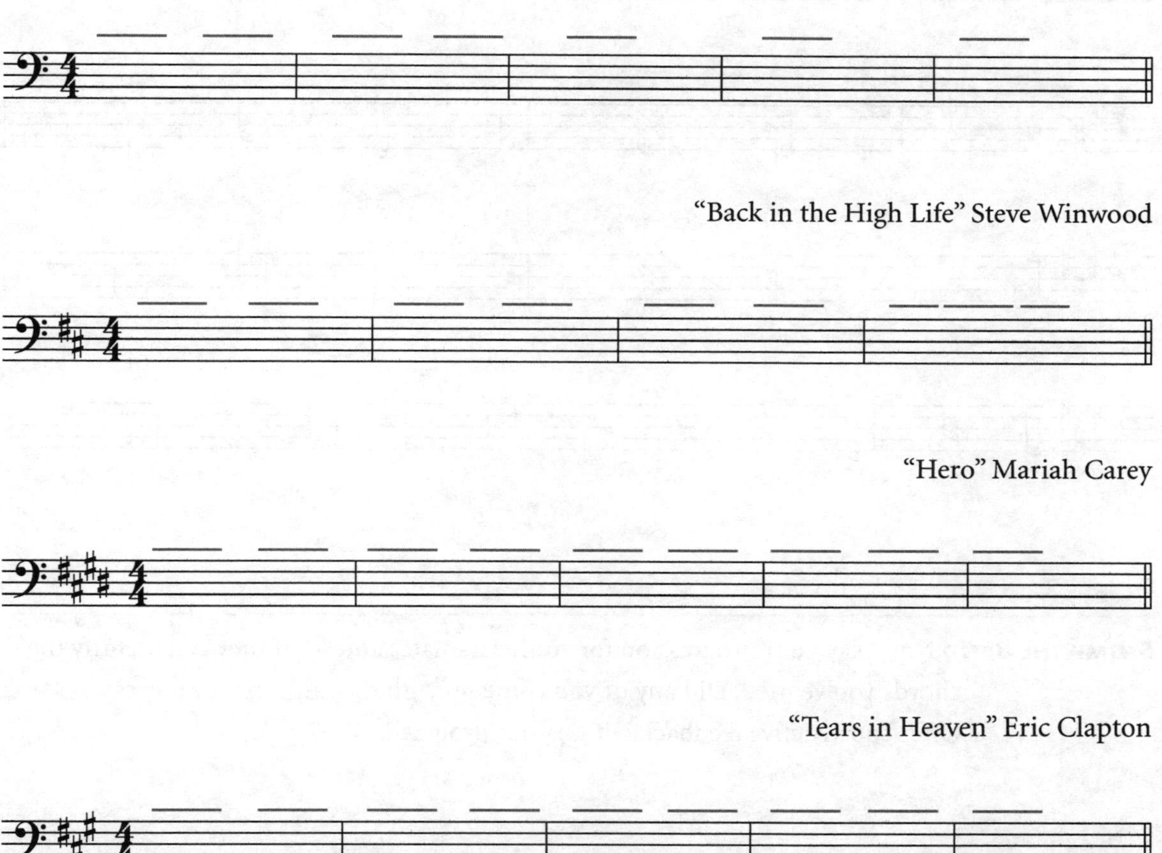

Activity Five *Write a Chord Progression, Including Inversions*

Write a chord progression to the following bass line, using a mix of both root position chords and inversions. As you attend to each individual bass note, also consider how the chords flow from one to the next within the phrase, creating a good balance of tension and rest. And remember, if you use inversions, they work best where the bass notes connect by stepwise motion. There are many good answers to this activity; I offer one possible solution in the answer key (Appendix: p. 131, Activity Five). Have fun!

Stump the Band Now play your progression for your classmates and see if they can identify the chords you've used. Did any of you come up with the same exact progression? Offer constructive feedback within your group.

Activity Six *Rewind... Determining the Changes from the Bass Line*

Determine the chords that are suggested by the following bass line. Pay particular attention to the notes on the downbeat of each measure, and look for arpeggios. Most bass notes will be chord tones, but not all. Check with the answer key (Appendix: p. 131, Activity Six.) to see if you match. Then try writing your own walking bass line to the same chord progression. Have the bass player in your band play through your line. How does it sound? Does it clearly outline the changes?

You've come a long way since Chapter One! At this point, you've explored the many ways diatonic triads can act in the chord progression, and have done a thorough workout with both the vertical (bottom-up) and horizontal (melodic) approaches to hearing the changes. In the next chapter we'll take a look and listen to how closely the melody and harmony relate to each other, and explore using the "top-down" approach to determine the accompanying chords. In many cases, melody is harmony, and harmony is melody. They go hand in hand, let's give a listen!

For Your Consideration Discuss with your classmates the benefits of using inversions in the chord progression. How can inversions play a role in reharmonizing song arrangements?

Making It Your Own Discover songs that use inversions in the chord progression. Look at lead sheets, or better yet, transcribe examples. It has been my experience that folk, country, pop and rock music have lots of examples of inversions; they are not so common in jazz standards.

Melody and Harmony Relationship

Introduction

In previous chapters, we've used the vertical ("bottom-up") and horizontal approaches for figuring out the chord changes. In this chapter, we'll take a "top-down" approach, listening to how the melody relates to the harmony. In most cases, important melody notes are chord tones of the accompanying chord progression. Rather than having to dig deep into the inner voices of the chord progression, let's see what the top line, the melody, has to say. Often, the melody is shouting out the harmonic answer; let's take a look and a listen.

Melody Is Harmony

Melody and harmony work together like ebony and ivory. In most songs, the majority of melody notes will be chord tones of the accompanying harmony. In fact, composers most often create the melody of the song first, and then develop a chord progression to support this melody as the second step. The melody notes will "invite," or strongly suggest what chords to use in the harmony. Let's take a look and a listen to the following examples, noting how many of the melody notes are chord tones.

Activity One *Identify the Chord Tones in the Melody*

1. Indicate the melody notes that represent chord tones of the accompanying progressions by labeling whether these chord tones are the root, third or fifth of the chord.
2. Listen to how easily the melody and chords work together, sharing a similar harmonic intention.
3. When checking the answer key (Appendix: p. 132, Activity One, CD1, track 65), notice that the majority of melody notes are chord tones.

Activity One *(cont'd)*

* non-diatonic chord

You might have noticed that not every melody note is a chord tone. But typically the "important" melody notes may be. What makes melody notes important? They may have long durations, may fall on strong beats (particularly beat one), and they may be leapt away from, or not always connected by stepwise motion. In other words, these are the melodic notes that stand out to your ear when listening.

Bonus Take a look and a listen to songs you're familiar with and analyze the relationship of the melody to the chords. Without a doubt, you'll notice how the majority of the melody notes will be chord tones. Looking at the "real thing" will make a believer out of you, as it did me. In addition to the melodies we looked at in Chapter Five ("All of Me," "Goodbye to Yellow Brick Road," "Blueberry Hill," and "Here, There and Everywhere"), the following song excerpts leave little doubt as to the accompanying chords.

"Because" Lennon & McCartney

"Up, Up and Away" Jimmy Webb

HOOKING UP WITH *THE REAL EASY BOOK* Pick any song in the book and investigate the relationship between melody notes and accompanying chords. You'll find that the majority of melody notes represent chord tones. Check out the following songs for a particularly tight relationship between melody and harmony: "Jo Jo Calypso," "Listen Here," "Little Sunflower," "Shoshana," and "When the Saints Go Marching In."

At times, composers will create the chord progression first, and then write the melody. Or when players improvise, they will often create a line that accesses the chord progression for inspiration, outlining the harmony. Once again, here are examples of how tight the relationship is between melody and harmony, this time with the harmony taking the lead.

ACTIVITY TWO *Improvise Over the Changes*

Here is a short solo I wrote over the following changes. Let's "trade some eights" and see what you can come up with as well. Here's my solo…

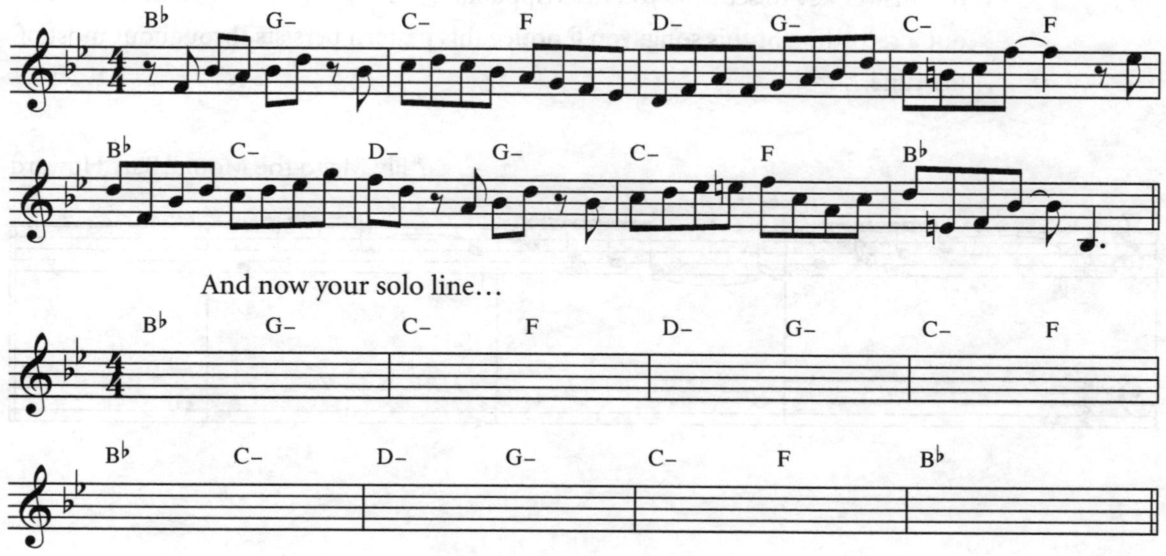

Trade your solos from Activity Two with classmates or band members. Start with your written solo lines and then branch out from there, playing some improvised lines on the spot. Go a few rounds and let your ears get warmed up to the changes.

Transcribing the Melody for Harmonic Information

Considering how closely melody and harmony work hand in hand, the melody can often provide important clues about the accompanying chord changes. When transcribing a song from a recording, it can be very difficult to hear what the changes are simply from listening to the rhythm section. There's so much sound to "sift" through, and making sense of it all can be both ear and mind boggling. Often the melody shouts out the answer, if we'd only pay attention to it, making our ear training lives just a little bit brighter!

Using the "top-down" approach, it can be helpful to first transcribe the melody, looking for harmonic clues. This is especially true with melodies that clearly arpeggiate the chords, as we have seen earlier. The melody, coupled with the bass line, is often enough information for determining much of the harmony of the song. Let's try this approach with the following three examples where we hear only the melody and bass lines.

Activity Three *Transcribe the Melody and Bass Line to Determine the Chords*

1. Listen to the following three examples on CD1, track 66 and transcribe the melody and bass lines. These examples are in three different keys: #1 in G, #2 in C and #3 in E♭.
2. Then, determine what these two lines suggest for the chord changes.
3. Don't get fancy, go with the obviously suggested chords for your answer; we can reharmonize on another day.
4. Check with the answer key (Appendix: p. 132, Activity Three, CD1, track 66) to see how you did.

Bonus Here is the melody and root motion to the opening four bars of "Fly Me to the Moon." Can you figure out the changes? Hint: you'll see a consistent pattern between the downbeat melody notes and the accompanying bass line. Check with the answer key to see how you did (Appendix: p. 133, Bonus). If you can, check out a recording of this song; you'll notice this pattern persists throughout most of the tune.

"Fly Me to the Moon" Bart Howard

Harmonizing the Melody

Now let's get creative and come up with the chord changes to the following melody. Here are some things to consider in the process. First, think simple! Simple melodies most often invite simple harmonies. Look for chord choices the melody suggests; in other words, look for possible chord tones in the melody. Second, consider how the chords hook up with each other in the chord phrase. Is there a good flow of tension and rest in the chord progression itself? Third, if the melody suggests a point of rest, have you chosen a tonic chord? If the melody suggests unrest, have you chosen a subdominant or dominant functioning chord? Fourth, how does the bass line sound; have you used any inversions?

There is no one absolute correct answer to this activity, but there are some general guidelines that thread through the variety of good choices. The answer key (Appendix: p. 134, Activity Four, CD1, track 68) will suggest a couple of possibilities. Have some fun with this!

Activity Four *Create a Chord Progression to the Following Melody*

1. Keeping in mind all of the above considerations, harmonize the following melody (CD1, track 67).
2. Make sure to play through your choices of chords with the melody; some will work better than others if you give a listen. This is not simply a theoretical exercise—get your ears involved!
3. Compare your version with the answer key (Appendix: p. 134, Activity Four, CD1, track 68). Remember there is no one perfect answer, and it is often more interesting to see how different versions are equally good choices.
4. Have some creative fun with this, but above all, listen to what the melody has to say!

Stump the Band Play your set of changes for your classmates to identify. Did some of them have a similar version to what you came up with? Were there any that were quite different? Perform this song with your band, using your changes.

Activity Five *Determine the Changes to a Song from Memory*

Figure out the chords to song melodies you're familiar with. Using your listening memory of the song, you'll have the added advantage of a sense of what the answer is. Follow the steps you used in Activity Four, but also use your memory. When playing through your choices, your listening memory might say, "Yes, that's exactly the chord," or it might say, "Hmm, no, that's not it, I think it should be a minor chord here rather than major."

When in doubt, remember to keep it simple, "Less is more" is a good rule of thumb, and use the obvious choices when possible. You will definitely need to play through your choices, letting your aural memory of the song decide if you've come up with the right chords. Though there may be several theoretical possibilities, there is probably only one "right" answer that will match your memory of the way the song goes.

Here is what I've come up with for the changes to everyone's favorite song: "Happy Birthday!"

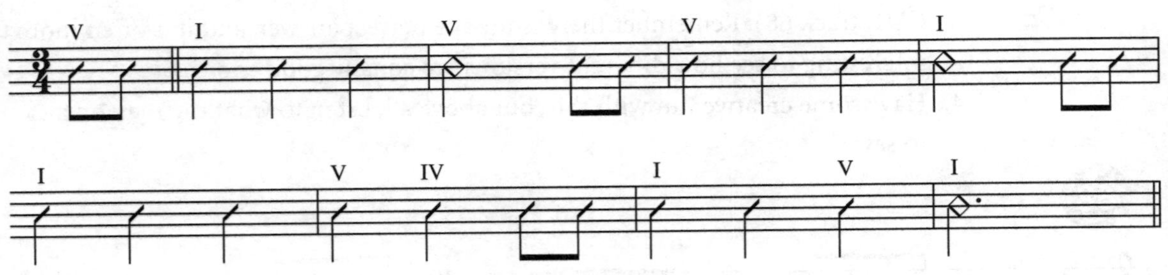

Activity Six *Rewind... Inversions*

1. Listen to the following "chorale style" progression in the key of G on CD1, track 69.
2. Using the template provided on the next page, transcribe each of the four lines. I recommend you first determine the bass and soprano lines, then the inner lines (alto and tenor). The outside lines (bass and melody) are easier to hear, and will give clues about what the inner lines might be.
3. Then label the resulting chords with chord symbols and Roman numeral analysis; indicate inversions when they occur. As is typical in this chorale style arrangement, you'll find many inversions.
4. Check with the answer key to see how you did (Appendix: p. 134, Activity Six, CD1, track 69).
5. Finally, sing the chorale with classmates. Because most lines are voice-led, you will find the lines easy to sing.

In the next two chapters, we will add one more chord tone to the mix, the 7th. In this lesson's work, some of the melody notes that you did not identify as members of triads are in fact the 7th of seventh chords.

FOR YOUR CONSIDERATION Talk with your classmates about composing. When writing a song, do you create the melody or harmony first, or a little bit of both?

MAKING IT YOUR OWN Continue to figure out the changes to song melodies you're familiar with, using the techniques recommended in Activity Five.

9 Hearing Seventh Chords

Introduction

In this chapter we will be adding one more note to the chord structure, developing the triad into a seventh chord. Knowing your triads inside out at this point will serve you well as we work on building and recognizing seventh chords. It's much more than simply adding one more note to the mix: there are several different kinds of seventh chords to become familiar with. Also, it will often be challenging to distinguish between triads and seventh chords.

We will pull out all the stops with our work with seventh chords in these next two chapters: examining seventh chords from both a vertical and horizontal approach; recognizing the seven diatonic seventh chords in the major scale; voice-leading guide tone lines that incorporate both the 3rd and 7th of the chords; introducing the passing 7th in the bass line that continues our work with inversions; and, recognizing the tight bond between the melody and seventh chord harmony. This is quite an "earful" to tackle and will require many weeks (months!) to fully accomplish, so hang in there as we begin our work with hearing seventh chords.

Hearing the Major 7th and Dominant 7th Chords

We have spent the last several weeks working with triads, and by this point I imagine you're starting to feel pretty confident about your ability to recognize diatonic triadic harmony. Now let's expand our knowledge by learning to hear diatonic seventh chord harmony. Essentially, seventh chords are extensions of triads, adding either a major or minor seventh interval above the root of the triad. Let's begin by working with major 7th and dominant 7th chord structures, and how they function in the major key as Imaj7, IVmaj7 and V7.

The Major 7th Chord Sound

To build a major 7th chord, we start with a major triad, and then add a major seventh interval above the root.

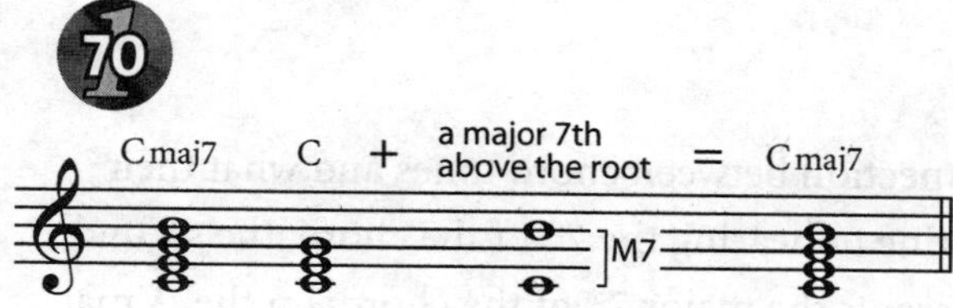

Note With major 7th chords, we will use the following chord symbol:

C (the triad) plus maj7 = Cmaj7.

At times, you might see CM7 or CΔ7 as alternative chord symbols.

In a major key, we find two diatonic major 7th chords: Imaj7 (Do, Mi, Sol, Ti) and IVmaj7 (Fa, La, Do, Mi).

Activity One *Write Out the Imaj7 and IVmaj7 Chords*

1. Write out the Imaj7 and IVmaj7 chords in the following keys. As you write, sing the solfege for each chord: "do, mi, sol, ti" for Imaj7; "fa, la, do, mi" for IVmaj7.
2. Play these major 7th chords on your instrument or keyboard and sing the root position arpeggios, again, using solfege.
3. Compare playing the triad version and major 7th chords, listening for the more "dissonant" sound of the major 7th chord. You will discover that certain musical styles, such as jazz, will make frequent use of this richer, major 7th chord sound.

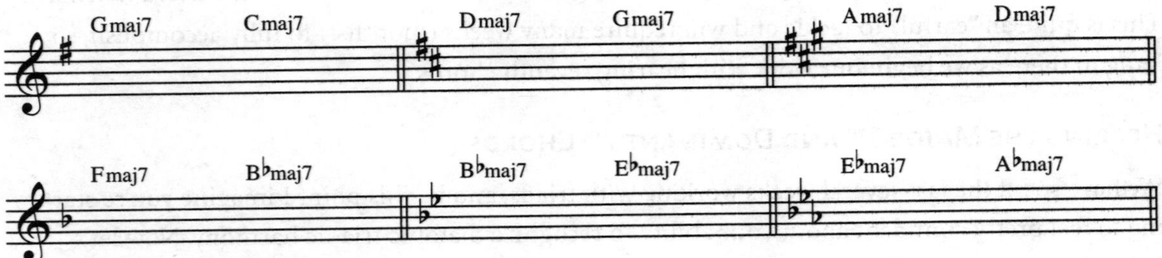

Note Here are a few songs that feature the major 7th sound for your listening pleasure: "Litha," Chick Corea; "Inner Urge," Joe Henderson; "Imagine," John Lennon; "Little Sunflower," Freddie Hubbard; "It's Too Late," Carol King; "Watch What Happens," Michel Legrand; "Dindi," Antonio Jobim; and "Lady Bird," Tadd Dameron (which features standard turn-around changes: Imaj7, ♭IIImaj7, ♭VImaj7, ♭IImaj7).

The 7th as a Second Guide Tone

You can never get enough practice making the connection between chord tones and what their sound represents in the key. We will apply this routine to hearing the 7th of the chord, the second guide tone. On the Imaj7 chord, Ti of the key represents the major 7th of the chord; on the IVmaj7 chord, Mi represents the major 7th chord tone. Along with the 3rd of each chord, we will be adding the 7th as a second guide tone that defines the essential sound of the chord.

Listen to the following voice-led progression between the Imaj7 and IVmaj7 chords, paying particular attention to the two guide tone lines that incorporate the 3rds and 7ths: Ti (7th) to La (3rd) back to Ti (7th), and Mi sustaining throughout as the 3rd, then becoming the 7th, and back to the 3rd.

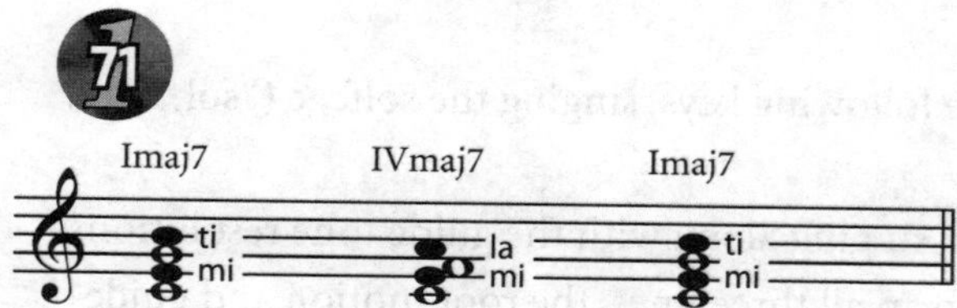

The Dominant 7th Chord Sound

The dominant 7th chord is the most popular seventh chord structure: in the major scale, it occurs as the V7 chord, and is especially prominent in blues harmony.

To build a dominant 7th chord, we start with a major triad, and then add a minor seventh interval above the root.

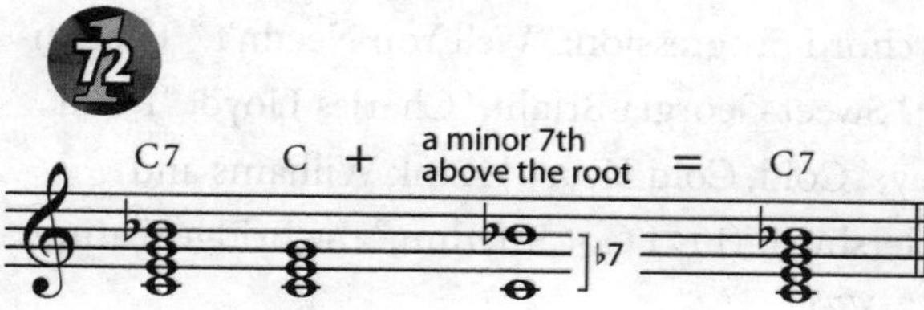

Note There is only one standard chord symbol for the dominant 7th chord: C (the triad) plus 7 (which assumes to be a ♭7 interval above the root) = C7.

In a major scale, we find one diatonic dominant 7th chord, V7, which contains Sol, Ti, Re and Fa of the key.

The Tritone Interval

On a dominant 7th chord, the ♭7 joins the 3rd as a second guide tone. The interval created between the 3rd and ♭7 is called the "tritone" because of the three whole steps that exist between these two notes. It is this dissonant tritone interval that best defines the sound of the dominant 7th chord. In the major scale, Fa of the key represents the ♭7 on the V7 chord. In the dominant cadence of V7 to I, Ti resolves up to Do as Fa resolves down to Mi.

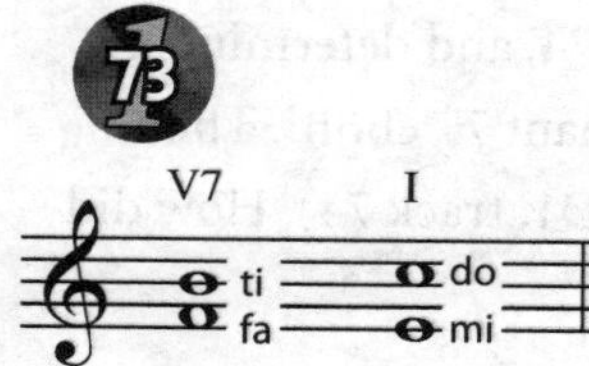

Activity Two *Write Out the V7 Chord*

1. Write out the V7 chords in the following keys, singing the solfege ("sol, ti, re, fa") as you write.
2. Now play V7 to I in these keys, singing along with the guide tone resolutions of Ti to Do and Fa to Mi. Perform all three lines, the root motion and guide tone line resolutions along with classmates, "chorale" style, for the complete experience.

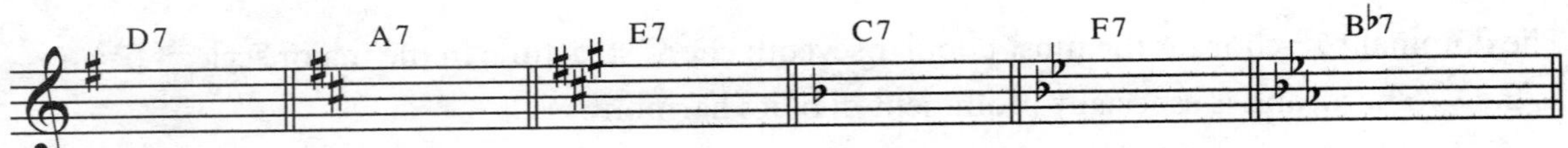

Note Along with the blues, here are many other songs that feature the dominant 7th sound exclusively throughout the chord progression: "Well You Needn't," Thelonious Monk; "Doxy," Sonny Rollins; "Sweet Georgia Bright," Charles Lloyd; "I Call Your Name," Lennon & McCartney; "Cold, Cold Heart," Hank Williams and "I Got Rhythm," George and Ira Gershwin (in "I Got Rhythm," the bridge features cycle 5 dominant 7ths: III7, VI7, II7, V7).

Bonus Play through the standard 12 bar blues form first using triads, and then dominant 7th chords, hearing how the seventh chord version takes on a richer, and in some ways, more authentic sound.

Hooking Up with *The Real Easy Book* Listen and play through the many blues selections featured throughout *The Real Easy Book.* Notice how the melody also highlights the dominant 7th sound, particularly in the following songs: "Blue Seven," Sonny Rollins; "Blues By Five," Red Garland; and "Red's Good Groove," Red Garland.

Tip Here's a helpful strategy to follow when figuring out if the chord is a triad or a seventh chord, or if the 7th is a major or minor 7th. Listen for the 7th as a step below the root. A major seventh interval inverts to a minor second; a minor seventh interval inverts to a major second.

If the chord progression is moving by quickly, we need to use the easiest and quickest approach to determine the answer. It is easier, and therefore faster, to identify small vs. large intervals.

Activity Three *Identify Major Triad, Major 7th or Dominant 7th Chords*

Listen to the following ten chord examples on CD1, track 74, and determine if you're hearing a major triad, a major 7th chord, or a dominant 7th chord. Then check the answer key (Appendix: p. 135, Activity Three, CD1, track 74). How did you do? Did you find the Tip helpful?

The V7sus4 chord follows a similar construction pattern as the V7. It is a sus4 triad with a minor seventh interval added above the root.

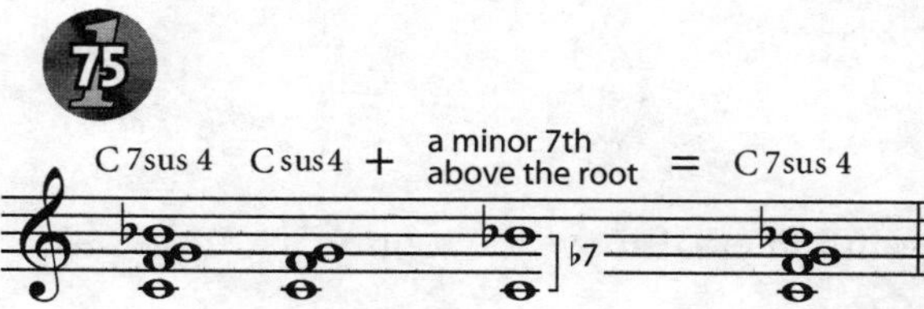

Note Check out the following songs that feature the V7sus4 sound: "Maiden Voyage," Herbie Hancock; "My Cherie Amour," Stevie Wonder; "Passion Dance," McCoy Tyner; and "Red Clay," Freddie Hubbard.

Now let's do some dictation work that will incorporate these three new seventh chords Imaj7, IVmaj7, and V7 into the diatonic mix.

Activity Four *Progression Dictation Including Imaj7, IVmaj7 and V7*

Listen to the following ten examples in the key of G on CD1, track 76 and identify the chords. Each example is four measures long. As is our usual routine, start with identifying the bass line, then…

1. Using the vertical approach, do you hear the simplicity of a triad or something richer in the chord texture?
2. If you detect a richer sound, sing down a half step (for the maj7) or a whole step (for the dominant 7th) to determine if a 7th exists, and if so, which one.
3. Using the horizontal approach, do you hear Ti of the key for Imaj7; do you hear Mi of the key for IVmaj7; do you hear Fa of the key for V7? Don't wait until the last minute to ask these questions; prepare ahead of time so that you'll be ready to receive the answer when the chord in question comes along.
4. And remember, for now we're only adding the possibility of these three diatonic seventh chords to the mix, the remaining chords will be triads (II–, III–, VI–, VII°).
5. Now check the answer key to see how you did (Appendix: p. 135, Activity Four, CD1, track 76).

Hearing the Minor 7th and Min7♭5 Chords

We will continue using the same approach to building minor 7th and minor 7♭5 chords as we did with major 7th and dominant 7th chords, and thus complete our palette of diatonic seventh chords in the major scale.

The Minor 7th Chord Sound

A minor 7th chord is a minor triad plus a minor seventh interval above the root.

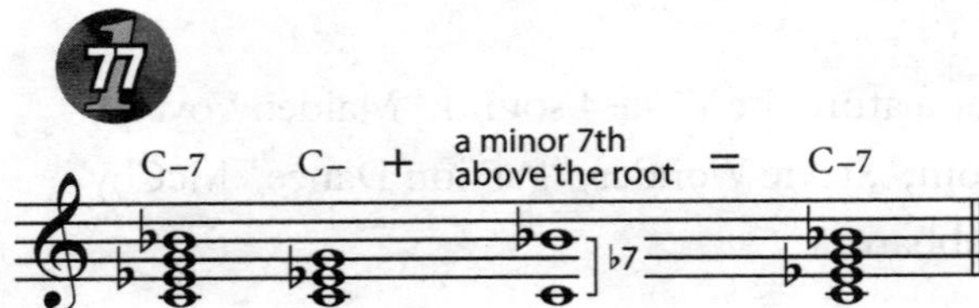

Note We will use C–7 to indicate minor 7th chords:

C– (the triad) plus 7 (assumed to be ♭7) = C–7.

At times you might see Cm7 , Cmi7, or Cmin7 as alternate chord symbols.

There are three diatonic minor 7th chords in the major scale: II–7, III–7 and VI–7. Once again, it is good practice to write out these three new seventh chords in the additional keys of G, D, A, F, B♭ and E♭, singing the solfege as you write to reinforce the connection between sound and solfege names for the chord tones.

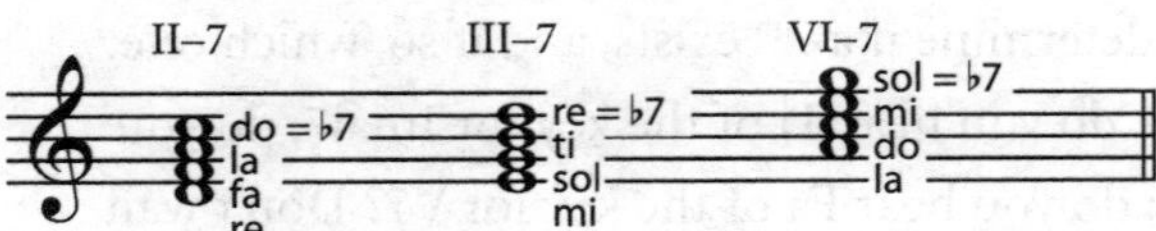

Memorize the ♭7 guide tone for each of these minor 7th chords: Do is the ♭7 on the II–7; Re is the ♭7 on the III–7; Sol is the ♭7 on the VI–7. Remember, these ♭7's can be heard as a whole step below the root of each chord, rather than taking the time to climb up the full chord structure (1, ♭3, 5, ♭7). By that time, it's often too late as the chord has gone by already in the progression.

Note The following songs feature the minor 7th sound: "Impressions," John Coltrane; "Lately," Stevie Wonder; "Little B's Poem," Bobby Hutcherson; "Stolen Moments," Oliver Nelson; "Time Remembered," Bill Evans; and "Take Five," Dave Brubeck.

The Minor 7♭5 Chord Sound

Let's complete our palette of diatonic seventh chords with the minor 7♭5 chord. It consists of a diminished triad plus a minor seventh interval above the root.

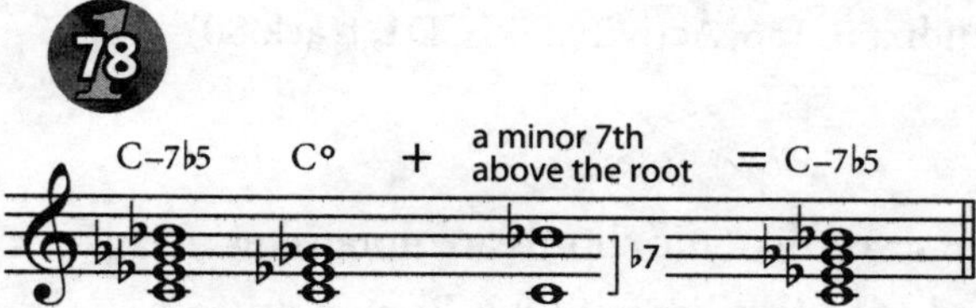

Note C–7♭5 is the standard chord symbol for a minor 7♭5 chord. It is sometimes, though rarely, notated as a "half-diminished" chord (Cø7).

This chord appears only once in the major scale: it is VII–7♭5 (Ti, Re, Fa, La of the key).

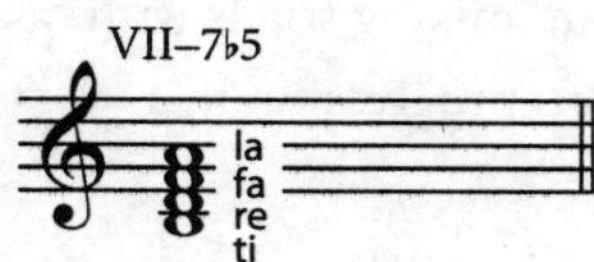

In the case of the minor 7♭5 chord, we often add ♭5 as a third guide tone along with the ♭3 and ♭7, to bring out its uniqueness. With VII–7♭5, Fa of the key represents this ♭5 chord tone.

Note Listen to the following songs for examples of the minor 7♭5 sound: "Gloria's Step," Scott LaFaro; "What Is This Thing Called Love?" Cole Porter; "Woody'n You," Dizzie Gillespie; "Alone Again (Naturally)," Gilbert O'Sullivan; and "If I Were A Bell," Frank Loesser.

Tip Before doing Activity Five, spend some time comparing the sound of minor and diminished triads to their seventh chord partners. This distinction can be tricky at times. I often hear students say that they're not sure whether they actually hear the added ♭7 or are imagining it as a cooperative sound to the triad. It is hearing these subtle differences between triads and seventh chords that can test our patience at times!

Activity Five *Identify Minor or Diminished Triads, Minor 7th or Minor 7♭5 Chords*

Listen to the following ten chord examples on CD1, track 79 and determine if you're hearing a minor triad, a minor 7th chord, a diminished triad or a minor 7♭5 chord. Then check in with the answer key for results (Appendix: p. 135, Activity Five, CD1, track 79).

Let's put all the diatonic seventh chords to work in the next activity!

Activity Six *Progression Dictation Including All Diatonic Seventh Chords*

Listen to the following ten examples in the key of F on CD1, track 80. Each example is four measures long. Identify the chords with both chord symbols and Roman numerals. For now, all chords will be diatonic seventh chords, no triads. Then check the answer key (Appendix: p. 136, Activity Six, CD1, track 80) to see how you did.

Note In the classical harmony world, the seven diatonic chords are notated as : I7, ii7, iii7, IV7, V7, vi7, and vii7. It is good to be familiar with this Roman numeral approach as well; it will enable you to communicate with musicians who have been trained in this traditional system of chord analysis.

Activity Seven *Comparing Triads with Seventh Chords*

Play the following progression, first as only triads, then as all seventh chords, and finally mixing them up for comparison and variety. This will set the table for the next chapter where we will do a thorough dictation workout, mixing triads with seventh chords throughout the progressions. Try playing this progression in a variety of keys as well.

I | VI– | II– | V | I | III– | IV | V | I | IV | VII° | III– | VI– | II– | Vsus4 | V | I

Stump the Band Play your mixed version of this progression and see if your classmates or band members can identify what you're playing. Triads or seventh chords, that is the question.

Activity Eight *Rewind... Harmonize the Melody*

Harmonize the following 16 bar melody, incorporating a mix of diatonic triads and seventh chords. As a result, the majority of melody notes should represent chord tones. There are several correct solutions to this assignment. Compare your version with those of classmates and band members. Play them!

For You Consideration Discuss with your classmates your own strategies for hearing the differences between triadic and seventh chord harmonies. What styles of music would you recommend listening to for examples of seventh chord harmony?

Making It Your Own In order to put the sound of seventh chord harmony into your ears, put them under your fingers and into your playing as much as possible. There is no substitute for "hands-on" practice!

10 More on Hearing Seventh Chords

Introduction

In Chapter Nine we began building and recognizing major 7th, dominant 7th, minor 7th and minor 7♭5 chords, and identifying them within the major key as: Imaj7, II–7, III–7, IVmaj7, V7, VI–7 and VII–7♭5. Along with the 3rd of each chord, we added the 7th as the second "guide tone" for recognizing the chord quality. Applying the horizontal approach, we learned to identify this second guide tone via its solfege placement within the key. Often the trickiest challenge is determining whether a particular chord is a triad or seventh chord! We then wrapped up Chapter Nine with some progression dictation work, "a drop in the bucket's worth." There's much more dictation practice to come in this chapter.

In addition to more dictation practice with progressions which mix triads with seventh chords, we will delve more deeply into voice-leading the guide tones of seventh chords, add the concept of the "passing 7th" to our work with inversions, and continue our discussion of the relationship of melody and harmony, this time involving seventh chords. Let's begin our work with voice-leading the guide tone lines of seventh chords.

Voice-Leading the Guide Tones, the 3rd and 7th, of Seventh Chords

First, let's use the following chart to review what notes in the key (via solfege) represent the guide tones. With lots of practice and experience, you will eventually have this information memorized, but for now, having this chart handy for referral will be very helpful.

Seventh Chord Guide Tone Chart

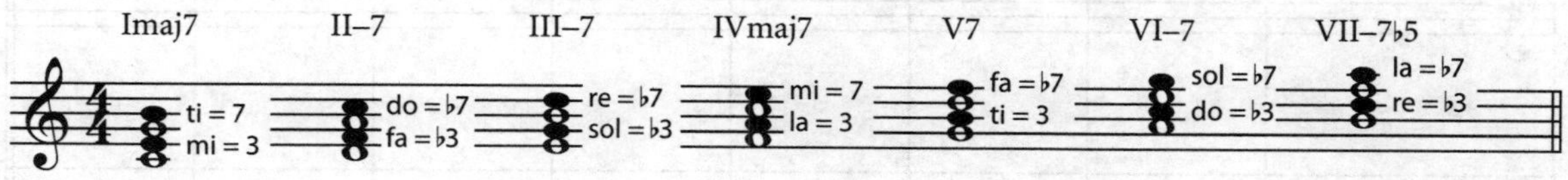

Activity One *Voice-Leading Guide Tone Lines with the Cycle 5 Pattern*

Here are the seven diatonic seventh chords organized with the familiar cycle 5 pattern. This time, we will only work with hearing the root motion and the voice-led guide tone lines, the 3rds and 7ths of each chord. With this particular cycle, you will notice the "perfect" voice-leading pattern that results, with either common tone or stepwise motion occurring from guide tone to guide tone. You will also notice in this chord pattern that the guide tones alternate between being the 3rd and then the 7th.

(Activity One cont'd)

1. Listen to the example above that uses voice-led guide tone lines, noticing the smooth connection from one chord to the next.
2. Now sing along with each line, using solfege syllables. You will notice that the voice-led guide tone lines are easy to sing because of the common tone or stepwise motion that results. With classmates, perform all three lines as an ensemble.
3. Using solfege, now transpose this pattern to two other keys. Use the blank staves below, choosing keys you find "user," or "instrumentally" friendly.
4. Memorize this pattern and try to play it in different keys without reading.

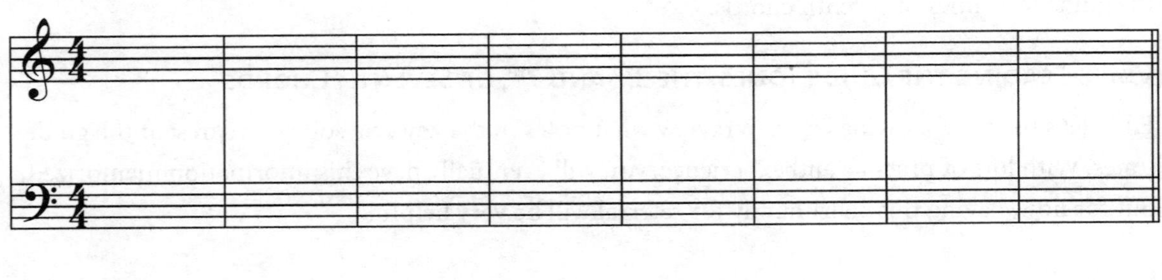

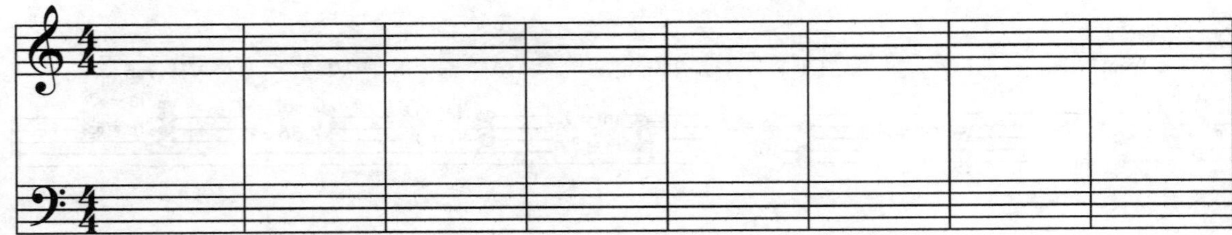

Bonus Sing this voice-led pattern along with recordings of some of the cycle 5 songs we've worked with previously: "Autumn Leaves," "Alice in Wonderland" (start the cycle with II–7); "You Never Give Me Your Money," "Fly Me to the Moon" and "I Will Survive"(start the cycle with VI–7).

In earlier chapters, we addressed only the triads, but in fact, the majority of the chords are seventh chords in these song selections. Singing along with the guide tone lines will help the ear "pull out" the sound of the 7ths from the recording. These 7ths might otherwise remain hidden, buried within the overall sound.

Note This "perfect" (cycle 5) voice-leading situation does not occur with all chord patterns. At times you'll need to choose between smooth voice-leading (incorporating chord tones other than the 3rd or 7th), or using only the guide tones, which might not result in such smooth voice-leading.

Activity Two *Root and Guide Tone Dictation of Seventh Chords*

Listen to the following ten progressions in the key of B♭ on CD2, track 2. Each example is four measures long. Only the root and voice-led guide tone lines will be played. Transcribe all three lines and indicate the resulting chord symbols. For the ultimate workout, label the guide tones with solfege as well.

1. First, identify the bass line. For these examples, only root position chords will be used.
2. Some of you will recognize the overall color of the chord first, which will then help lead you to hearing the specific guide tone notes, the 3rds and 7ths. In this case, the vertical approach is taking the lead.
3. Others will use the horizontal approach first, identifying the two guide tone lines, the specific notes, and then concluding what the overall chord sound is. In this case, I recommend listening to the top line first, then the middle line. It is my experience that many students have the toughest time hearing the inner line. If you have the two outside lines established, then with a little help from your theory knowledge, you can almost predict what the middle line will be.
4. Check with the answer key (Appendix: p. 136, Activity Two, CD2, track 2) to see how well you did. Now it's time to sing and/or play through these examples for additional practice.

Bonus Write out the voice-led guide tone lines to one of your favorite songs that uses seventh chord harmony. Then play these lines along with a recording of the song. These voice-led guide tone lines make for wonderful beginnings for background vocal or horn lines in arrangements. For examples, listen to jazz quintet and sextet recordings from the 1950's and 60's. Many of the background horn lines are simple guide tone lines, often made up on the spot by ear by these wonderfully talented musicians. Join the club, and try this with your own band.

Activity Three *Singing Root Position Arpeggios of Seventh Chords*

Sing and play through the following cycle 5 patterns. The first progression features root position arpeggios that are linked from root to root. The second pattern "voice-leads" the arpeggios, going up one chord and then down the next, producing a more melodic result. These arpeggios are the beginnings of hearing seventh chords as melodic phrases rather than as vertical structures.

Bonus Experiment with embellishing these arpeggios with passing tones, and other approach note patterns, as a way to develop improvisational ideas "over the changes." As an example, here's something I came up with, this time in the key of C.

Now let's check out how melody and the chord changes go hand in hand with seventh chord harmonies.

Relationship of Melody and Harmony

As with triads, the melody will often give us many clues about the accompanying chords. Many melodies will feature the 7th of the chord, and in some cases even present the full arpeggio. Let's take a look at a few examples.

The following melodic excerpts feature the major 7th chord sound.

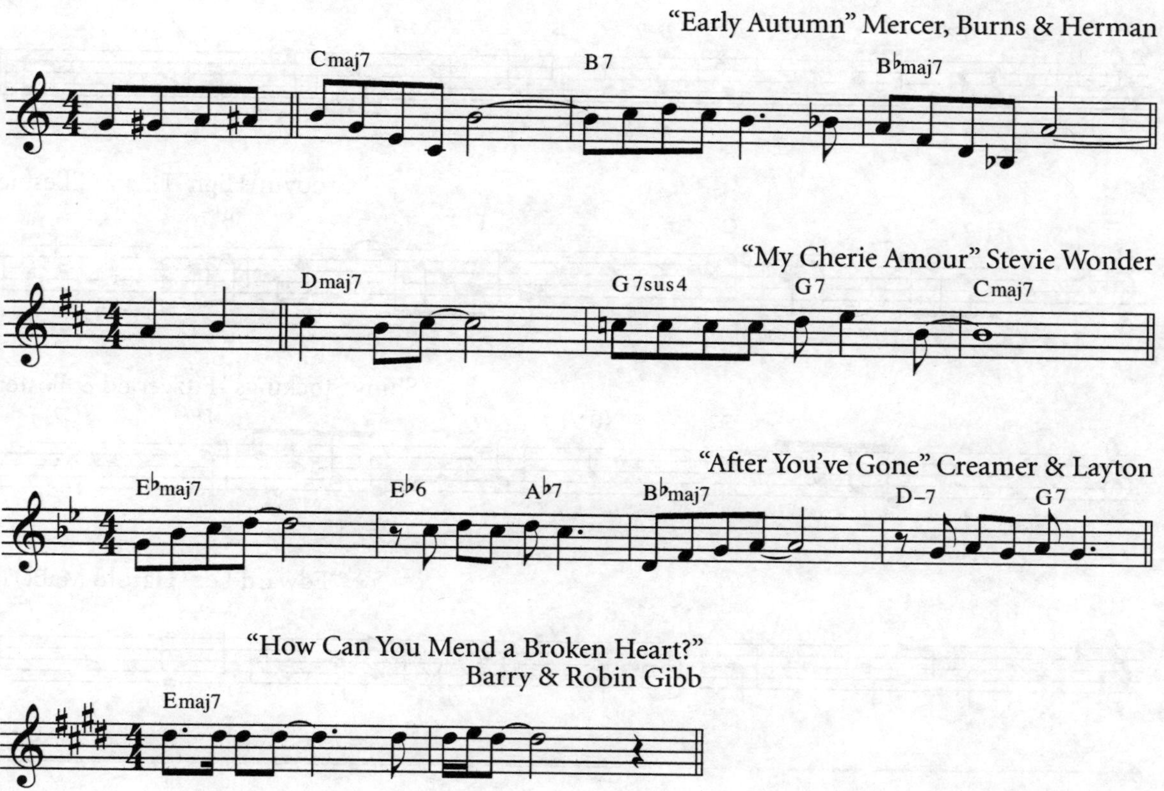

The following melodic excerpts feature the entire arpeggio of the dominant 7th chord sound.

"For the Longest Time" Billy Joel

And the following melodic excerpts highlight the minor 7th chord sound.

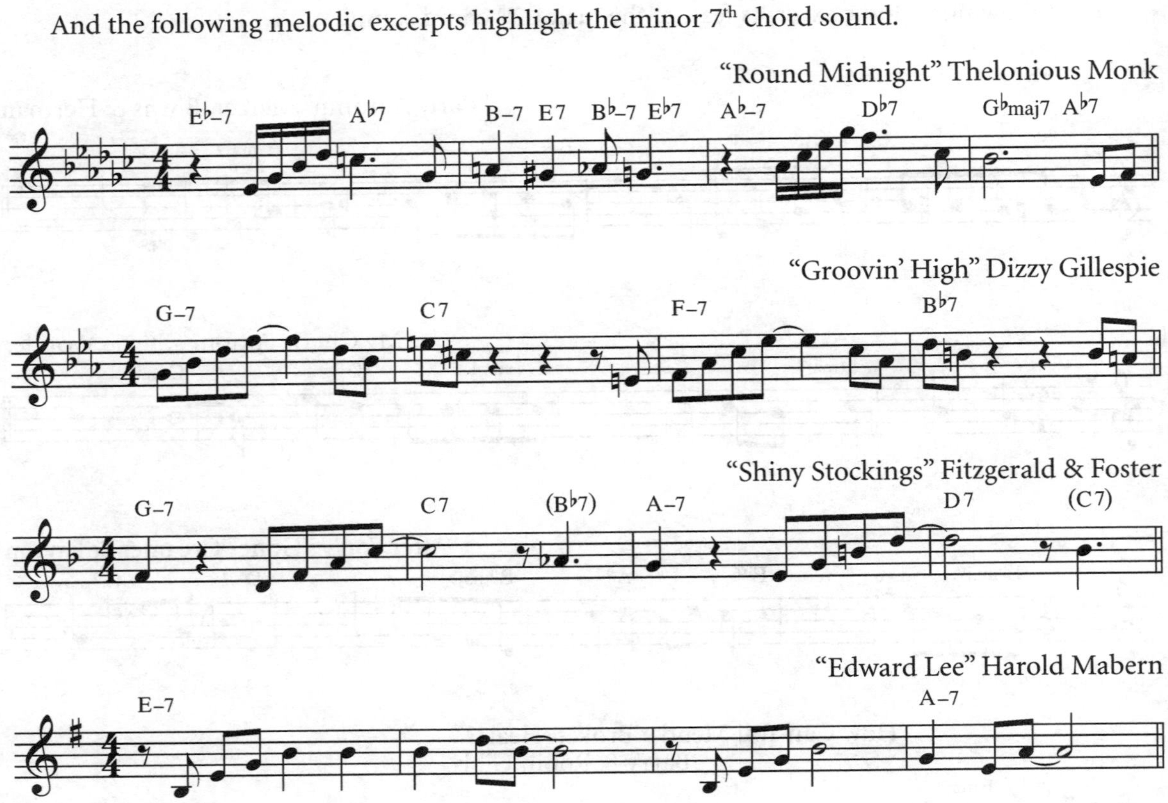

Activity Four *Identify the Chord Tones in the Melody*

The excerpts below feature embellished voice-led guide tone lines within the melodic phrase. Label all chord tones with numbers, corresponding to each individual chord. Pay particular attention to the guide tone lines that thread through each melody. You'll also notice that some of the melody notes are non-diatonic. More about these "out of key" notes and how to label them with chromatic solfege syllables in Chapter Twelve. Check with the answer key (Appendix: p. 139, Activity Four) to see how you did.

Hooking Up with *The Real Easy Book* Return to the written bass lines you've worked with previously, now recognizing the chord tones that are 7ths. They are already labeled in numbers regarding each individual chord. The remaining non-chord tones are "approach notes." Notice how these approach notes usually resolve by stepwise motion to a following chord tone.

Let's continue our discussion of the bass line with the next topic, the "passing 7th."

Hearing the Passing 7th

In Chapter Seven we began our work of hearing inversions of the I, IV and V triads. Inversions of seventh chords are also possible. In particular, having the "passing 7th" as the bass note is a common use of inversions for seventh chords. Let's see how this works.

The "passing 7th" will serve as a passing note from the original chord in root position to the following bass note. Its function is mainly melodic, linking the two end points by stepwise motion and creating a smooth transition from one chord to the next.

How do you know it's the "passing 7th" and not the root of a new chord? Because you will hear the upper voicing of the chord remain exactly the same, while the bass note moves down by step. Listen to the two examples on the next page for comparison.

It is quite common to see passing 7[th]s incorporated into progressions that also include several other chord inversions. In the next activity, we'll put our ears to the test with this very situation.

Activity Five *Recognizing the Passing 7th*

Listen to the following four song excerpts on CD2, track 6, that feature the passing 7th. Use the templates provided below to fill in your answers. These progressions will also include several other chord inversions to identify (including a few non-diatonic chords), keeping us practicing with the old as we tackle the new. If possible, listen to the original recordings of these tunes for the "real life" experience. Enjoy! Then check with the answer key to see how you did (Appendix: p. 139, Activity Five, CD2, track 6).

"The Spirit Carries On" Dream Theater

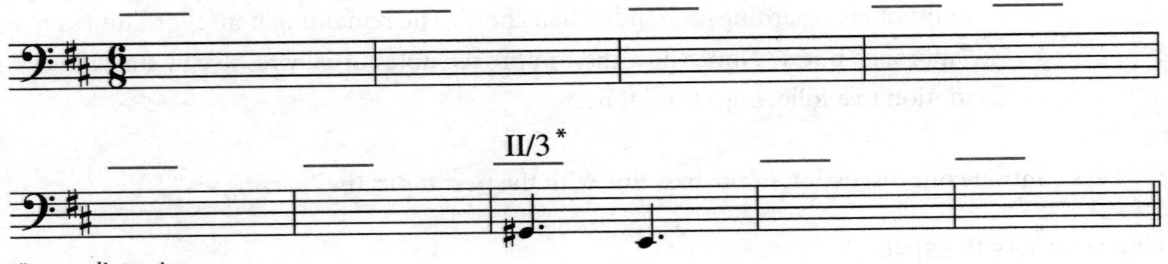

* non-diatonic

"Never Saw Blue Like That Before" Shawn Colvin

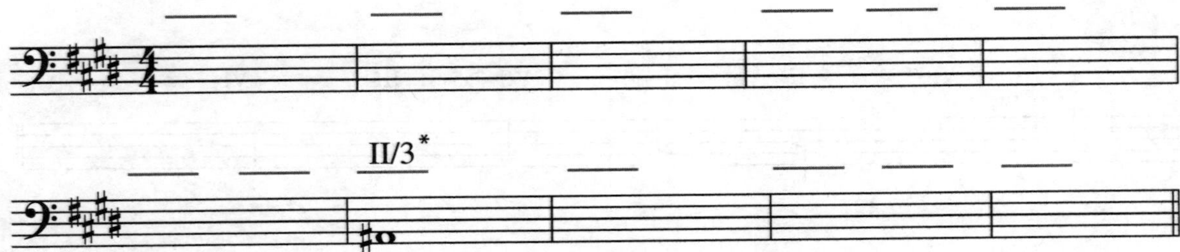

* non-diatonic

"Don't Let the Sun Go Down on Me" Elton John

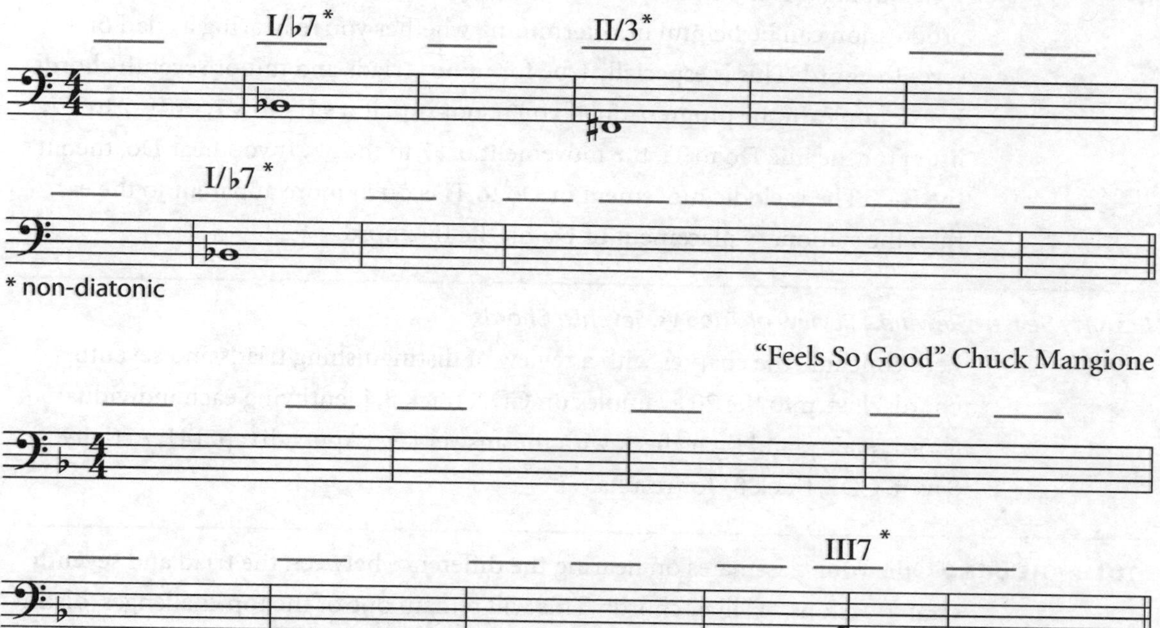

Now it's time to put it all together: triads, seventh chords, inversions, and passing 7ths into the mix for the final dictation activity of the chapter. Are you ready?

Activity Six *Complete Dictation Workout with Diatonic Triads and Seventh Chords*

You've come a long way these last two chapters hearing seventh chord harmonies. Let's put it to the test with the following ten examples in the key of C on CD2, track 7 (all examples are five measures long). Here are a few tips to keep in mind.

1. Always go for the bass line first.
2. "Kick in" with the brainwork. What are the possibilities suggested by the bass line? For example, if you hear stepwise motion in the bass, consider the options of inversions or passing 7ths.
3. If it's a root position chord, is it a triad or a seventh chord? Does the texture seem simple or rich?
4. If the vertical approach of step 3 doesn't work, use the horizontal approach, listening for the guide tone 7th as a solfege note in the key.
5. Use your instrument if you need some help, playing the different options and seeing what matches best with the dictation example.
6. Don't do all ten examples in one sitting. This work requires intense concentration; avoid overloading, burning out, and getting discouraged.
7. Absolutely give this the "24-hour rule," double-checking your work on the next day with a fresh set of ears.
8. If this work is still overwhelming, spend some time listening to the examples while looking at the answer key.
9. Give yourself a pat on the back; this stuff is hard!
10. Now check in with the answer key to see how well you've done (Appendix: p. 140, Activity Six, CD2, track 7).

Tip When doing dictation or transcription, preparing to hear a voice-led line in the progression can be helpful in determining whether you're hearing a triad or a seventh chord. This is especially true for minor triads and minor seventh chords. For example, in the progression, if you're not sure if it's II– to V7, or II–7 to V7, listen for the line Do to Ti, the movement of ♭7 to the 3rd. If you hear Do, then it's the II–7. The melodic movement of Do to Ti is often more apparent to the ear than the stationary placement of Do on the II– chord.

Activity Seven *Rewind... Review of Triad vs. Seventh Chords*

Let's conclude the chapter with a review of distinguishing triads and seventh chords. Listen to the 20 examples on CD2, track 8, identifying each individual chord quality, and then check with the answer key (Appendix: p. 141, Activity Seven, CD2, track 8) for results.

Stump the Band Quiz your classmates on hearing the difference between the triad and seventh chord versions of "like" chords. This will remain one of the top challenges, distinguishing the subtle differences of "To be or not to be...": is it a triad or a seventh chord?

For Your Consideration We have covered quite a bit of material over these last ten chapters! How do you keep it all straight? Discuss with your classmates the strategies and approaches you're finding helpful when figuring out the changes. What are some of the challenges you're still facing? Maybe a classmate can offer some tips. If two heads are better than one, then imagine what *four ears* can do. At times, team up with a friend for dictation work, putting those four ears to the task.

Making It Your Own Continue to find examples of seventh chord harmony in the "real world." Whether it's reading lead sheets, listening and transcribing tunes from recordings, or playing songs that incorporate lots of seventh chords, find ways to "own it."

11 Hearing Minor Key Harmony

Introduction

In this chapter, we'll become familiar with some of the popular chord progressions found in the minor key. We'll use the same listening approaches developed so far for identifying chords in the major key: listening to the bass line, and using a combination of the vertical and horizontal approaches for recognizing the chords. First we'll learn the new solfege syllables for the minor scale, and then become familiar with the diatonic chords. Once our vocabulary list is established, then we'll move on to recognizing the changes in minor key progressions. Why wait, let's get started!

Minor Scale Solfege

Let's begin with a look and listen to the C natural minor scale. Notice the three new solfege syllables: Me (♭3), Le (♭6) and Te (♭7). The "e" sound is pronounced like "ay" in the word "say."

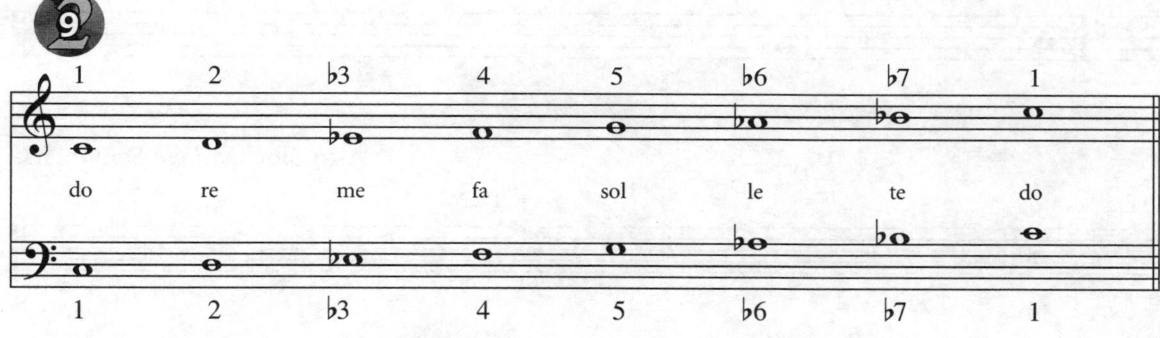

Activity One *Building Natural Minor Scales*

Write out the natural minor scales listed below. For now, write accidentals before each scale tone rather than using the key signature. This will help emphasize the intervallic relationship of each scale tone back to Do. Make sure to sing along as you write to internalize the sound of this new scale.

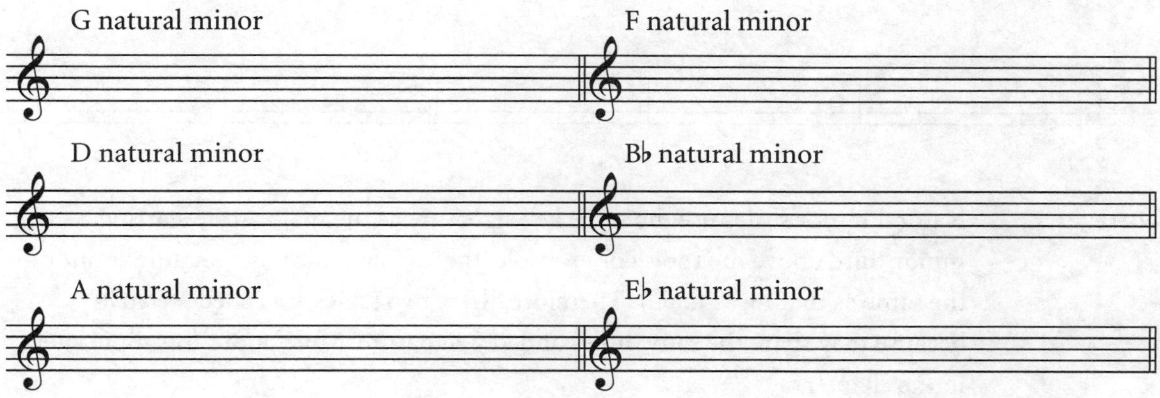

Bonus Here are the bass lines to "Serenade to a Cuckoo," Roland Kirk; "Fragile," Sting; "Afro Blue," Mongo Santamaria; and "Hotel California," The Eagles. Try sight-reading these natural minor bass lines. We will return to these songs later in the chapter for a complete workout with hearing the changes.

"Serenade to a Cuckoo" Roland Kirk

"Fragile" Sting

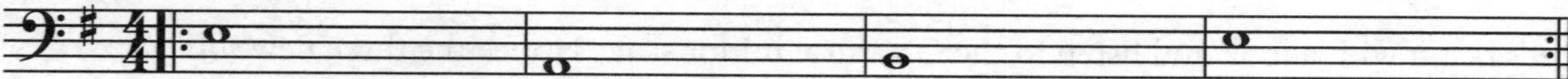

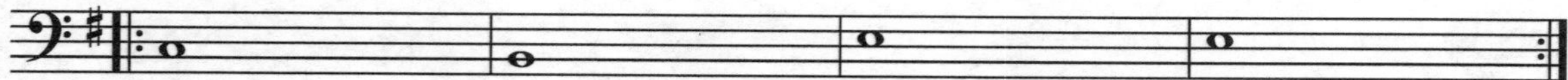

"Afro Blue" Mongo Santamaria

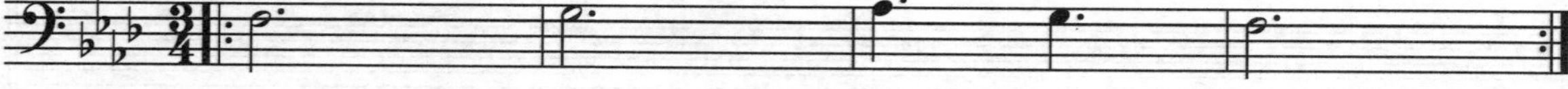

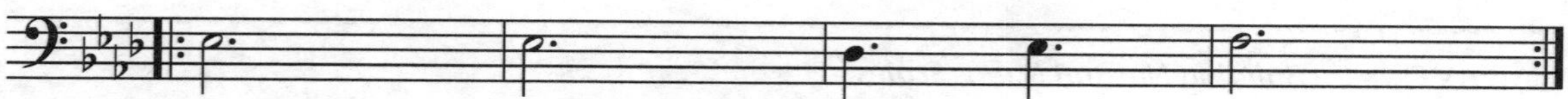

"Hotel California" The Eagles

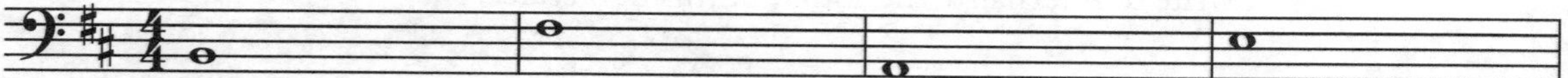

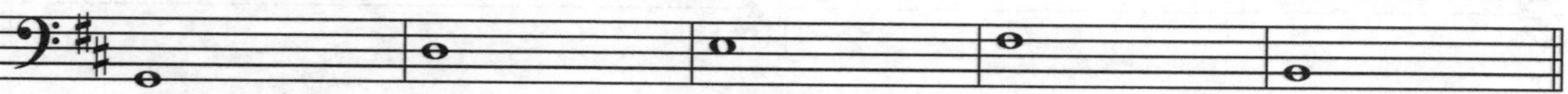

Note Natural minor scales use the same key signature as the major scale starting a minor third above the root. For example, the key signature for A natural minor is the same as that for C major. Therefore, these two scales are called "relative" because they share the same notes and key signature. More about this topic later in the chapter.

Let's now compare the sounds of the C major and C natural minor scales. They are called "parallel" scales because they both start with the same root note. Sing both scales back to back, paying particular attention to how the sounds of the 3rd, 6th and 7th degrees of the major and minor scales differ. Comparing and contrasting the sounds of these two parallel scales is excellent practice.

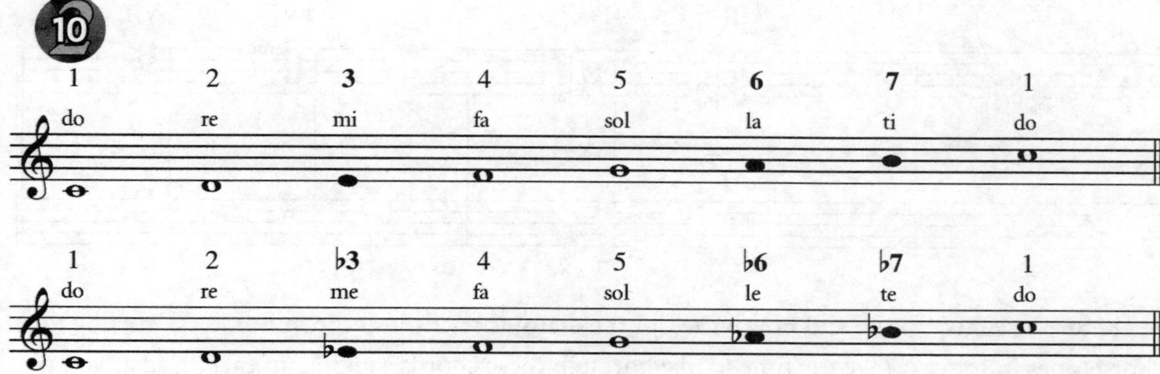

BONUS Listen to the following songs which demonstrate the relationship between parallel major and minor keys: "Best of What's Around," Dave Matthews; "My Favorite Things," recorded by John Coltrane; "What Are You Doing the Rest of Your Life," Michel Legrand; "While My Guitar Gently Weeps," George Harrison; and "Chega de Saudade," Antonio Jobim. Can you find some examples of your own?

ACTIVITY TWO *Minor Bass Line Dictation*

Let's jump right in and get some practice with hearing diatonic bass lines in the natural minor key. Listen to the following ten examples in the key of C natural minor (CD2, track 11) and transcribe the bass lines. Each example is four measures long. You can notate your answers in a variety of ways: music notation in the bass clef, solfege syllables or numbers. Considering all three interpretations is the ultimate workout.

Check with the key (Appendix: p. 141, Activity Two, CD2, track 11) which includes all three versions of the answers: notated pitches, solfege syllables and numbers.

BONUS Now sing back these bass lines in both C natural minor and parallel C major, changing Me's, Le's and Te's to Mi's, La's and Ti's. You can never get enough singing practice to internalize the sounds. Back to back contrast of hearing minor vs. major brings out each one's uniqueness.

STUMP THE BAND Write your own natural minor bass lines, exploring some keys other than C minor. Then sing or play them for your classmates for dictation practice. How did they do?

Diatonic Chords in Natural Minor

Let's examine the diatonic chords in the natural minor key. The example below lists these diatonic triads in root position, labeled with Roman numerals and solfege.

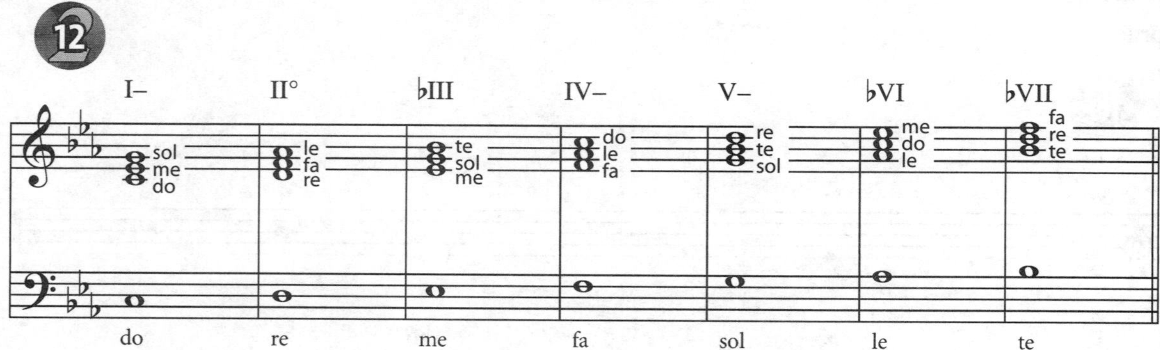

Return to Activity One and now write out the diatonic triads in those minor keys, labeling the chord tones in solfege. Take the time to play through these chords, singing up each triad as you go along. Sing, sing, sing!

Bonus Classics such as "Ain't No Sunshine When She's Gone," Bill Withers; "Wrapped Around Your Finger," The Police; "Miss You Fever," Delbert McClinton; "Money For Nothing," Dire Straits; and "Smooth Operator," Sade, are great examples of songs that are 100% natural minor. Have a listen! Can you transcribe the changes?

About Relative Minor

Do the chords above look familiar? Yes, they're the same diatonic chords as in the key of E♭ major. The C natural minor scale and the E♭ major scale are called "relative" scales because they both contain the same notes, but have different starting pitches. Singing the C natural minor scale is like singing the E♭ major scale, only starting on La instead. It is true that these relative scales contain the same notes, but it is important to hear the differences. Remember, we call the first note of the scale Do in the movable Do solfege system, whether we're in a major or minor key. In this case, we call C Do and not La in the key of C minor.

At times it's tricky to tell whether a song is in the major or relative minor key, because they both have the same "look." These relative scales have the same notes, and therefore the same key signature. Many songs will modulate between major and relative minor, making it even trickier to tell the difference. My best advice is to listen. What note sounds like the tonal center, the Do? In most cases the ear can be a better judge than the eye in determining the answer.

Activity Three *Major or Minor?*

Have a discussion with classmates about whether you hear the following song, "Autumn Leaves," in a major or minor key, or perhaps a little bit of both. Play through the changes, and if possible, listen to a recording of the song to hear how the melody influences your decision. There is no one absolute right answer to this question, but it's important to support your opinion. When all words and explanations fail, simply sing what you hear as the Do. Did you sing G or E?

"Autumn Leaves" Prévert, Kosma & Mercer

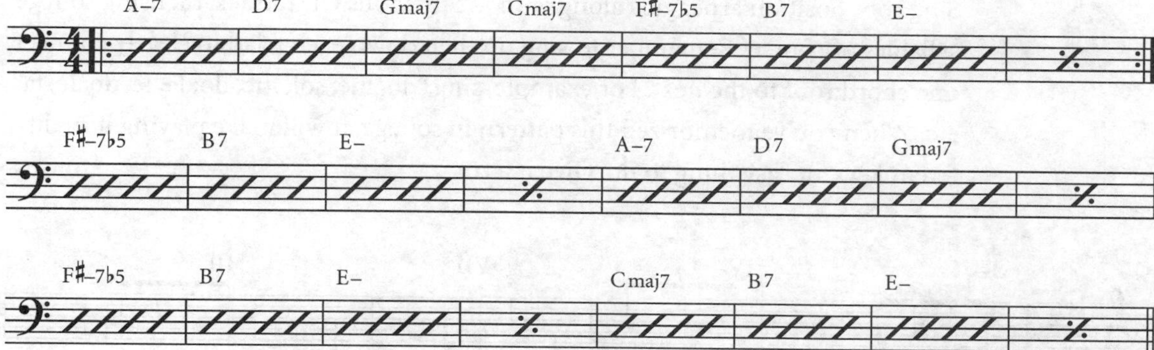

Note The lead sheet to "Autumn Leaves" uses seventh chords, as we have studied in Chapters Nine and Ten. We will continue our discussion of seventh chords in the minor key later in this chapter. Stay tuned!

Bonus Listen to the following songs that demonstrate modulation between relative major and minor keys: "Georgia," Hoagy Carmichael; "God Bless the Child," Billie Holiday; "There is No Greater Love," Symes & Jones; "Tico Tico," Zequinha Abreu; "Yesterday," The Beatles; "Black Orpheus," Luiz Bonfá; and "You've Got a Friend," Carol King.

Notice that in some of these songs, the dividing line between keys is obvious, and with others, even debatable whether a modulation has occurred. What do your ears tell you? Does placement of the chords within the form play a role in making these decisions? Is the melody an important factor in determining what note sounds like Do in the song? Discuss these questions with your classmates.

Root Position Diatonic Triads in the Cycle 5 Pattern

The progression below organizes these same diatonic root position triads using the cycle 5 pattern. Similar to our workout in the major key, listen up each chord structure using the vertical approach, paying particular attention to the relationship of the root to the third of each triad. Don't just listen; sing the root to the third of each chord for additional practice.

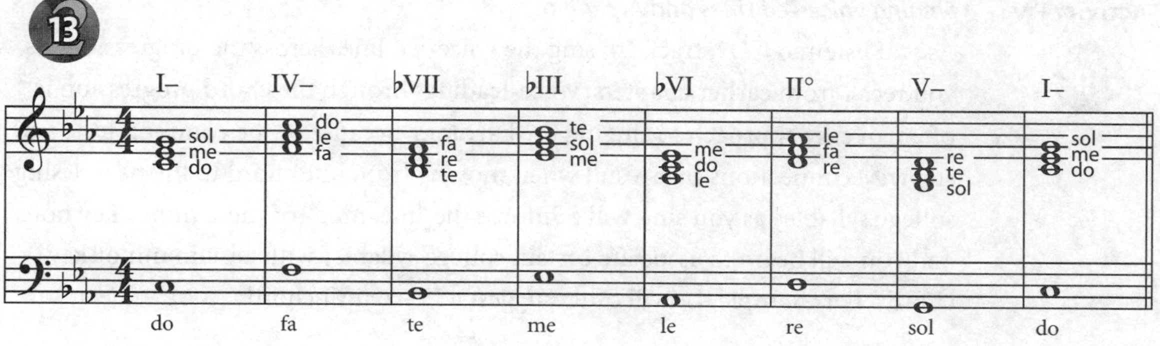

Activity Four *Singing Root Position Arpeggios*

Sing root position arpeggios along with the previous CD2, track 13, using solfege syllables of course! Remember to sing up then down each triad to clearly connect one chord root to the next. For example, sing "do, me, sol, me, do; fa, le, do, le, fa," etc. When you've memorized this pattern in solfege, it will make playing it in different keys an easy thing to do. Give it a try.

Voice-Leading Diatonic Triads in the Cycle 5 Pattern

Again, we can use all of the same routines we used to work out in the major key with minor key progressions. Let's listen to the cycle 5 pattern, this time using the voice-leading technique. First, let's just give it a listen.

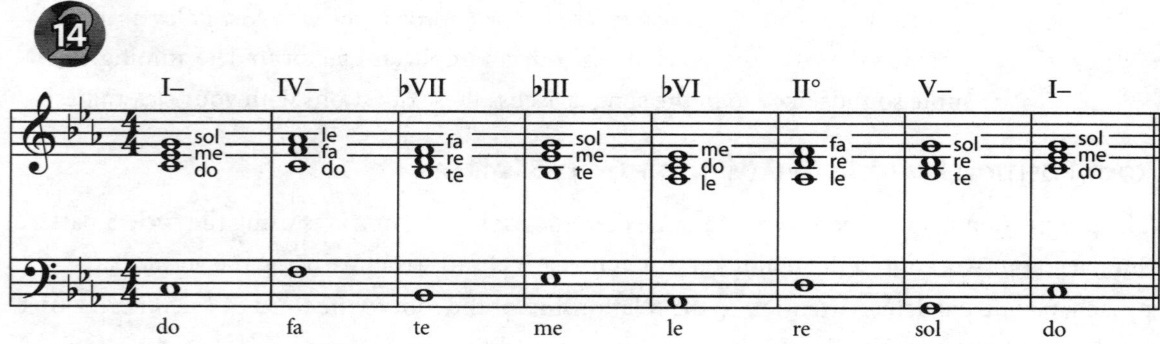

Activity Five *Singing Voice-Led Lines and Arpeggios*

As you listen to CD2, track 14, sing the voice-led lines across the progression. As you recall from earlier chapters, voice-leading through the chord progression is often an easy approach to singing the harmony because of the common tone and stepwise connections that result when moving from one chord to the next. Using solfege syllables as you sing will reinforce the "meaning" of these minor key notes, and you will begin to associate certain solfege syllables with certain minor key chords. For example, Le will often suggest a IV– or ♭VI chord.

And if your voice is still holding up, try singing the following melodic arpeggios to the cycle 5 pattern. Don't forget to also practice these patterns in other minor keys. Transposing these lines will get you hearing the sound of the patterns, and will be great practice with your new minor key solfege syllables, Me, Le and Te.

About Harmonic Minor

There are many kinds of major and minor scales; in this book we're focusing on the two most popular ones, the major scale and it's relative, or natural minor scale. Another scale that is often used for the harmonic component of a minor song is, logically enough, called the "harmonic minor" scale. This scale is very similar to the natural minor scale, but contains a major 7th degree, Ti, in place of Te, the ♭7. In other words: Do Re Me Fa Sol Le Ti Do.

With this Ti, we now have the strong cadence of V back to I–, with Ti resolving up to Do by a half step. You can spot the harmonic minor scale, because Ti will always need an accidental before it to cancel out the ♭7 found in the key signature. This is one instance where the eye has an advantage over the ear in detecting if the song is in a major or minor key, and in this case, harmonic minor specifically.

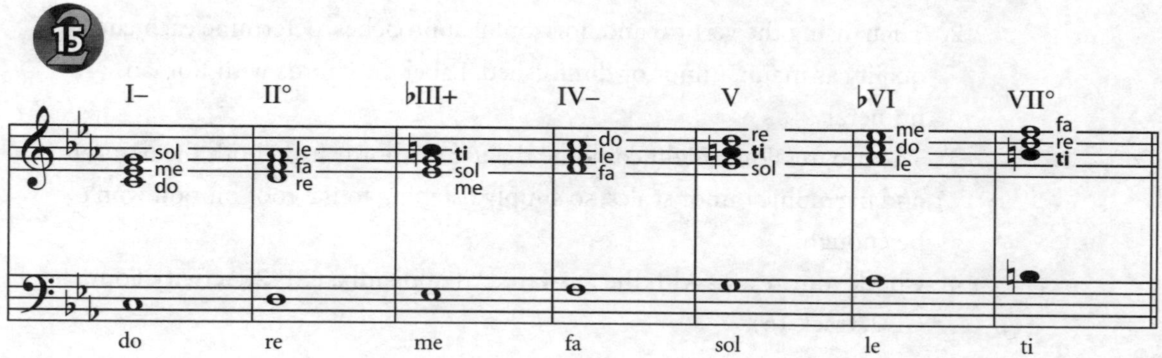

Activity Six *Singing Voice-Led Lines to a Harmonic Minor Progression*

Sing the root motion and slightly embellished voice-led lines to the following song, "Fragile," by Sting. For the full experience, join classmates in singing all the parts, "chorale" style. And if possible, sing the parts along with the original recording of the song. Enjoy!

Wow! There's a lot to keep straight with minor scales and keys. I promise you no more brain-work. Let's do some dictation.

Activity Seven *Minor Key Chord Progression Dictation*

Listen to the following ten examples in the key of C minor (CD2, track 16) and identify the chords. Each example is four measures long. Remember to apply the same familiar routines we've used when listening to major key examples.

1. First identify the bass line. Most bass notes will be roots in these examples.
2. Then, using the vertical and horizontal approaches, determine each chord quality as major, minor or diminished. Label the chords with Roman numerals.
3. The progressions might combine the use of chords from both the natural and harmonic minor scales, so simply listening to the root motion won't be enough.
4. Check your results with the answer key (Appendix: p. 142, Activity Four, CD2, track 16).

Bonus

Let's continue our work with the song selection, "Hotel California," on CD2, track 17. Using the vertical approach, sing up from the root to the third of each triad, determining whether you hear a major or minor third interval. Keep in mind that the chords are borrowed from a variety of minor scales, so listen carefully to the quality of the third. Use the template provided on the top of page 103 to fill in your answers, then check with the answer key to see how you did (Appendix: p. 143, CD2, track 17).

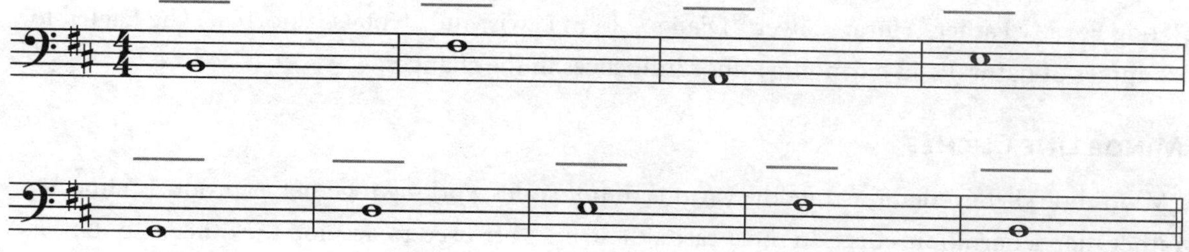

Working with Seventh Chords in the Minor Key

Now let's look and listen to the diatonic seventh chords in both natural and harmonic minor. The list below combines the chords from both scales, and shows the resulting differences that ♭7 and 7 play in their construction.

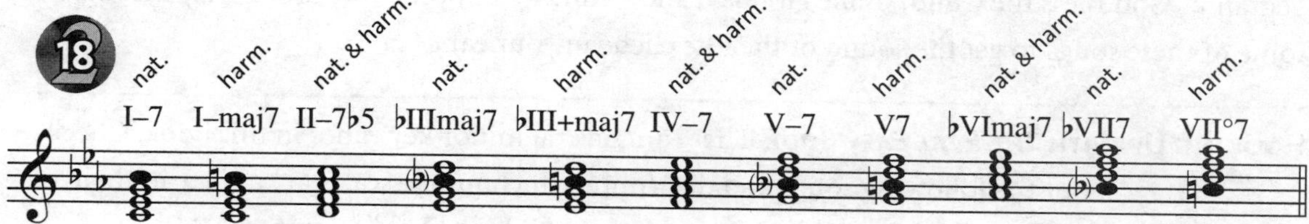

Apply all the same practice routines to these minor key seventh chords as you have with triads: writing them out in a variety of keys; playing them and singing along with solfege; researching songs that demonstrate minor key seventh chord harmony; applying both the vertical and horizontal approaches for determining chord quality; hearing the guide tone details (3rds and 7ths) of the chord progression, as well as recognizing the role of the melody in determining the chord changes.

Minor Scale Combinations

Unlike major key songs, minor songs are often a combination of natural and harmonic minor scales working together. Sometimes the melody is 100% natural minor, accompanied by harmonic minor changes. This is the case with "The Thrill is Gone," BB King; "Summertime," George and Ira Gershwin; "Serenade to a Cuckoo," Roland Kirk; "House of the Rising Sun," Alan Price; and "You Never Give Me Your Money," The Beatles. Check these songs out, whether you read through a lead sheet, or listen to a recording, or ideally, do both.

Note We studied the Beatles' tune, "You Never Give Me Your Money," in earlier chapters as an example of the cycle 5 pattern starting with the VI– chord. Similar to our discussion about "Autumn Leaves," it is debatable whether this song is in major, starting on the VI– chord, or perhaps in the key of the relative minor, starting on the I– chord. Listen to the song and let your ears decide for themselves.

Sometimes the chord progression itself is a combination of these two minor scales. Check out "Song For My Father," Horace Silver; "Django," John Lewis; and "Hotel California," The Eagles, for examples of natural and harmonic minor influences in the changes.

Minor Line Clichés

"Minor line clichés" demonstrate the various minor scales working together to produce a linear, rather than a harmonic effect. In most cases, these lines are used to develop the otherwise stationary sound of the I– chord, and are often played in the bass line, demonstrating another effective use of chord inversions. The most popular of these line clichés is the descending chromatic theme, Do, Ti, Te, La, while the I– chord sustains above. For example, in the key of C minor: C–, C–/B, C–/B♭, C–/A; or you might see it notated as: C–, C–maj7, C–7, C–6.

The following songs are good examples of this particular line cliché: "My Funny Valentine," Rogers & Hart; "Golden Lady," Stevie Wonder; "What Are You Doing the Rest of Your Life," Michel Legrand; "God Bless the Child," Billie Holiday; and "Time in a Bottle," Jim Croce. Play through some of these songs to get the sound of the line cliché in your ear.

Hooking Up with *The Real Easy Book* There are several minor key tunes in this book. Check out the following songs and determine which minor scales are at play in their makeup: "Big Bertha," "Contemplation," "Edward Lee," "Equinox," "Mr. P.C.," "One For Daddy-O," "Revelation," "Road Song," "Song For My Father," "St. James Infirmary" and "Work Song." You will see a variety of possibilities: some songs stay exclusively within one scale; some use natural minor for the melody and harmonic minor for the changes; some use a combination of minor scales for the changes, and some songs modulate to the relative major key. As you play through these songs, be aware of all these subtle features. It will give you some insights as to how to interpret the songs, particularly when soloing.

Voice-Leading Guide Tone Lines in the Minor Key

Let's continue our work with voicing leading the guide tones, the 3rds and 7ths, this time using minor key harmony. But what happens when the chord progression is a mix of both triads and seventh chords? In the case of the triads, we will continue to use the 3rd, but will have a choice, mainly determined by voice-leading, between using the root or the 5th as the second guide tone. Let's see this demonstrated in revisiting the song, "Hotel California." Notice that the top guide tone line is actually the chromatic line cliché we talked about earlier. Sing these voice-led guide tone lines along with CD2, track 19, or better yet, with the actual Eagles' recording.

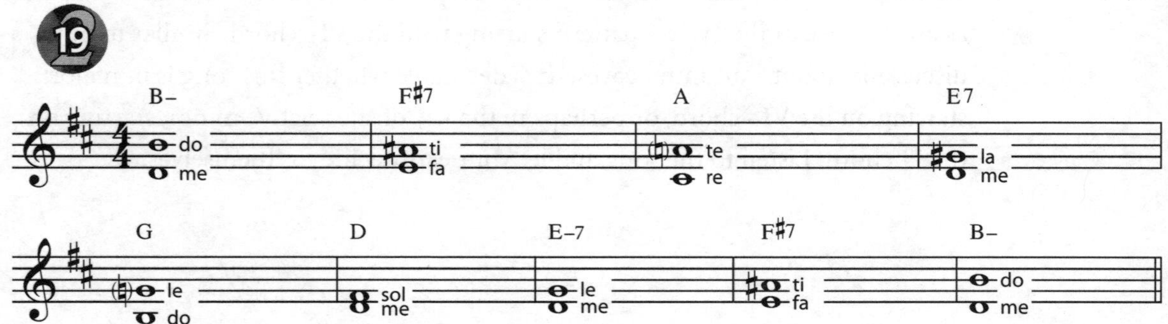

Activity Eight *Dictating the Voice-Led Guide Tone Lines*

Listen to the following excerpt from Roland Kirk's "Serenade to a Cuckoo" on CD2, track 20. At the beginning of the chapter you sight-read through the bass line to this song: now it's time to notate the voice-led guide tone lines and discover what the resulting changes are. Notice in the A section another popular minor line cliché being used, the descending Do, Te, Le, Sol pattern. Use the template below to fill in your answers, then check with the answer key (Appendix: p.144, CD2, track 20) for the results.

Activity Nine *Rewind... Harmonize the Bass Line*

Harmonize the following bass line with your own set of changes. You can explore major or minor key harmonies, or perhaps a little bit of both. Because there are so many good solutions, there is no answer key listed for this activity in the Appendix. Then write out the voice-led guide tone lines to your progression (remember, these can be the simple beginnings of tasty horn or vocal background lines). If you want to really get creative, compose a melody as well. Perform the arrangement of your composition with classmates or band members, getting feedback. Did others come up with a similar set of changes to yours, or perhaps something quite different? By the way, I borrowed this bass line from John Lewis' "Django." Check out this wonderful tune when you get a chance!

In the next and final chapter of this book, we will explore further ways in which major and minor harmonies combine to create interesting chord progressions. Let's move on and see what the possibilities are.

FOR YOUR CONSIDERATION Discuss with your classmates how to determine whether a song is in a major or minor key. What criteria do you use to determine the answer?

MAKING IT YOUR OWN Review many songs you're familiar with. Are they in a major or minor key? Do you know some songs that modulate between major and minor?

12 Hearing Non-Diatonic Harmony

Introduction

In this final chapter, we'll study the chromatic scale and its associated solfege syllables in order to prepare for identifying non-diatonic harmony in the chord progressions. So far we've learned the diatonic solfege syllables for the major, natural minor and harmonic minor scales, leaving still a few new syllables to become familiar with. I'm sure in your playing and listening experiences you've encountered some out-of-key, or "non-diatonic" chords in the music. The list of non-diatonic harmonic possibilities is long, but we can at least begin to develop a method for becoming familiar with some of them. Adding the chromatic solfege syllables to our vocabulary list is a good place to begin.

Introducing the Chromatic Scale and Its Solfege Syllables

The chromatic scale contains all twelve notes, each a half step apart. But in fact there are seventeen possible solfege names! How is this possible? Let's take a look at the chromatic scale below and discuss the musical reasons for why some notes have two solfege names. But first, let's practice singing the chromatic scale, getting familiar with these new solfege syllables.

* Ra is pronounced "rah"

Note Just to refresh your memory on pronouncing the solfege vowels: "i" is pronounced "ee" and "e" is pronounced "ay."

Activity One *Sing the Chromatic Scale Using Solfege Syllables*

Practice singing up and down the chromatic scale using solfege. For starters, sing along with CD2, track 21 to help you stay on pitch with all these half steps. When you're ready, try singing the scale on your own. It's a tongue twister, so go slowly!

Why Two Names for the Same Pitch?

Each non-diatonic chromatic pitch has the potential of two names. For example, in a melody, or in a bass line, if the notes are moving up by half step, you use the ascending solfege name (Fa, Fi, Sol, etc.); if the notes are moving down by half step, you use the descending solfege name (Mi, Me, Re, etc.). In this way, the solfege syllables truly indicate their function, or their intended direction of resolution.

Activity Two *Use Solfege to Label the Chromatic Approach Notes*

Label all notes in the following five melodies with solfege, including both chord tones and approach notes. Consider the direction of resolution of the approach notes when choosing the appropriate chromatic solfege syllables. Then sing the melodies for additional practice with these new syllables. Check with the answer key (Appendix: p. 144, Activity Two) for results.

Here's another situation to consider, this time involving the chords rather than the melody. If you're in the key of C, and you encounter an E triad, you would write the third of that chord as a G♯, calling it Si, (♯5 of the key). If you have an F– triad, you would call the third of that chord an A♭, labeling it as Le (♭6 of the key). In these examples, the solfege syllable directly relates to the letter name of the note.

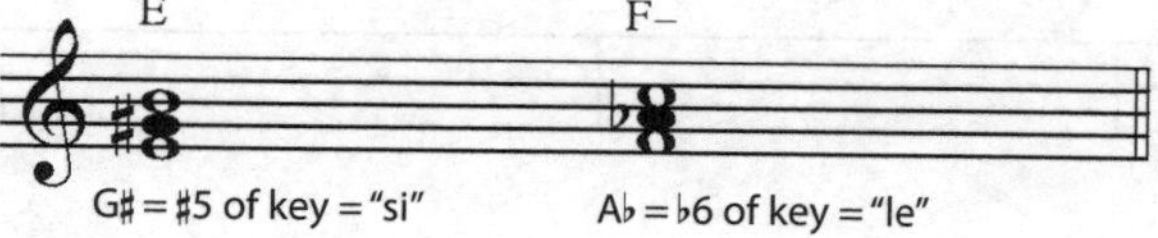

Activity Three *Label the Non-Diatonic Chord Tones with Solfege*

Label all chord tones with solfege. Remember to use the appropriate harmonic solfege syllable; we will assume we're in the key of C major for all examples. Then check with the answer key (Appendix: p. 145, Activity Three) to see how you did.

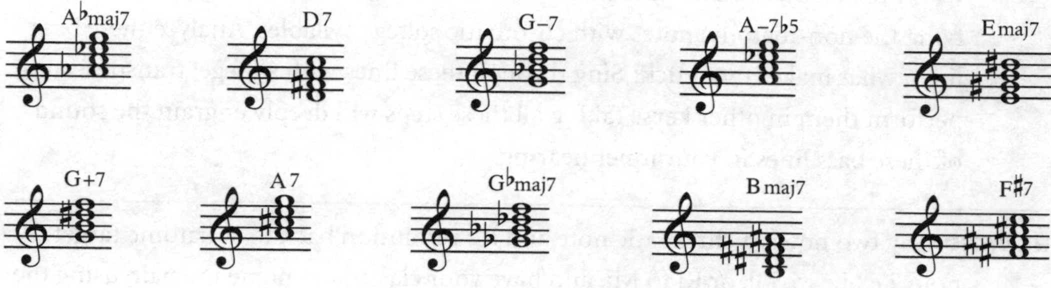

Bonus Lets put it all together. Using solfege, label each note, including the chromatic approach notes and non-diatonic chord tones, in the following blues bass line. Then check your work with the answer key (Appendix, p.145, Bonus).

Can you sing the line without using your instrument for reference? The solfege syllables will help you sing the line. Then (using the blank staves on the top of page 110) transpose this bass line to the key of F for an additional workout using the chromatic solfege syllables.

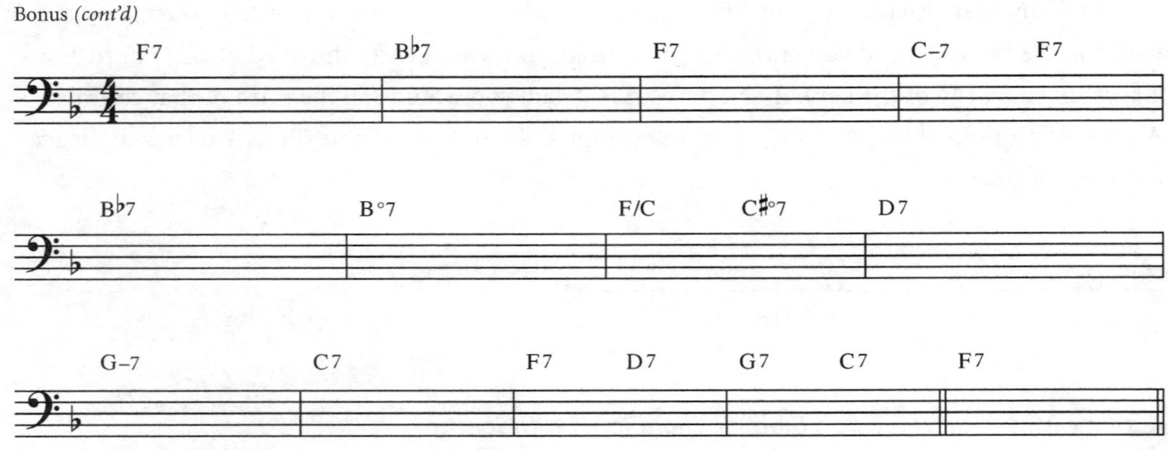

HOOKING UP WITH *THE REAL EASY BOOK* Return to some of the written bass lines you've worked with previously, but this time you'll be able to complete the solfege puzzle, identifying the non-diatonic notes with chromatic solfege syllables. Analyze these bass lines; what makes them tick? Sing through these lines with solfege; transpose and perform them in other keys. Taking all these steps will deeply engrain the sound of these bass lines in your inner hearing.

STUMP THE BAND Play two notes, a chromatic note and it's resolution back to a diatonic target note, i.e., Le to Sol, or Ri to Mi, and have your classmates name the pair, using the correct solfege. Frequently refer back to the I chord to help keep everyone's ears focused on the sound of the overall key.

Listening for the Non-Diatonic Chords

Sometimes the non-diatonic chord will stand out in the harmonic crowd. You might not know exactly what the chord is, but you'll know that it sounds out of the key. In fact, sometimes it's easier to pick out the "outsider" than distinguish the subtle differences between diatonic chords. Let's put this to the test. In the following examples, identify the non-diatonic chords by putting a check mark by them.

ACTIVITY FOUR *Locate the Non-Diatonic Chords*

Listen to the following ten four-measure progressions (CD2, track 23) and put a check mark where you hear the non-diatonic chord. There is only one "outsider" per example. We will revisit these same progressions in Activity Eight for a complete dictation workout. For now, let's just identify where the non-diatonic chords occur. Refer to the answer key (Appendix: p.145, Activity Four, CD2, track 23) to check your answers.

I imagine you didn't have too much difficulty finding the "outsider." The real challenge is in determining the particulars. What exactly is this non-diatonic chord? As I mentioned in the introduction, we can't cover all the possibilities, but there are two groups of non-diatonic chords that are popular. Let's explore them.

Modal Interchange Chords

There are many sources of "modal interchange" chords: one source uses chords borrowed from the parallel natural minor scale in the context of the major key. These "borrowed" chords are called "modal interchange" chords. For example, check out the progression below:

As a reminder, the diatonic triads in natural minor are: I–, II°, ♭III, IV–, V–, ♭VI, and ♭VII. With this topic being brand new, let's only use triads for the following exercises, and limit our modal interchange choices to IV–, ♭VI and ♭VII for now.

Activity Five *Identify the Modal Interchange Chords*

Listen to the following five progressions on CD2, track 25 and identify the chords. Each example is five measures long, including at least one modal interchange chord (IV–, ♭VI, ♭VII). Don't forget to apply both the vertical (listening to the root/3rd relationship) and horizontal (listening for the non-diatonic chord tone via solfege) approaches when determining the chord qualities. These examples are in C major, but answer with Roman numerals to emphasize the functional aspect of the chords. Then check with the answer key (Appendix: p. 146, Activity Five, CD2, track 25) for the results.

Hooking Up with *The Real Easy Book* Check out the following songs which include modal interchange chords in their harmonic progressions: "Cold Duck Time," "Killer Joe," "Midnight Waltz," "Short Stuff" and "Straight Life."

Secondary Dominant Chords

The other source of non-diatonic chords uses major triads, or dominant 7th chords built on diatonic roots. These chords most often resolve down a perfect 5th to a diatonic target chord, much like the V or V7 chords resolve back to the I chord. These chords are called "secondary dominants." Listen to the example below:

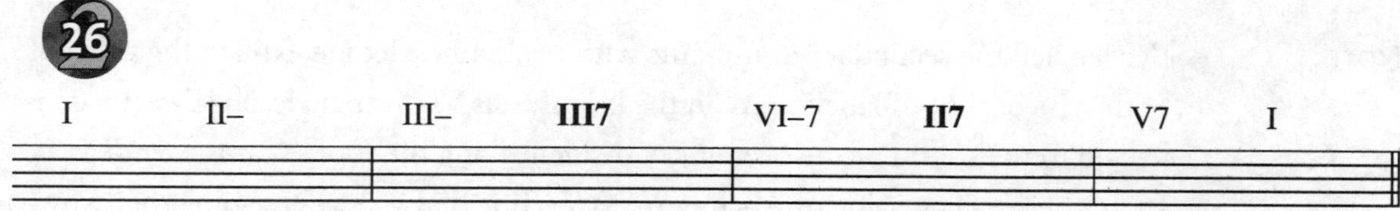

It is good practice to compare, back to back, the sound of the diatonic chord and the dominant 7th chord built on the same root. Listen to the following cycle 5 pattern that includes both chords, side by side. This is an excellent opportunity to apply the vertical approach, paying particular attention to the contrasting root/minor 3rd, root/major 3rd relationship that results between most partner chords.

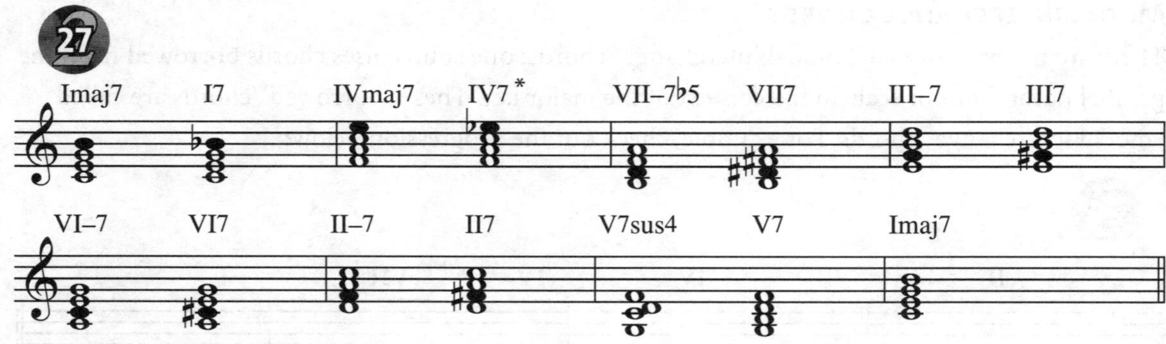

* IV7 is usually a blues chord, not a secondary dominant

Activity Six *Identify the Secondary Dominant Chords*

Listen to the following six progressions on CD2, track 28 and identify the chords. Each example is five measures long and includes at least one secondary dominant. If you hear something that's out of the key, it's probably a secondary dominant chord. Make sure by singing up from the root to the third, listening for a major third interval. Again, answer with Roman numerals to highlight the functional feature of each chord. Check the answer key to see how you did (Appendix: p. 146, Activity Six, CD2, track 28).

Recognizing the Guide Tones of Secondary Dominants

Let's address the guide tones, the 3rds and 7ths of secondary dominants, paying particular attention to the ones which are non-diatonic. It is the non-diatonic guide tone that will give our ears the biggest clue that we've heard a secondary dominant chord. But sometimes the biggest challenge is—which secondary dominant? The chart below lists each secondary dominant and its specific non-diatonic guide tone in solfege. Using the horizontal approach, let's become familiar with recognizing each secondary dominant by its unique chromatic solfege syllable. For example, if you hear Di of the key, you've heard VI7, or V7/II. Or, if you hear Si of the key, you've heard III7, or V7/VI. This is a good chance to work out with our new chromatic solfege syllables once again.

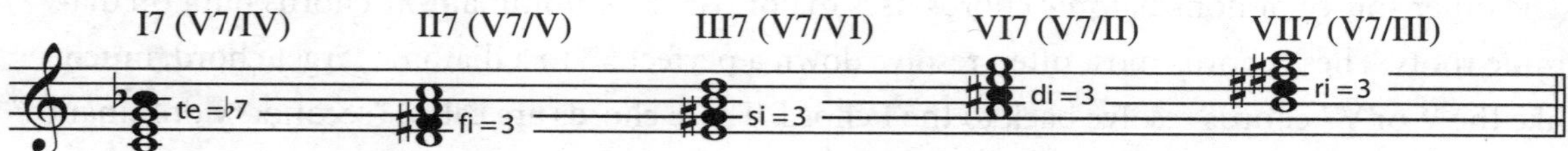

Note I've labeled the secondary dominants with two names; let me explain the value of both. The benefit of labeling A^7 in the key of C as VI^7 is that we stay directly connected to the sound of the overall key by identifying the root, A, as the 6th degree, La, in the key. The value of labeling A^7 as V^7/II is that we're describing the "why," the function of A^7 as a secondary dominant, and its need to resolve to D–, the II– chord in the key. Experiment with both labels; they are both helpful in their own ways in identifying the secondary dominant sound.

Voice-Leading the Secondary Dominant Guide Tone Lines

Listen to the cycle of secondary dominant resolution pairs below. This time, focus in on the voice-led guide tone lines, paying particular attention to the non-diatonic guide tone of each secondary dominant. Practice singing the root motion and the two voice-led guide tone lines along with classmates, "ensemble" style, and of course, with solfege syllables to reinforce the meaning of the notes. In time, and with experience, you will make an immediate connection between the chromatic solfege syllable and it's translation to a specific secondary dominant.

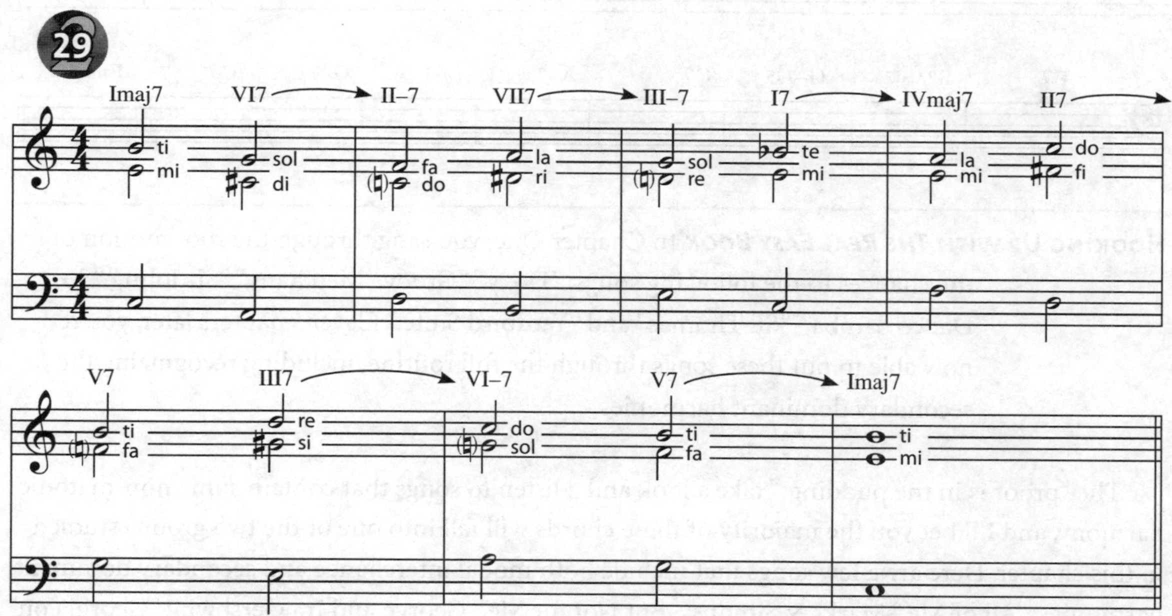

Stump the Band Play a secondary dominant resolution pair and see if your classmates can identify which pair you're playing. Remember to frequently reference the I chord to re-establish the sound of the key.

Activity Seven *Transcribe the Voice-Led Guide Tone Lines*

Using the template below, transcribe the root motion and voice-led guide tone lines to the following progression; include the resulting chord symbols. Upon completion, do you recognize this "mystery tune" by its changes? Check with the answer key (Appendix: p. 147 Activity Seven, CD2, track 30) to solve the mystery!

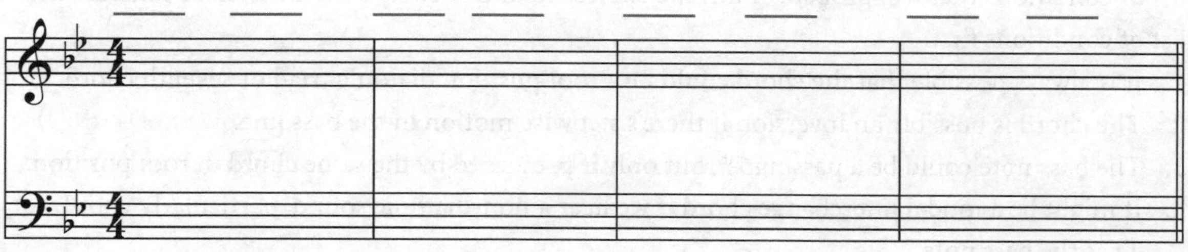

BONUS

Here are the changes to Bill Evans' "Waltz For Debby." Transcribe the bass line as performed by the late great, Scott LaFaro. Here's a hint: most of the bass line is a voice-led guide tone line. Check with the answer key (Appendix: p. 147, Bonus, CD2, track 31) for results. Then sing the bass line, using the new chromatic solfege syllables, for additional practice.

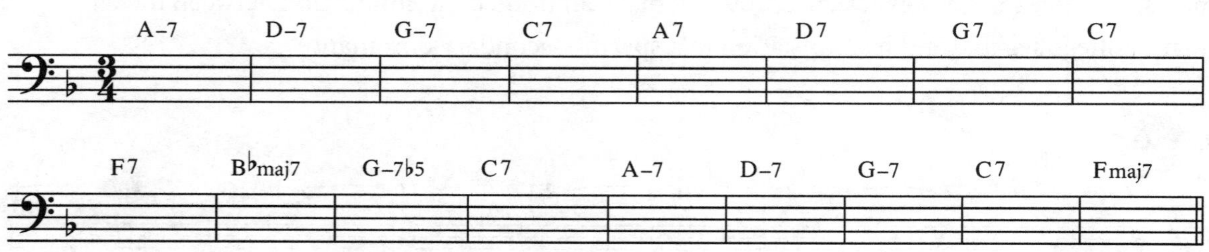

HOOKING UP WITH *THE REAL EASY BOOK* In Chapter One, you sang through the root motion of the changes to the following songs: "Doxy," "Groove Merchant," "Sir John," "So Danco Samba," "St. Thomas" and "Yardbird Suite." Eleven chapters later, you're now able to put these songs through the full routine, including recognizing the secondary dominant harmonies.

The "proof is in the pudding;" take a look and a listen to songs that contain some non-diatonic harmony, and I'll bet you the majority of these chords will fall into one of the two groups studied in this chapter. Here are a few songs that include both modal interchange and secondary dominant harmonies: "All of Me," Marks & Simons; "But Not for Me," George and Ira Gershwin; "Georgia on My Mind," Hoagy Carmichael; "Hello," Lionel Ritchie; "How Deep is Your Love," Barry, Maurice and Robin Gibb; "In My Life," Lennon & McCartney; "What a Wonderful World," Thiele & Weiss; and "You Never Give Me Your Money," Lennon & McCartney.

HELPING OUT THE EARS WITH THEORY

Knowing some harmonic theory offers an expectation of what *could* occur harmonically: a great help when analyzing chord changes. The ears can always use some extra help from the brain, and limiting the likely choices can save us a lot of listening time. Since Chapter One, we've built quite a large list of harmonic possibilities to choose from: triads or seventh chords; root position or inversions; diatonic or non-diatonic harmony. I think you'll find the following chart helpful in organizing your decisions about hearing the changes. It's organized by which diatonic note is in the bass, and all the possible chord choices (thus far) that bass note might suggest. More importantly is a list of conditions that will probably limit the choices to one or two possibilities. Let's consider the list of conditions first.

1. It is always possible that the chord could be a root position diatonic triad or seventh chord.
2. The chord is possibly an inversion if there's stepwise motion in the bass line.
3. The bass note could be a passing 7th, but only if preceeded by the same chord in root position.
4. It might be a modal interchange chord if we hear a non-diatonic sound, particularly with Le or Te as the bass note.
5. It could be a secondary dominant if it is non-diatonic, and there is root motion of down a perfect 5th to the next chord.

Chord Possibilities — Diatonic Bass Notes

Diatonic Bass Note	Root Position Diatonic	Inversion	Passing 7th	Modal Interchange	Secondary Dominant
DO	I, Imaj7	IV/5	II–/♭7	none	I7, V7/IV
RE	II–, II–7	V/5	III–/♭7	none	II7, V7/V
MI	III–, III–7	I/3	IV/7	none	III7, V7/VI
FA	IV, IVmaj7	none	V/♭7	IV–	none
SOL	V, V7, V7sus4	I/5	VI–/♭7	none	none (it's the V7)
LA	VI–, VI–7	IV/3	VII°/♭7	none	VI7, V7/II
TI	VII°, VII–7♭5	V/3	I/7	none	VII7, V7/III

Keep this chart handy as you work through the following dictation exercises and when you're transcribing the changes to tunes. It's a lot to remember!

But our real job is to *hear*, not *think* what the chords might be. We can employ both the vertical and horizontal approaches to hearing non-diatonic chords as well. Let's test the waters with the next activity.

Activity Eight *Non-Diatonic Dictation*

Listen once again to the same ten progressions in the key of C major from Activity Four (CD2, track 23). This time we will identify all the details along the way. Each example will incorporate one non-diatonic chord. Identify all the chords (again, with Roman numerals) using the following familiar routines.

1. First, listen to the bass line. Some of these notes might be non-diatonic, and some of these bass notes might not be roots.
2. Using the Theory Chart, consider the likely chord choices based on the action in the bass line. This is where brainwork is extremely helpful in limiting choices.
3. Apply the vertical approach, listening up from the root to the third of each chord. Is it major or minor?
4. Perhaps most challenging is determining whether you hear a triad or seventh chord; applying the horizontal approach can fine-tune your decision on this matter.
5. Check your results with the answer key (Appendix: p. 147, Activity Eight, CD2, track 23).

Activity Nine *Rewind... Putting It All Together*

Transcribe the changes to the classic Beatles' tune, "Blackbird." It contains all the harmonic features we've studied throughout this book and is an excellent way to wrap up our work of hearing the changes. Then check in with the answer key for final results (Appendix: p. 148, Activity Nine, CD2, track 32).

If you get a chance, listen to the original recording of this song, it's a real gem! You'll notice there's a tonic pedal tone (G) that threads throughout this harmonic passage, which is not played on the CD2, track 32 version.

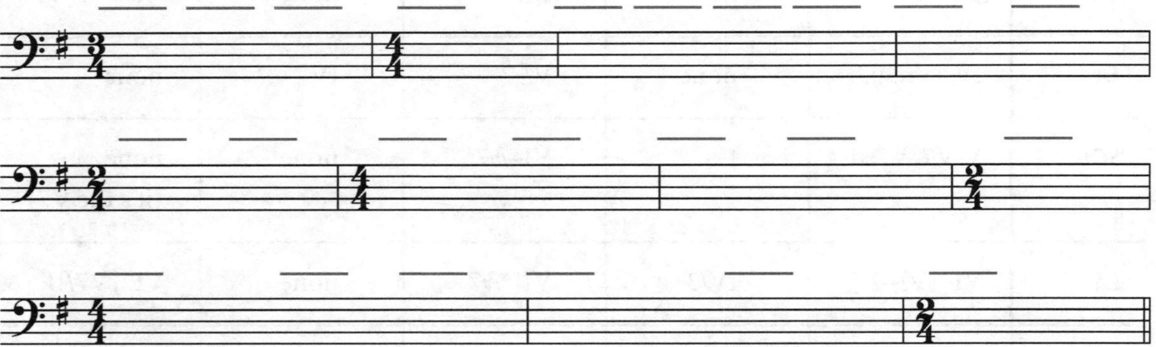

You certainly have come a long way since the first chapter in developing your abilities to hear the changes! In fact, if you return to the seven lead sheets presented in Chapter One, you are now capable of understanding the inner workings of those chord progressions far beyond simply singing through the root motion. Everything is there: diatonic triads and seventh chords; inversions and passing 7ths; modal interchange and secondary dominant harmonies. We've come full circle.

Give these seven songs the complete harmonic workout: reviewing the bass lines with numbers and solfege; singing the root to third relationships; recognizing the guide tones, the 3rds and 7ths, via solfege syllables; voice-leading through the changes; memorizing the chord progressions and playing them in a variety of keys. Doing this will provide a good benchmark of the significant progress you've made with hearing the changes over these past few months. Congratulations!

For Your Consideration Discuss with your classmates the various practice routines you find helpful with recognizing non-diatonic harmonies within the chord progression.

Making It Your Own Look for songs that contain some non-diatonic chords. Do some of these "outsiders" now look and sound familiar after learning the chord patterns we've studied here?

Summary

Congratulations! Having come this far, you've gained considerable harmonic listening skills.

We began with hearing the bass line as a diatonic melody, using numbers and solfege syllables as our tonal translators. From there, we gradually built our harmonic vocabulary, identifying major, minor, diminished, augmented, and sus4 triads; then we added major 7th, dominant 7th, minor 7th and minor 7♭5 chords to the mix. Continue your study of recognizing these individual chord types—the more you recognize chord quality automatically, the easier and faster it will be to recognize chord changes in progressions.

We spent time building our diatonic vocabulary in the major key, starting with the I, IV and V major triads, and then progressed to the remaining diatonic minor and diminished triads: II–, III–, VI– and VII°. From there, we extended our studies to include recognition of diatonic seventh chord patterns. In the final chapters we explored minor key diatonic harmony, and then investigated the chromatic scale to identify some non-diatonic chords, highlighting modal interchange and secondary dominant possibilities.

We developed two approaches to hearing chord changes and analyzing chord progressions: "vertical" and "horizontal." Working up from the bass line, we used the vertical approach to identify the quality of the third of the chord as being major or minor. We referred to the third as the "guide tone." With the inclusion of seventh chords, we then added the seventh as a second guide tone. As our harmonic vocabulary expanded, particularly with the addition of hearing chord inversions, we added the horizontal approach.

Using the horizontal approach combined with solfege syllables, we learned to identify chord tones in relation to the key. Referencing the key allowed us to prepare specific questions to "ask" the chord. For example, in the key of C major, investigating whether the chord is the diatonic A minor, or the non-diatonic A major, we could prepare to hear either C (Do) or C♯ (Di) of the key. If we heard Do, we would conclude we heard the diatonic A minor triad; if we heard Di, it had to be a non-diatonic A major chord. Using this horizontal approach becomes particularly helpful when the chords are changing quickly in progressions.

We spent time learning how to voice-lead through a chord progression, listening to the chord tones in relation to the key, again using solfege syllables. This was our first attempt at listening to the chord progression in a linear fashion, and hearing the common-tone and stepwise connections from one set of chord tones to the next.

We sang as much as possible throughout our studies, because singing is an excellent way to "feed" our inner hearing memory bank. It's also a terrific way to confirm "out loud" what our inner hearing is actually hearing. "If you can sing it, you most likely can hear it," is one of my mottos.

Using numbers and solfege syllables made transposition an easy task. As your ears grow more familiar with listening to repeated bass line and chord patterns, your ability to transpose and play chord progressions in different keys increases.

The importance of understanding how melody and harmony work together was emphasized. The melody often contains chord tones of the accompanying harmony, and thus offers clues as to what that harmony is.

Your knowledge of basic theory has been put to excellent use, allowing you to identify and organize what you're hearing harmonically. Our primary goal in this book was to improve your ability to recognize "the changes" quickly and easily. The theory presented provides the musical vocabulary to do so.

You have much harmonic vocabulary to absorb and practice at this point. There are thousands of songs in the real musical world which provide opportunities to practice hearing diatonic harmonies in major and minor keys. Add to those the possibility of non-diatonic chords, and there are thousands more. Keep practicing with these harmonic ingredients, remembering that the ear grows in time—it is not an overnight success story.

Now that you've learned to recognize diatonic and non-diatonic harmony and the melody's relationship to those harmonies, the next step is to incorporate this knowledge into every aspect of your musical experience. When playing songs, memorizing and/or transcribing them, improvising, composing, arranging, or just listening to music, let your newly-educated inner ear work for you: let it be your first tool for analysis. Then use your instrument if you need to verify what your ear tells you about the music. Take the techniques you've practiced in this book "to the street," and get some hands-on experience with all you've learned.

Good luck!

Roberta Radley

November, 2008

Appendix

Chapter 1

Activity Five, CD1, track 2

Chapter 2

Activity Three, CD1, track 5

1. Yes 2. Yes 3. No 4. Yes 5. No 6. No 7. Yes 8. No 9. Yes 10. Yes

Activity Five, CD1, track 9

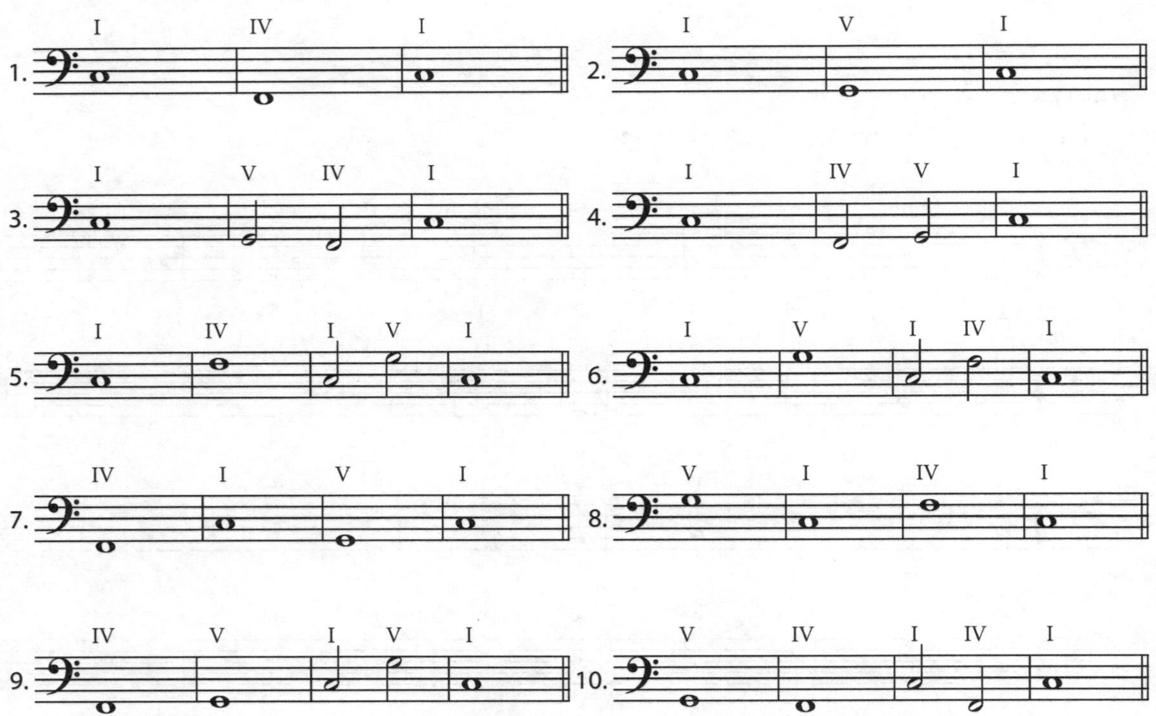

Activity Six

2.
3.
F
C
F
B♭
F
B♭
F
B♭
E♭
B♭
E♭
B♭
E♭
A♭
E♭
G
D
G
C
G
D
A
D
G
D
A
E
A
D
A

Chapter 2

Activity Six *(cont'd)*

Activity Seven, CD1, track 12

1.	do 1	re 2	mi 3	la 6	re 2	mi 3	fa 4	sol 5	do 1
2.	do 1	mi 3	la 6	re 2	sol 5	ti 7	do 1	fa 4	do 1
3.	do 1	la 6	re 2	sol 5	mi 3	do 1	fa 4	sol 5	do 1
4.	do 1	ti 7	la 6	re 2	sol 5	do 1	fa 4	ti 7	do 1
5.	do 1	fa 4	ti 7	mi 3	la 6	re 2	sol 5	ti 7	do 1

Chapter 3

Activity Three, CD1, track 15

1. minor 2. minor 3. major 4. minor 5. major
6. major 7. minor 8. major 9. minor 10. major

Chapter 4

Activity One, CD1, track 23

1. dim 2. minor 3. minor 4. dim 5. dim
6. dim 7. minor 8. dim 9. minor 10. dim

Activity Two, CD1, track 27

1. major 2. aug 3. major 4. major 5. aug
6. aug 7. major 8. aug 9. major 10. aug

Activity Three, CD1, track 28

1. major 2. minor 3. major 4. aug 5. dim 6. minor 7. dim 8. aug 9. major
10. major 11. minor 12. aug 13. aug 14. major 15. minor 16. dim 17. minor
18. dim 19. major 20. minor

Activity Five, CD1, track 31

Key of C

1. I / C   II– / D– | III– / E–   IV / F | V / G   IV / F | I / C ||

2. I / C   II– / D– | III– / E–   VI– / A– | IV / F   V / G | I / C ||

3. I / C   VI– / A– | IV / F   V / G | I / C   IV / F | I / C ||

4. I / C   VI– / A– | II– / D–   V / G | I / C   VII° / B° | I / C ||

5. I / C   VI– / A– | IV / F   II– / D– | V / G   VII° / B° | I / C ||

Chapter 4

Activity Five *(cont'd)*

Key of D

6.	I D	VI– B–	IV G	III– F♯–	II– E–	V A	I D
7.	I D	III– F♯–	VI– B–	V A	IV G	V A	I D
8.	I D	III– F♯–	VI– B–	IV G	V A	VII° C♯°	I D
9.	I D	IV G	I D	VI– B–	V A	IV G	I D
10.	I D	IV G	III– F♯–	II– E–	VI– B–	VII° C♯°	I D

Key of B♭

11.	I B♭	IV E♭	III– D–	VI– G–	II– C–	V F	I B♭
12.	I B♭	V F	VI– G–	III– D–	II– C–	VII° A°	I B♭
13.	I B♭	VII° A°	VI– G–	II– C–	V F	IV E♭	I B♭
14.	I B♭	VII° A°	VI– G–	IV E♭	II– C–	V F	I B♭
15.	I B♭	IV E♭	VII° A°	III– D–	VI– G–	II– C–	I B♭

Bonus, CD1, track 32

"Come Away with Me" Norah Jones

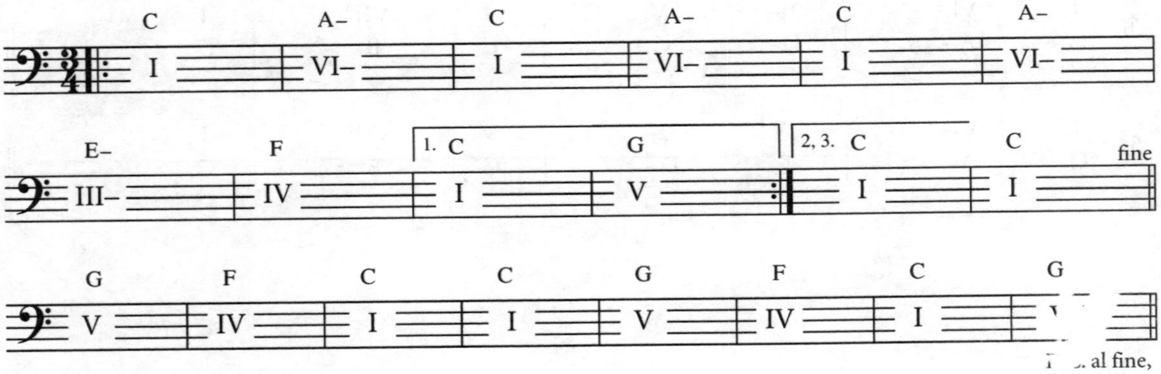

3/4 ||: C: I | A–: VI– | C: I | A–: VI– | C: I | A–: VI– |

E–: III– | F: IV | 1. C: I | G: V :|| 2, 3. C: I | C: I || fine

G: V | F: IV | C: I | C: I | G: V | F: IV | C: I | G: V ||

... al fine,
...rd ending

Chapter 5

Bonus

Activity Four

Chapter 5

Activity Six, CD1, track 39

"Golden Slumbers" The Beatles

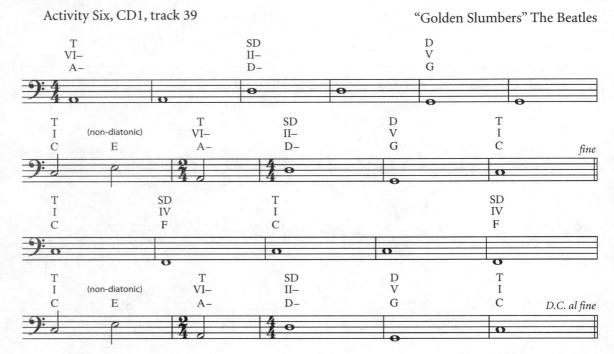

T VI– A– | SD II– D– | D V G

T I C | (non-diatonic) E | T VI– A– | SD II– D– | D V G | T I C *fine*

T I C | SD IV F | T I C | SD IV F

T I C | (non-diatonic) E | T VI– A– | SD II– D– | D V G | T I C *D.C. al fine*

Chapter 6

Activity One, CD1, track 41

Activity Two, CD1, track 42

1. V 2. I 3. III– 4. VI– 5. IV 6. V 7. III– 8. II– 9. VI– 10. I

Activity Three, CD1, track 43

Chapter 6

Bonus, CD1, track 44

"One Hand, One Heart" Leonard Bernstein

G C D G E– B– F C G

Activity Four, CD1, track 48

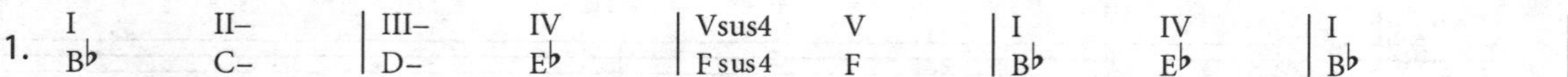

1. I / B♭ | II– / C– | III– / D– | IV / E♭ | Vsus4 / F sus4 | V / F | I / B♭ | IV / E♭ | I / B♭ ||

2. I / B♭ | VI– / G– | II– / C– | Vsus4 / F sus4 | III– / D– | VI– / G– | II– / C– | V / F | I / B♭ ||

3. I / B♭ | III– / D– | VI– / G– | Vsus4 / F sus4 | I / B♭ | VI– / G– | IV / E♭ | Vsus4 / F sus4 | I / B♭ ||

4. I / B♭ | IV / E♭ | I / B♭ | Vsus4 / F sus4 | I / B♭ | V / F | VI– / G– | Vsus4 / F sus4 | I / B♭ ||

5. I / B♭ | IV / E♭ | VII° / A° | III– / D– | VI– / G– | II– / C– | Vsus4 / F sus4 | V / F | I / B♭ ||

Bonus, CD1, track 49

"Europa" Carlos Santana

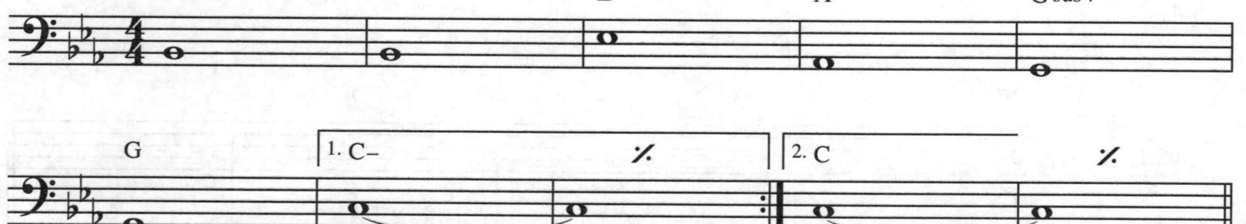

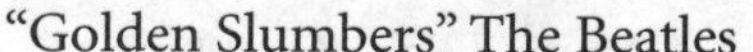

Activity Five, CD1, track 49

"Golden Slumbers" The Beatles

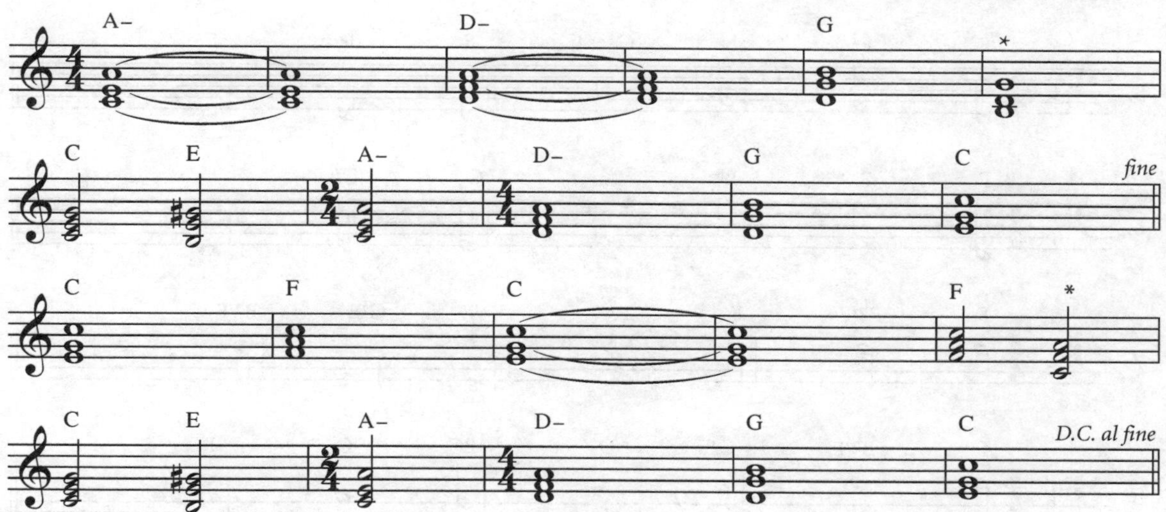

* voicing has been inverted here

Chapter 7

Activity One, CD1, track 53

1. I/3 2. III– 3. V 4. I/5 5. III– 6. I/5 7. I/3 8. V 9. III– 10. I/3

Activity Two, CD1, track 57

1. I 2. IV/5 3. IV/3 4. VI– 5. IV/5 6. I 7. VI– 8. IV/3 9. IV/5 10. I

Activity Three, CD1, track 61

1. V/3 2. VII° 3. II– 4. V/5 5. VII° 6. V/5 7. V/3 8. II– 9. V/3 10. VII°

Activity Four, CD1, track 63

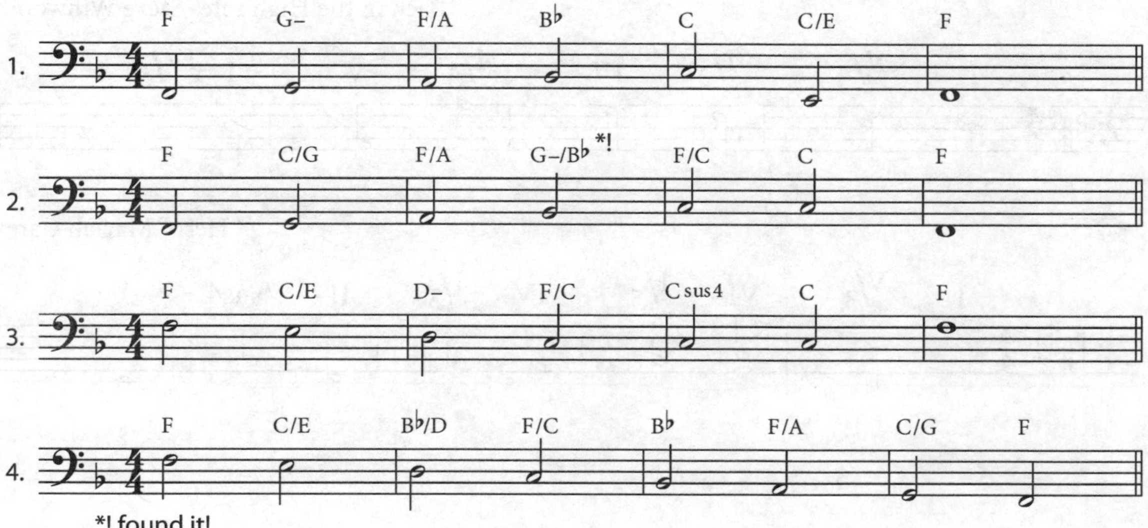

*! found it!

Chapter 7

Activity Four *(cont'd)*

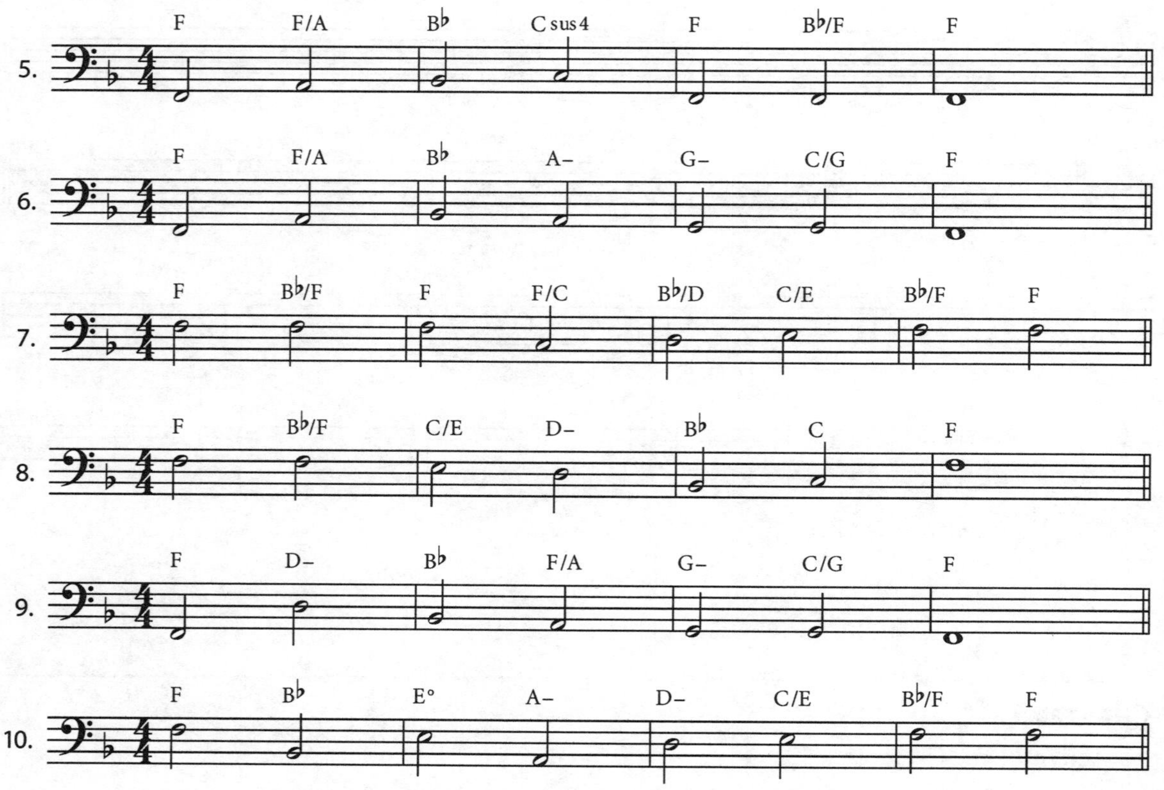

Bonus, CD1, track 64

"Like a Rolling Stone" Bob Dylan

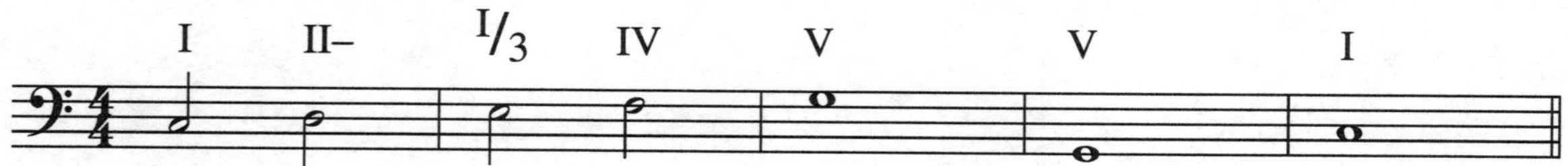

"Back in the High Life" Steve Winwood

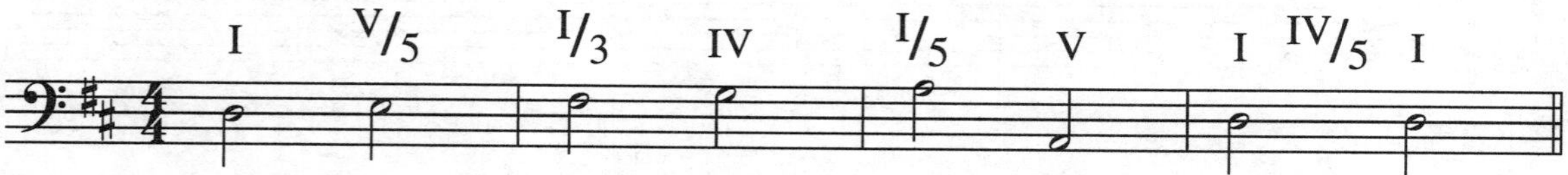

"Hero" Mariah Carey

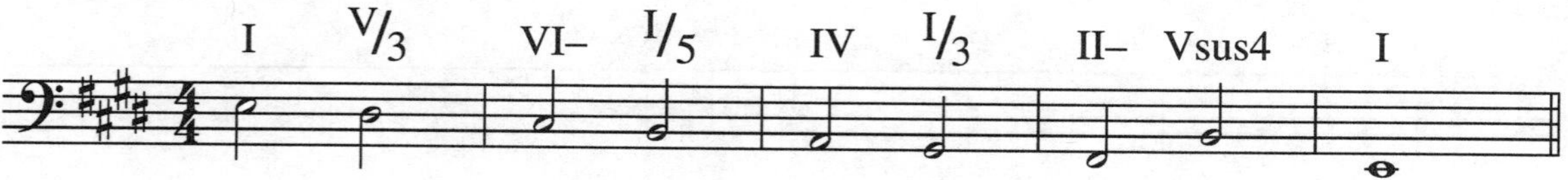

"Tears in Heaven" Eric Clapton

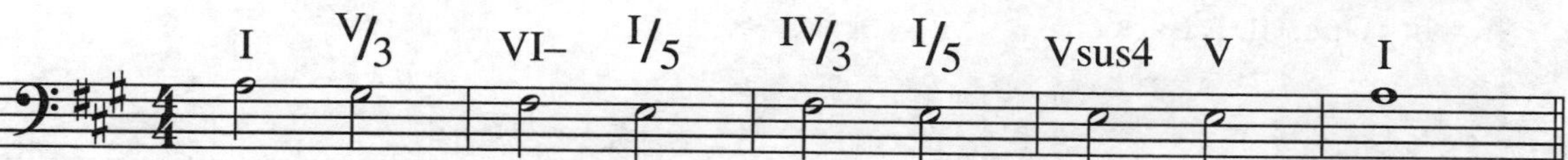

Activity Five

Activity Six

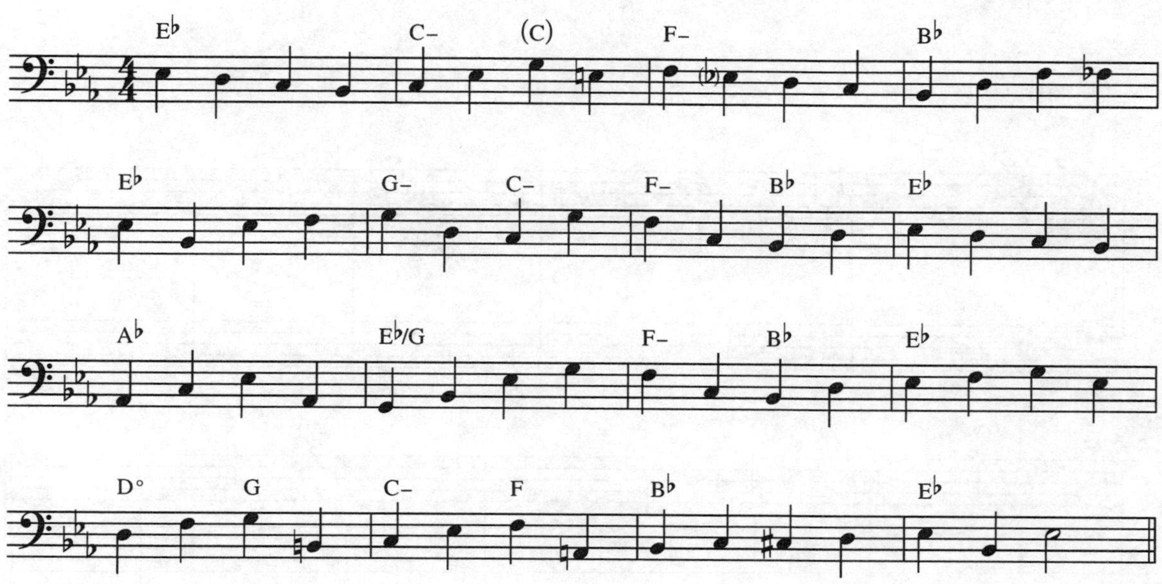

Chapter 8

Activity One, CD1, track 65

1.
C D– E– A– F C 
1 3 5 5 ♭3 5 ♭3 5 5 ♭3 5 1 5 3 5 3 1
F G C F/C C C
1 3 5 3 1 3 5 1 1 5 3 1 3 1 1 1 3 5 1

2.
D B– E– F♯– 
5 1 1 1 5 ♭3 1 ♭3 5 1 1 ♭3 5 1
G B– A/C♯ D D
1 3 5 1 1 3 1 3 1 5 3 1 1 1

3.
B♭ E♭ B♭/D D*
5 1 5 1 5 3 5 3 5 3 5 1 5 1 5 3 1 3
G– C– F B♭
1 ♭3 1 ♭3 1 5 1 5 1 5 3 5 3 1 3 5 1 5 1 1

* non-diatonic chord

Activity Three, CD1, track 66

2.

C G/B F/A C/G F G

E– A– D– G G/B C F C

3.

E♭ G– A♭ B♭ G– G C– E♭/B♭

A♭ B♭ G– C– F– F E♭/B♭ G A♭ B♭ E♭

Bonus

"Fly Me to the Moon" Bart Howard

Chapter 8

Activity Four, CD1, track 68

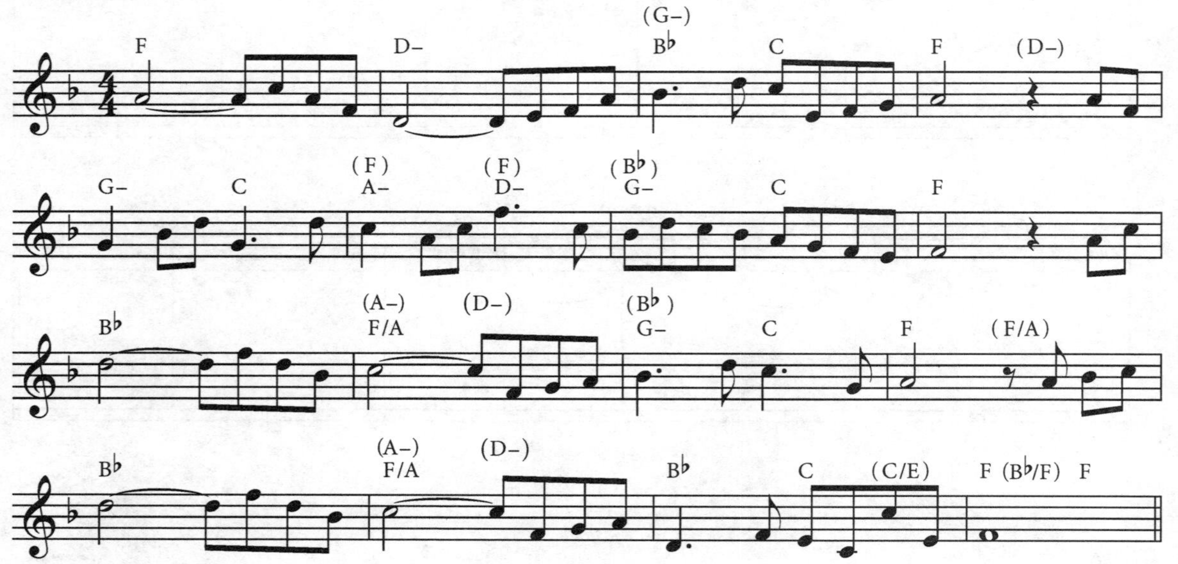

Activity Six, CD1, track 69

Chapter 9

Activity Three, CD1, track 74

1. major 2. dom7 3. maj7 4. dom7 5. major
6. maj7 7. maj7 8. dom7 9. major 10. dom7

Activity Four, CD1, track 76

1.	I G	Imaj7 Gmaj7	IV C	IVmaj7 Cmaj7	V D	V7 D7	Imaj7 Gmaj7	‖
2.	I G	II– A–	III– B–	IV C	V D	V7 D7	I G	‖
3.	I G	VI– E–	IVmaj7 Cmaj7	V7 D7	Imaj7 Gmaj7	IVmaj7 Cmaj7	I G	‖
4.	Imaj7 Gmaj7	IVmaj7 Cmaj7	III– B–	VI– E–	II– A–	V7 D7	Imaj7 Gmaj7	‖
5.	I G	IVmaj7 Cmaj7	VII° F♯°	III– B–	VI– E–	V7 D7	Imaj7 Gmaj7	‖
6.	I G	III– B–	VI– E–	II– A–	V D	V7 D7	I G	‖
7.	I G	V/3 D/F♯	VI– E–	IV C	II– A–	V7 D7	I G	‖
8.	I G	III– B–	VI– E–	I/5 G/D	IVmaj7 Cmaj7	V7 D7	I G	‖
9.	I G	I/3 G/B	IV C	IVmaj7 Cmaj7	V D	V7 D7	Imaj7 Gmaj7	‖
10.	I G	V/3 D/F♯	IV/3 C/E	I/5 G/D	IV C	V7 D7	Imaj7 Gmaj7	‖

Activity Five, CD1, track 79

1. minor 2. min7 3. min7♭5 4. min7 5. dim
6. min7♭5 7. minor 8. min7 9. dim 10. minor

Chapter 9

Activity Six, CD1, track 80

	Bar 1		Bar 2		Bar 3		Bar 4
1.	Imaj7	IVmaj7	Imaj7	V7sus4	Imaj7	V7	Imaj7
	Fmaj7	B♭maj7	Fmaj7	C7sus4	Fmaj7	C7	Fmaj7
2.	Imaj7	II–7	III–7	VI–7	II–7	V7	Imaj7
	Fmaj7	G–7	A–7	D–7	G–7	C7	Fmaj7
3.	Imaj7	VI–7	II–7	III–7	IVmaj7	V7sus4	Imaj7
	Fmaj7	D–7	G–7	A–7	B♭maj7	C7sus4	Fmaj7
4.	Imaj7	III–7	IVmaj7	II–7	V7sus4	V7	Imaj7
	Fmaj7	A–7	B♭maj7	G–7	C7sus4	C7	Fmaj7
5.	Imaj7	VI–7	II–7	V7	Imaj7	IVmaj7	Imaj7
	Fmaj7	D–7	G–7	C7	Fmaj7	B♭maj7	Fmaj7
6.	Imaj7	II–7	III–7	IVmaj7	II–7	V7	Imaj7
	Fmaj7	G–7	A–7	B♭maj7	G–7	C7	Fmaj7
7.	Imaj7	VI–7	IVmaj7	II–7	V7sus4	VII–7♭5	Imaj7
	Fmaj7	D–7	B♭maj7	G–7	C7sus4	E–7♭5	Fmaj7
8.	Imaj7	IVmaj7	III–7	II–7	IVmaj7	V7	Imaj7
	Fmaj7	B♭maj7	A–7	G–7	B♭maj7	C7	Fmaj7
9.	Imaj7	VI–7	II–7	V7sus4	IVmaj7	VII–7♭5	Imaj7
	Fmaj7	D–7	G–7	C7sus4	B♭maj7	E–7♭5	Fmaj7
10.	Imaj7	IVmaj7	VII–7♭5	III–7	VI–7	V7sus4	Imaj7
	Fmaj7	B♭maj7	E–7♭5	A–7	D–7	C7sus4	Fmaj7

Chapter 10

Activity Two, CD2, track 2

1.

2.
B♭maj7 G–7 C–7 F7sus4 B♭maj7 E♭maj7 B♭maj7
ti do do do ti la ti
mi sol fa fa mi mi mi

3.
B♭maj7 F7 G–7 E♭maj7 C–7 F7 B♭maj7
ti ti do la do ti ti
mi fa sol mi fa fa mi

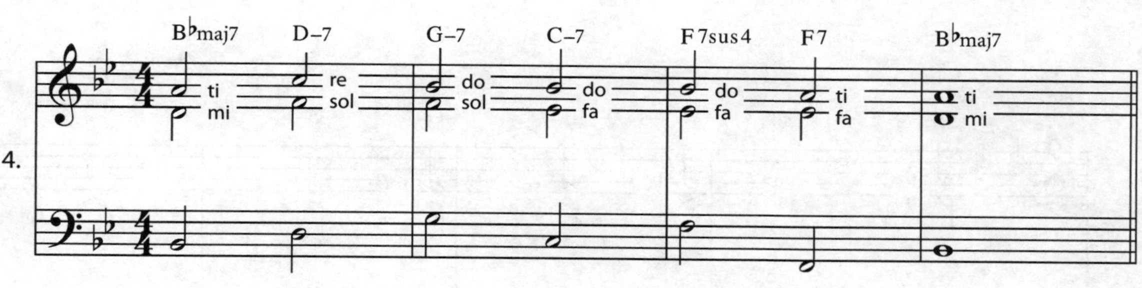
4.
B♭maj7 D–7 G–7 C–7 F7sus4 F7 B♭maj7
ti re do do do ti ti
mi sol sol fa fa fa mi

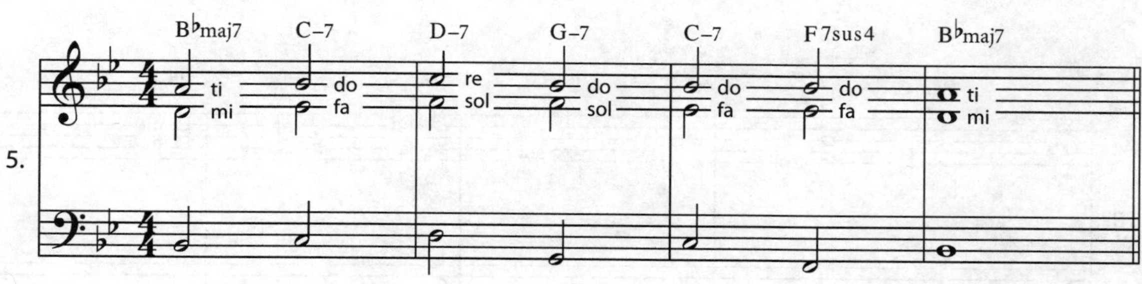
5.
B♭maj7 C–7 D–7 G–7 C–7 F7sus4 B♭maj7
ti do re do do do ti
mi fa sol sol fa fa mi

6.
B♭maj7 E♭maj7 D–7 C–7 F7sus4 F7 B♭maj7
ti la sol fa fa fa mi
mi mi re do do ti ti

Chapter 10

Activity Two *(cont'd)*

Activity Four

Chapter 10

Activity Five *(cont'd)*

"Never Saw Blue Like That Before" Shawn Colvin

"Don't Let the Sun Go Down on Me" Elton John

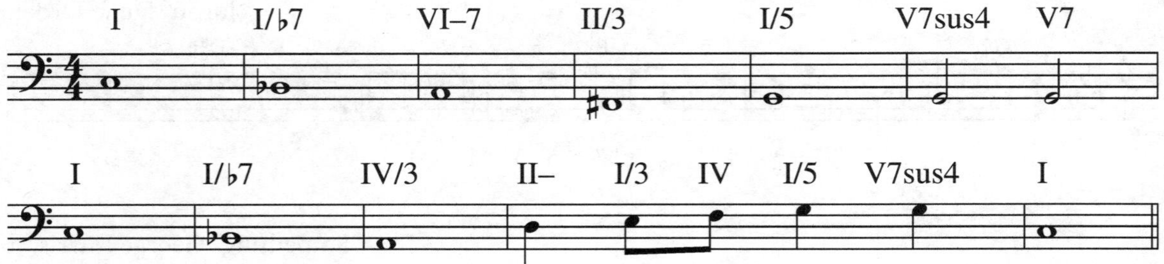

"Feels So Good" Chuck Mangione

Activity Six, CD2, track 7

Activity Seven, CD2, track 8

1. minor 2. maj7 3. major 4. dom7 5. min7 6. major 7. minor 8. min7♭5 9. dom7 10. maj7 11. minor 12. min7♭5 13. major 14. min7 15. dom7 16. minor 17. maj7 18. diminished 19. dom7 20. major

Chapter 11

Activity Two, CD2, track 11

Chapter 11

Activity Two *(cont'd)*

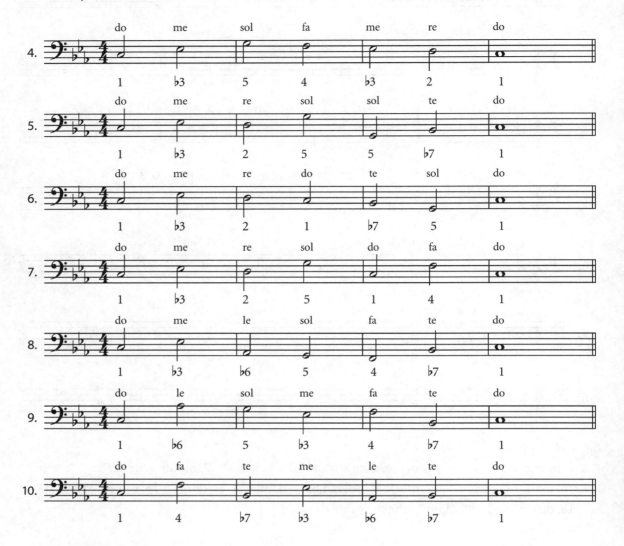

4.
do me sol fa me re do
1 ♭3 5 4 ♭3 2 1

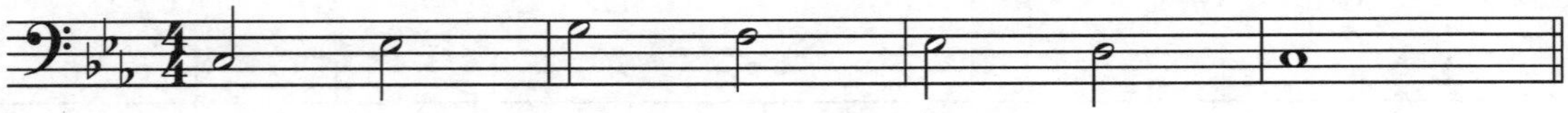

5.
do me re sol sol te do
1 ♭3 2 5 5 ♭7 1

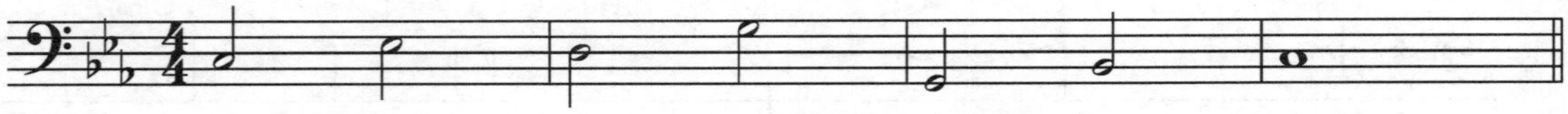

6.
do me re do te sol do
1 ♭3 2 1 ♭7 5 1

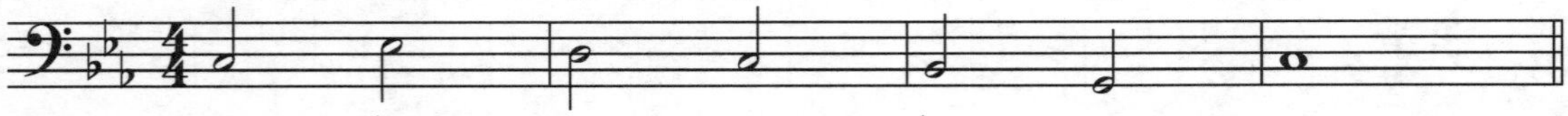

7.
do me re sol do fa do
1 ♭3 2 5 1 4 1

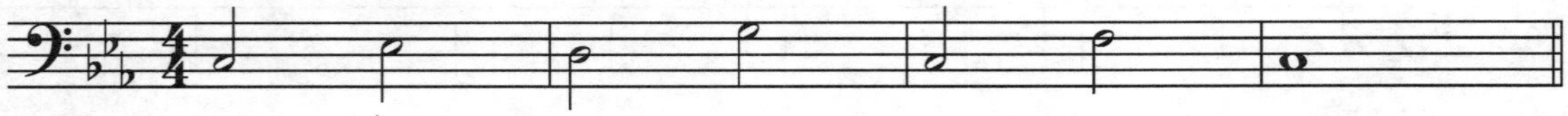

8.
do me le sol fa te do
1 ♭3 ♭6 5 4 ♭7 1

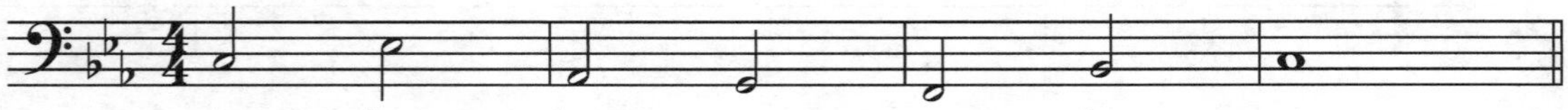

9.
do le sol me fa te do
1 ♭6 5 ♭3 4 ♭7 1

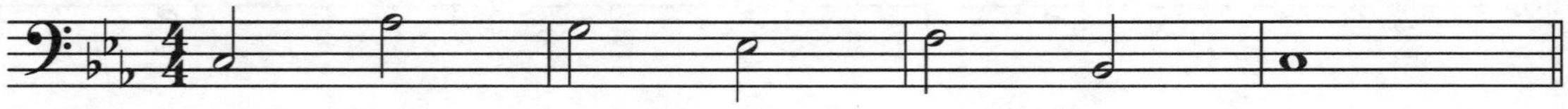

10.
do fa te me le te do
1 4 ♭7 ♭3 ♭6 ♭7 1

Activity Seven, CD2, track 16

1.
I– IV– I– V– I– V I–

2.
I– IV– ♭VII ♭III II° V– I–

3.
I– IV– V– I– ♭VI ♭VII I–

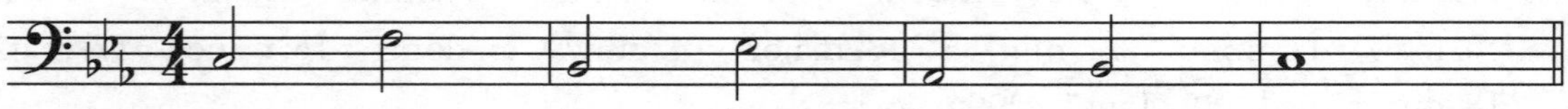

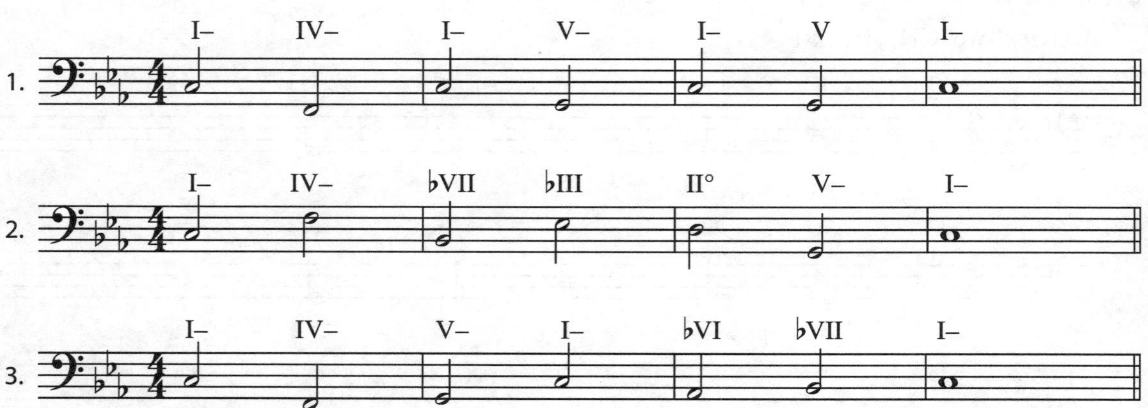

Bonus, CD2, track 17

"Hotel California" The Eagles

Activity Eight, CD2, track 20 — "Serenade to a Cuckoo" Roland Kirk

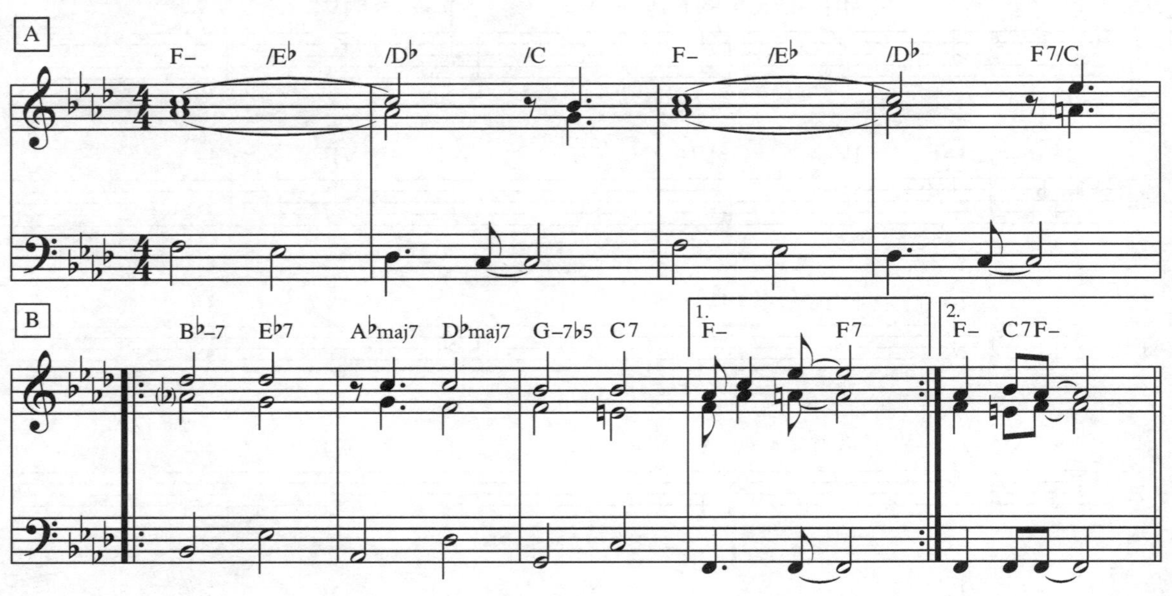

Chapter 12

Activity Two

Activity Three

Bonus

Activity Four, CD2, track 23

Chapter 12

Activity Four *(cont'd)*

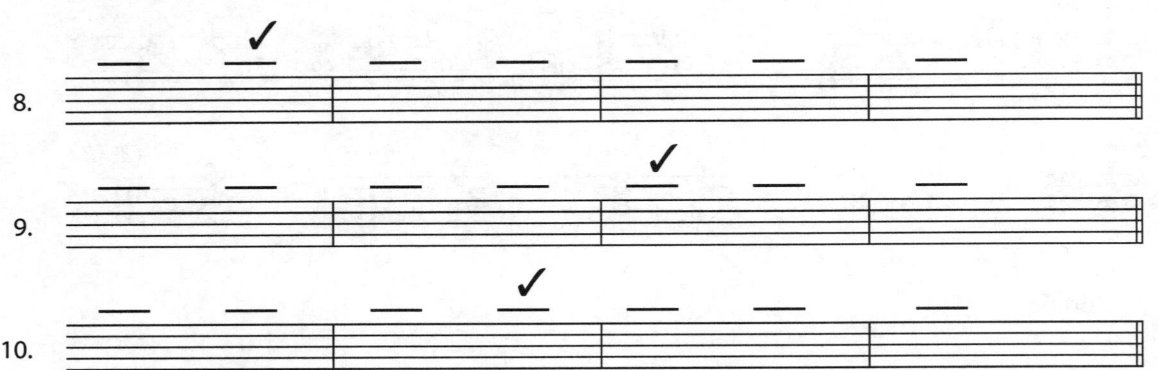

Activity Five, CD2, track 25

Activity Six, CD2, track 28

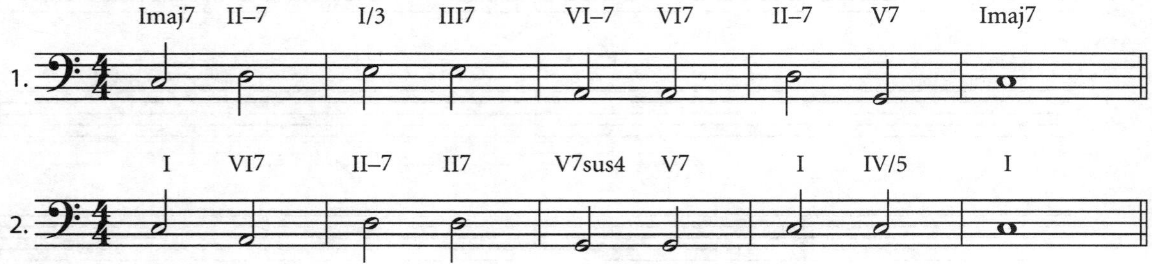

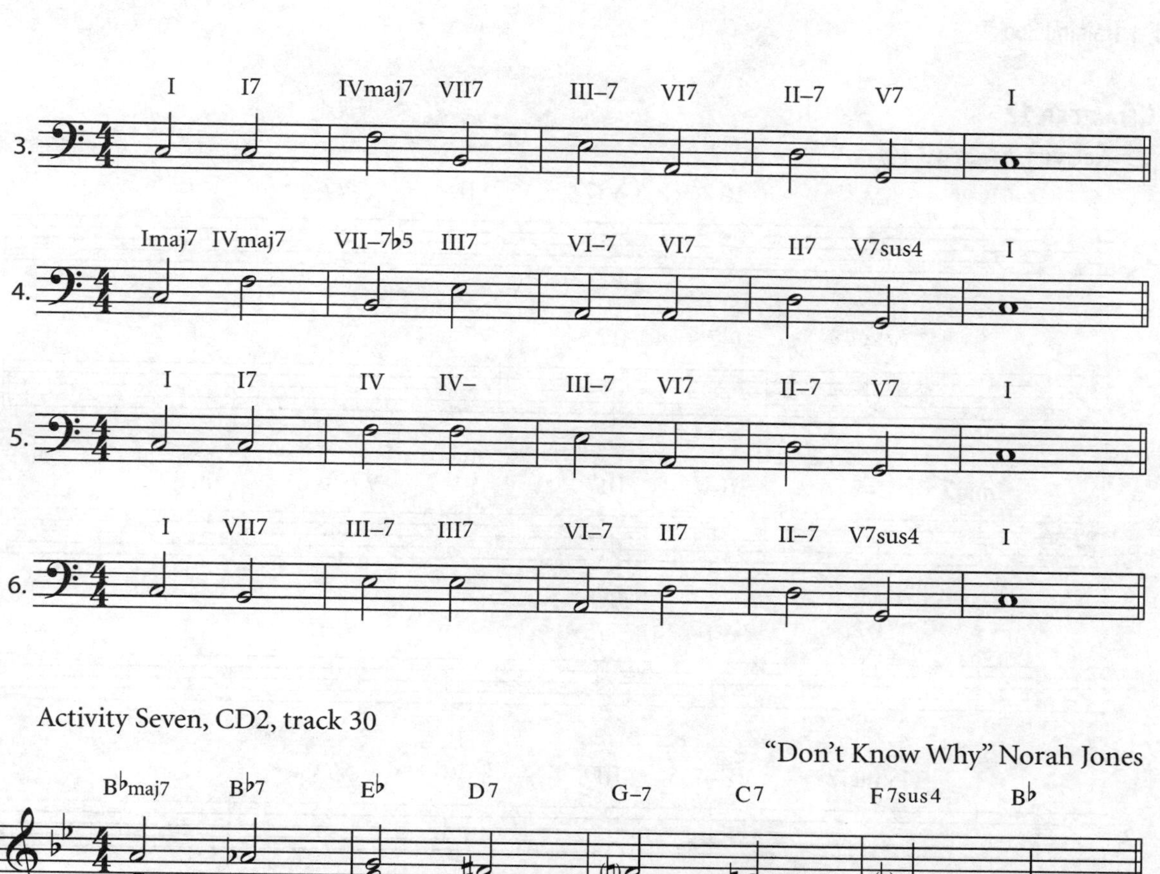

Activity Seven, CD2, track 30

"Don't Know Why" Norah Jones

Bonus, CD2, track 31

"Waltz for Debby" Bill Evans

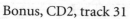

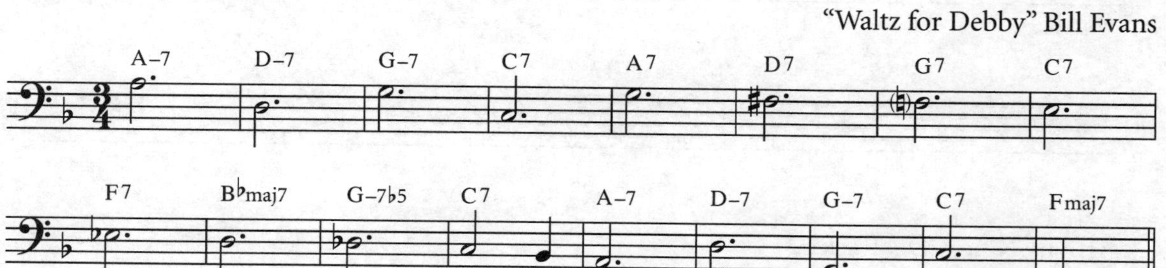

Activity Eight, CD2, track 23

Chapter 12

Activity Eight *(cont'd)*

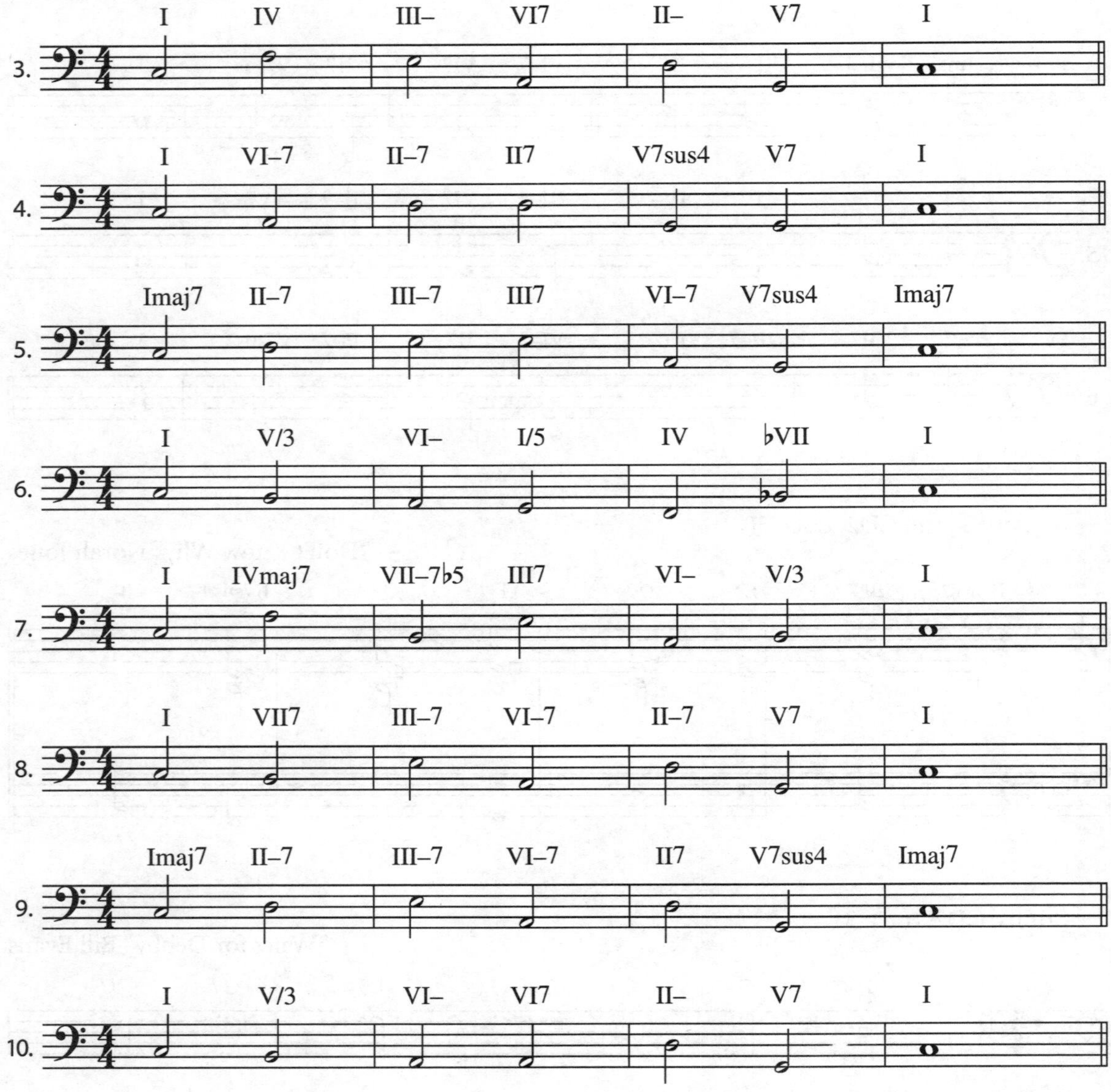

3. I IV III– VI7 II– V7 I
4. I VI–7 II–7 II7 V7sus4 V7 I
5. Imaj7 II–7 III–7 III7 VI–7 V7sus4 Imaj7
6. I V/3 VI– I/5 IV ♭VII I
7. I IVmaj7 VII–7♭5 III7 VI– V/3 I
8. I VII7 III–7 VI–7 II–7 V7 I
9. Imaj7 II–7 III–7 VI–7 II7 V7sus4 Imaj7
10. I V/3 VI– VI7 II– V7 I

Activity Nine, CD2, track 32

"Blackbird" The Beatles

G A–7 G/B G C A7/C♯ D B7/D♯ E– E♭
Gmaj7/D A7/C♯ C C– G/B A7 D7sus4
G C G/B A7 D7sus4 G

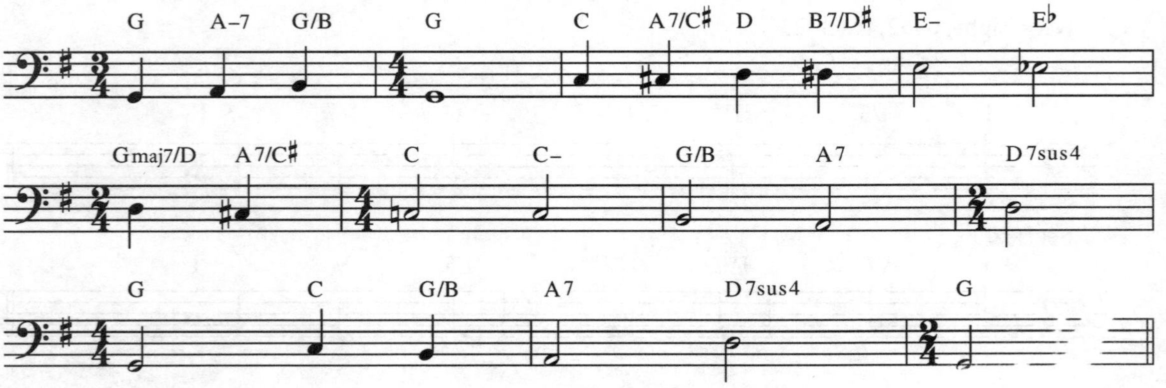

Discography

Song	*Composer*	*Artist/Album*
Afro Blue	Mongo Santamaria	Abbey Lincoln: "Abbey Is Blue"
Ain't No Sunshine When She's Gone	Bill Withers	Bill Withers: "The Best of Bill Withers"
Alice in Wonderland	Fain and Hilliard	Bill Evans Trio: "Sunday at the Village Vanguard"
All I Have to Do Is Dream	Boudleaux Bryant	The Everly Brothers: "The Very Best of the Everly Brothers"
All of Me	Simons and Marks	Dinah Washington: "Compact Jazz: Dinah Washington"
Alone Again (Naturally)	Gilbert O'Sullivan	Gilbert O'Sullivan: "The Virgin Suicides"
And When I Die	Laura Nyro	Blood, Sweat and Tears: "Blood, Sweat and Tears"
Autumn Leaves	Prévert, Kosma and Mercer	Frank Sinatra: "Where Are You?"
Back in the High Life	Jennings and Winwood	Steve Winwood: "Back in the High Life"
Bad Moon Rising	John Fogerty	Creedence Clearwater Revival: "The Concert"
Beauty and the Beast	Ashman and Menken	Walt Disney: "Beauty and the Beast" (soundtrack)
Best of What's Around	Dave Matthews	Dave Matthews Band: "Under the Table and Dreaming"
Beyond the Sea	Lawrence and Trenet	Bobby Darin: "The Ultimate Bobby Darin"
Black Orpheus	Luiz Bonfá	Wayne Shorter: "Shorter Moments"
Blackbird	Lennon and McCartney	Beatles: "The Beatles" (white album)
Blue Bayou	Orbison and Melson	Linda Ronstadt: "Linda Ronstadt"
Blue Sky	Dickey Betts	Allman Brothers: "Eat a Peach"
Brown Eyed Girl	Van Morrison	Van Morrison: "The Best of Van Morrison"
But Not For Me	George and Ira Gershwin	Kenny Burrell: "Introducing Kenny Burrell-The First Blue Note Sessions"
Chega de Saudade	Antonio Jobim	Joao Gilberto: "Prado Pereira de Oliveira"
Cold, Cold Heart	Hank Williams	Norah Jones: "Come Away With Me"
Come Away With Me	Norah Jones	Norah Jones: "Come Away With Me"
Crying	Roy Orbison	Roy Orbison: "The Essential Roy Orbison"
Daniel	John and Taupin	Elton John: "Don't Shoot the Piano Player"
Dindi	Antonio Jobim	Jon Lucien: "By Request"
Django	John Lewis	MJQ: "The Modern Jazz Quartet"
Do-Re-Mi	Richard Rodgers	Soundtrack from "The Sound of Music"
Don't Know Why	Jesse Harris	Norah Jones: "Come Away With Me"
Don't Let the Sun Go Down on Me	John and Taupin	Elton John: "Caribou"
Don't Play That Song	Ertegun and Nelson	Aretha Franklin: "Queen of Soul"

Song	*Composer*	*Artist/Album*
Don't Stop Believing	Cain, Perry, and Schon	Journey: "Escape"
Duke of Earl	Edwards, Dixon and Williams	Gene Chandler: "Original Solid Gold"
Europa	Costa and Santana	Carlos Santana: "Carlos Santana and Wayne Shorter Live at the Montreux Jazz Festival 1988"
Every Breath You Take	Sting	The Police: "Synchronicity"
Every Little Thing She Does Is Magic	Sting	The Police: "Every Breath You Take"
Every Time You Go Away	Paul Young	Paul Young: "Super Hits"
Feels So Good	Chuck Mangione	Chuck Mangione: "Live at the Hollywood Bowl"
Fly Me to the Moon	Bart Howard	Frank Sinatra: "Sinatra at the Sands"
Fragile	Sting	Sting: "Nothing Like the Sun"
Georgia On My Mind	Hoagy Carmichael	Ray Charles: "The Very Best of Ray Charles"
Gloria's Step	Scott LaFaro	Bill Evans Trio: "Sunday at the Village Vanguard"
God Bless the Child	Herzog and Holiday	Billy Holiday: "The Very Best of Billie Holiday"
Golden Lady	Stevie Wonder	Stevie Wonder: "Inner Visions"
Golden Slumbers	Lennon and McCartney	Beatles: "Abbey Road"
Groovin'	Caveliere and Brigati	The Young Rascals: "Groovin"
Have a Heart	Bonnie Hayes	Bonnie Raitt: "Nick of Time"
Have You Ever Seen the Rain	John Fogerty	Creedence Clearwater Revival: "The Long Road Home"
Heat Wave	Holland, Holland and Dozier	Martha and the Vandellas: "Soul Anthems 1"
Hello	Lionel Ritchie	Lionel Ritchie: "Can't Slow Down"
Here Comes the Sun	George Harrison	Beatles: "Abbey Road"
Here, There and Everywhere	Lennon and McCartney	Beatles: "Revolver"
Hero	Afanasieff and Carey	Mariah Carey: "Music Box"
Hold My Hand	Bryan, Felber and Rucker	Hootie and the Blowfish: "Cracked Rear View"
Hotel California	Felder and Henley	The Eagles: "Hotel California"
How Deep Is Your Love	Barry, Maurice and Robin Gibb	The Bee Gees: "Saturday Night Fever"
Hurts So Good	Green and Mellencamp	John Cougar: "American Fool"
I Call Your Name	Lennon and McCartney	Beatles: "Long Tall Sally"
I Can't Help Myself	Holland, Holland and Dozier	The Four Tops: "Motown 1's"
I Got Rhythm	George and Ira Gershwin	Django Reinhardt: "Djangology"
I Will	Lennon and McCartney	Beatles: "The Beatles" (white album)
I Will Survive	Ferakis and Perren	Gloria Gaynor: "I Will Survive-The Anthology"
I Won't Last a Day Without You	Williams and Nichols	The Carpenters: "Carpenters Gold: 35th Anniversary Edition"
I'm Old Fashioned	Kern and Mercer	John Coltrane: "Blue Train"
If I Were a Bell	Frank Loesser	Miles Davis: "Relaxin' With the Miles Davis Quintet"

Song	*Composer*	*Artist/Album*
Imagine	John Lennon	John Lennon: "Imagine"
Impressions	John Coltrane	John Coltrane: "The Very Best of John Coltrane"
In My Life	Lennon and McCartney	Beatles: "Rubber Soul"
In the Midnight Hour	Cropper and Pickett	Wilson Pickett: "In the Midnight Hour"
Inner Urge	Joe Henderson	Joe Henderson: "Inner Urge"
It's Too Late	King and Stern	Carol King: "Tapestry"
Just Like You	Keb' Mo'	Keb' Mo' "Just Like You"
La Bamba	Ritchie Valens	Los Lobos: "Party"
Lady Bird	Tadd Dameron	Bud Powell: "The Best of Bud Powell on Verve"
Lady in Red	Chris deBurgh	Chris deBurgh: "The Lady in Red-The Very Best of Chris deBurgh"
Lately	Stevie Wonder	Stevie Wonder: "Hotter Than July"
Lean On Me	Bill Withers	Bill Wither: "The Best of Bill Withers"
Let It Be	Lennon and McCartney	Beatles: "Let It Be"
Let There Be Love	Grant and Rand	Natalie Cole: "Take a Look"
Like a Rolling Stone	Bob Dylan	Bob Dylan: "Highway 61 Revisited"
Litha	Chick Corea	Stan Getz' "Sweet Rain"
Little B's Poem	Bobby Hutcherson	Bobby Hutcherson: "Components"
Little Sunflower	Freddie Hubbard	Freddie Hubbard: "Backlash"
Little Wing	Jimi Hendrix	The Jimi Hendrix Experience: "Axis: Bold As Love"
Maiden Voyage	Herbie Hancock	Herbie Handcock: "Maiden Voyage"
Mandeville	Bill Frisell	Bill Frisell: "Bill, Ron, Paul-A Frisell"
Me and Bobby McGee	Foster and Kristofferson	Janice Joplin: "Pearl"
Me and Julio	Paul Simon	Paul Simon: "Negotiations and Love Songs 1971–1986"
Mercy, Mercy, Mercy	Joe Zawinul	Cannonball Adderley: "Mercy, Mercy, Mercy"
Miss You Fever	Dennis Morgan	Delbert McClinton: "Never Been Rocked Enough"
Money For Nothing	Mark Knopfler	Dire Straits: ""Brothers in Arms"
My Cherie Amour	Stevie Wonder	Stevie Wonder: "My Cherie Amour"
My Favorite Things	Rodgers and Hammerstein	John Coltrane: "Live at Birdland"
My Funny Valentine	Rodgers and Hart	Miles Davis: "My Funny Valentine"
My Girl	Robinson and White	The Temptations: "All the Million Sellers"
Never Saw Blue Like That Before	Shawn Colvin	Shawn Colvin: "Songs from Dawson's Creek, Vol. 2"
New York State of Mind	Billy Joel	Billy Joel: "Turnstiles"
No Buts and No Maybes	Henry Byrd	Professor Long Hair: "House Party New Orleans Style"
No One	Brothers, Harry and Keys	Alicia Keys: "As I Am"
Nowhere Man	Lennon and McCartney	Beatles: "Rubber Soul"
Obladi, Oblada	Lennon and McCartney	Beatles: "The Beatles" (white album)

Song	*Composer*	*Artist/Album*
Octopus's Garden	Ringo Starr	Beatles "Abbey Road"
Old Time Rock and Roll	Bob Seger	Bob Seger: "A Tribute to Bob Seger"
On the Trail	Ferdinand Von Grofe	Wynton Kelly Trio: " It's All Right"
One Hand, One Heart	Bernstein and Sondheim	Bernstein: "West Side Story"
Passion Dance	McCoy Tyner	McCoy Tyner: "The Real McCoy"
Pinball Wizard	Peter Townshend	The Who: "Tommy"
Red Clay	Freddie Hubbard	Freddie Hubbard: "Red Clay"
Respect	Otis Redding	Aretha Franklin: "I Never Loved a Man the Way I Love You"
Saving All My Love For You	Goffin and Masser	Whitney Houston: "Whitney Houston"
Serenade to a Cuckoo	Roland Kirk	Jethro Tull: "This Was"
Shower the People	James Taylor	James Taylor: "In the Pocket"
Smooth Operator	Adu and St. John	Sade: "Diamond Life"
So Much Mine	Jonatha Brooke	The Story: "Angel in the House"
Song For My Father	Horace Silver	Horace Silver: "Song For My Father"
Stand By Me	King, Leiber and Stoller	Otis Redding: "Pain in My Heart"
Start Me Up	The Rolling Stones	Rolling Stones: "Tattoo You"
Stir It Up	Bob Marley	Bob Marley: "Legend"
Stolen Moments	Oliver Nelson	Oliver Nelson: "Blues and the Abstract Truth"
Summertime	George Gershwin	Janis Joplin: "Cheap Thrills"
Surrey With the Fringe on Top	Rodgers and Hammerstein	Miles Davis: "Steamin' with the Miles Davis Quintet"
Sweet Georgia Bright	Charles Lloyd	Charles Lloyd: "Rabo de Nube"
Take Five	Dave Brubeck	Dave Brubeck: "Time Out"
Tattoo	Dench, Eriksen, Ghost and Hermansen	Jordin Spark: "Jordin Spark"
Teach Your Children	Graham Nash	Crosby, Stills and Nash: "Déjà Vu"
Tears In Heaven	Clapton and Jennings	Eric Clapton: "Unplugged"
The House of the Rising Sun	unknown	The Animals: "The House of the Rising Sun"
The Spirit Carries On	Dream Theater	Dream Theater: "Metropolis, Pt 2: Scenes From a Memory"
The Thrill is Gone	Roy Hawkins and Rick Darnell	B.B. King: "Completely Well"
There Is No Greater Love	Jones and Symes	McCoy Tyner: "Inception"
This Boy	Lennon and McCartney	Beatles: "Love Songs"
Tico Tico	Zequinha de Abreu	Paquito d'Rivera: "Tico! Tico!"
Time In a Bottle	Jim Croce	Jim Croce: "Jim Croce Music, Vol. 2"
Time Remembered	Bill Evans	Bill Evans Trio: "Time Remembered"
Under the Boardwalk	Resnick and Young	The Drifters: "Under the Boardwalk"
Wake Me Up Before You Go-Go	George Michael	Wham!: "Make It Big"
Waltz For Debby	Bill Evans	Bill Evans: "Waltz for Debby"

Song	*Composer*	*Artist/Album*
Watch What Happens	Legrand and Gimbel	Wes Montgomery: "A Day in the Life"
We're in This Love Together	Murrah and Stegall	Al Jarreau: "Breakin' Away"
Wedding Bell Blues	Laura Nyro	The 5th Dimension: "The Age of Aquarius"
Well You Needn't	Thelonious Monk	Thelonious Monk: "The Thelonious Monk Story"
What a Wonderful World	Weiss and Thiele	Louis Armstrong: "What a Wonderful World"
What Are You Doing the Rest of Your Life?	Michel Legrand, Bergman and Bergman	Dusty Springfield: "Dusty in London"
What Is This Thing Called Love?	Cole Porter	Bill Evans Trio: "Portrait in Jazz"
When I'm Sixty Four	Lennon and McCartney	Beatles: "Sgt. Pepper's Lonely Hearts Club Band"
While My Guitar Gently Weeps	George Harrison	Beatles: "The Beatles" (white album)
Why Do Fools Fall in Love?	Levy and Lymon	Franky Lymon and the Teenagers: "Doo Wop Classics, Vol. 4"
With or Without You	U2	U2: "The Joshua Tree"
Woody'n You	Dizzy Gillespie	Dizzy Gillespie: "Have Trumpet, Will Excite"
Wrapped Around Your Finger	Sting	The Police: "Synchronicity"
Yesterday	Lennon and McCartney	Beatles: "Help"
You Are My Sunshine	Jimmie Davis	Norman Blake: "O Brother, Where Art Thou?"
You Are the Sunshine of My Life	Stevie Wonder	Stevie Wonder: "Talking Book"
You Don't Have To Be a Star	Glover and Dean	Billy Davis Jr. and Marilyn McCoo: "I Hope We Get to Love in Time"
You Never Give Me Your Money	Lennon and McCartney	Beatles: "Abbey Road"
You Send Me	Sam Cooke	Sam Cooke: "The Man and His Music"
You're Still the One	Lange and Twain	Shania Twain: "Come On Over"
You've Got a Friend	Carol King	James Taylor: "Mud Slide Slim and the Blue Horizon"

ABOUT THE AUTHOR

Roberta Radley is an accomplished performer and a seasoned educator. She "walks the walk," bringing professional experience as a jazz vocalist, pianist and arranger into her classrooms. It is her strong belief that true learning occurs when students can apply their new knowledge and skills to their own personal music-making. There is no substitute for experience.

Ms. Radley is currently the Assistant Chair of the Ear Training department at Berklee College of Music. A Berklee graduate herself, she has been a member of the faculty since 1976.

In many ways, the classroom is Roberta's best and favorite performance stage. Her outstanding accomplishments as an educator earned her the "Outstanding Achievement in Music Education" award from the College. She has taught a wide range of ear training classes, using innovative methods to help students hear music more analytically, and to inspire students to develop their own unique musical voice.

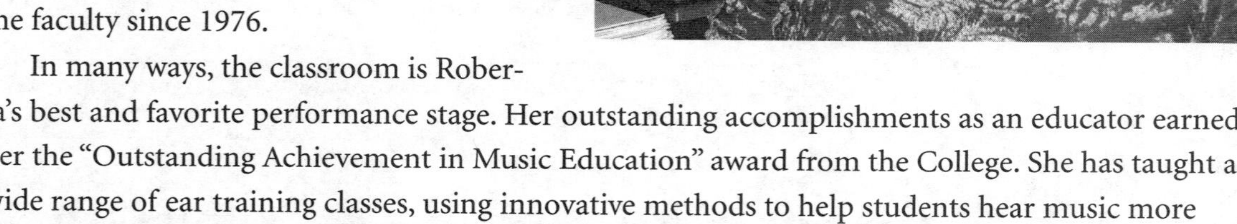

Roberta is currently performing with the jazz vocal trio The Sisters of Swing, featuring several of her own arrangements that give the jazz standards a fresh sound. You can visit the Sisters' website www.thesistersofswing.com, for more information. The group will soon release their first CD for your listening pleasure.

She has authored two online courses ("Basic Ear Training" and "Harmonic Ear Training," through Berkleemusic.com), a DVD, "Harmonic Ear Training," through Berklee Press, and co-authored the Ear Training department's *Core Ear Training Textbooks, Volumes 1–4.* Roberta has traveled across the US and internationally on behalf of the College, presenting seminars and performances.

She has given two presentations at the IAJE Conference: the first described how she presents her harmonic ear training pedagogy in a "live" classroom. The second presentation offered that same pedagogy, but this time in a "virtual" classroom (taught through Berklee's online program).

Now, finally, Ms. Radley is honored to present her specialty, harmonic ear training, in her debut book *The "Real Easy" Ear Training Book.*

LATIN MUSIC BOOKS, CDs, DVD

The Latin Real Book (C, Bb or Eb)

The only professional-level Latin fake book ever published! Over 570 pages. Detailed transcriptions exactly as recorded by:

Ray Barretto, Eddie Palmieri, Fania All-Stars, Tito Puente, Ruben Blades, Los Van Van, NG La Banda, Irakere, Celia Cruz, Arsenio Rodriguez, Tito Rodriguez, Orquesta Aragon, Beny Moré, Cal Tjader, Andy Narell, Mario Bauza, Dizzy Gilllespie, Mongo Santamaria, Manny Oquendo, Puerto Rico All-Stars, Issac Delgaldo, Ft. Apache Band, Dave Valentin, Paquito D'Rivera, Clare Fischer, Chick Corea, Sergio Mendes, Ivan Lins, Djavan, Tom Jobim, Toninho Horta, Joao Bosco, Milton Nascimento, Leila Pinheiro, Gal Costa, **And Many More!**

The Latin Real Book Sampler CD

12 of the greatest Latin Real Book tunes as played by the original artists: Tito Puente, Ray Barretto, Andy Narell, Puerto Rico Allstars, Bacacoto, etc.

$16 list price. Available in U.S.A. only.

The Conga Drummer's Guidebook By Michael Spiro

Includes CD - $28 list price. The only method book specifically designed for the intermediate to advanced conga drummer. It goes behind the superficial licks and explains how to approach any Afro-Latin rhythm with the right feel, so you can create a groove like the pros!.

"This book is awesome. Michael is completely knowledgable about his subject." – Dave Garibaldi

"A breakthrough book for all students of the conga drum." – Karl Perazzo

Introduction to the Conga Drum - DVD

By Michael Spiro

For beginners, or anyone needing a solid foundation in conga drum technique.

Jorge Alabe – "Mike Spiro is a great conga teacher. People can learn real conga technique from this DVD."

John Santos – "A great musician/teacher who's earned his stripes"

1 hour, 55 minutes running time. $25.

Muy Caliente!

Afro-Cuban Play-Along CD and Book

Rebeca Mauleón - Keyboard
Oscar Stagnaro - Bass
Orestes Vilató - Timbales
Carlos Caro - Bongos
Edgardo Cambon - Congas

Over 70 min. of smokin' Latin grooves!

Stereo separation so you can eliminate the bass or piano. Play-along with a rhythm section featuring some of the top Afro-Cuban musicians in the world! $18.

The True Cuban Bass

By Carlos Del Puerto, (bassist with Irakere) and **Silvio Vergara**, $22.

For acoustic or electric bass; English and Spanish text; Includes CDs of either historic Cuban recordings or Carlos playing each exercise; Many transcriptions of complete bass parts for tunes in different Cuban styles – the roots of Salsa.

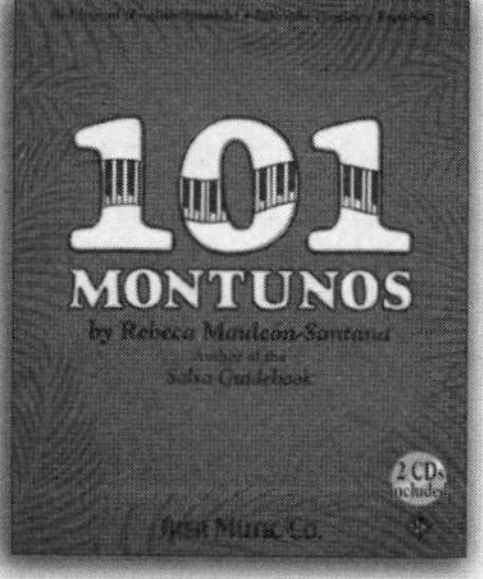

101 Montunos

By Rebeca Mauleón

The only comprehensive study of Latin piano playing ever published.

- Bi-lingual text (English/Spanish)
- 2 CDs of the author demonstrating each montuno
- Covers over 100 years of Afro-Cuban styles, including the danzón, guaracha, mambo, merengue and songo—from Peruchin to Eddie Palmieri. $28

The Salsa Guide Book

By Rebeca Mauleón

The only complete method book on salsa ever published! 260 pages. $25.

Carlos Santana – "A true treasure of knowledge and information about Afro-Cuban music."

Mark Levine, author of The Jazz Piano Book. – "This is the book on salsa."

Sonny Bravo, pianist with Tito Puente – "This will be the salsa 'bible' for years to come."

Oscar Hernández, pianist with Rubén Blades – "An excellent and much needed resource."

The Brazilian Guitar Book

By Nelson Faria, one of Brazil's best new guitarists.

- Over 140 pages of comping patterns, transcriptions and chord melodies for samba, bossa, baiaõ, etc.
- Complete chord voicings written out for each example.
- Comes with a CD of Nelson playing each example.
- The most complete Brazilian guitar method ever published! $28.

Joe Diorio – "Nelson Faria's book is a welcome addition to the guitar literature. I'm sure those who work with this volume wiill benefit greatly"

Inside The Brazilian Rhythm Section

By Nelson Faria and Cliff Korman

This is the first book/CD package ever published that provides an opportunity for bassists, guitarists, pianists and drummers to interact and play-along with a master Brazilian rhythm section. Perfect for practicing both accompanying and soloing.

$28 list price for book and 2 CDs - including the charts for the CD tracks and sample parts for each instrument, transcribed from the recording.

The Latin Bass Book

A PRACTICAL GUIDE

By Oscar Stagnaro

The only comprehensive book ever published on how to play bass in authentic Afro-Cuban, Brazilian, Caribbean, Latin Jazz & South American styles. $34.

Over 250 pages of transcriptions of Oscar Stagnaro playing each exercise. Learn from the best!

Includes: 3 Play-Along CDs to accompany each exercise, featuring world-class rhythm sections.

Afro-Caribbean Grooves for Drumset

By Jean-Philippe Fanfant, drummer with Andy narell's band, Sakesho.

Covers grooves from 10 Caribbean nations, arranged for drumset.

Endorsed by Peter Erskine, Horacio Hernandez, etc.

CD includes both audio and video files. $25.

MORE JAZZ PUBLICATIONS

SHER MUSIC CO. and Freehand Systems are proud to announce the publication of
THE DIGITAL REAL BOOK
Now you can download over 800 songs from Sher Music Co.'s world-renowned books:
Including some of the best songs by:
See SherMusic.com for details

The Digital Real Book

On the web

Over 850 downloadable tunes from all the Sher Music Co. fakebooks.

See www.shermusic.com for details.

Jazz Guitar Voicings The Drop 2 Book

By Randy Vincent, Everything you need to know to create full chord melody voicings like Jim Hall, Joe Pass, etc. Luscious voicings for chord melody playing based on the "Drop 2" principle of chord voicings.

You will find that this book covers this essential material in a unique way unlike any other guitar book available.

Endorsed by Julian Lage, John Stowell, Larry Koonse, etc.

$25, includes 2 CDs.

Three-Note Voicings and Beyond

By Randy Vincent, A complete guide to the construction and use of every kind of three-note voicing on guitar.

"Randy Vincent is an extraordinary musician. This book illuminates harmonies in the most sensible and transparent way." – **Pat Metheny**

"This book is full of essential information for jazz guitarists at any level. Wonderful!" – **Mike Stern**

194 pages, $28

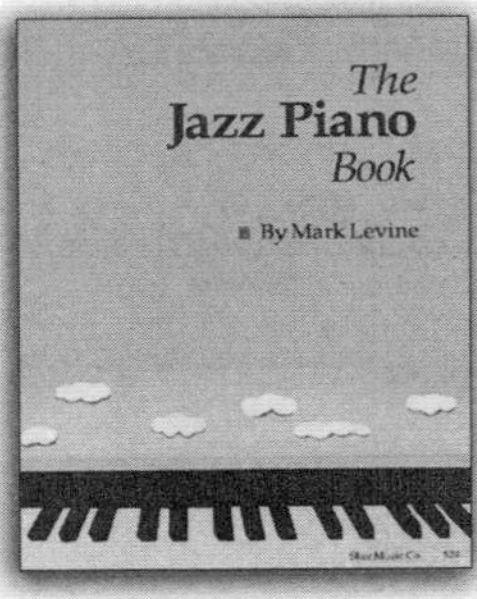

The Jazz Piano Book

By Mark Levine, Concord recording artist and pianist with Cal Tjader. For beginning to advanced pianists. The only truly comprehensive method ever published! Over 300 pages. $32

Richie Beirach – "The best new method book available."

Hal Galper – "This is a must!"

Jamey Aebersold – "This is an invaluable resource for any pianist."

James Williams – "One of the most complete anthologies on jazz piano."

Also available in Spanish! ¡El Libro del Jazz Piano!

The Blues Scales

ESSENTIAL TOOLS FOR JAZZ IMPROVISATION

By Dan Greenblatt

Great Transcriptions from Miles, Dizzy Gillespie, Lester Young, Oscar Peterson, Dave Sanborn, Michael Brecker and many more, showing how the Blues Scales are actually used in various styles of jazz.

Accompanying CD by author Dan Greenblatt and his swinging quartet of New York jazz musicians shows how each exercise should sound. And it also gives the student numerous play-along tracks to practice with. $22

Forward Motion

FROM BACH TO BEBOP

A Corrective Approach to Jazz Phrasing

By Hal Galper

- Perhaps the most important jazz book in a decade, Foward Motion shows the reader how to create jazz phrases that swing with authentic jazz feeling.
- Hal Galper was pianist with Cannonball Adderley, Phil Woods, Stan Getz, Chet Baker, John Scofield, and many other jazz legends.
- Each exercise available on an interactive website so that the reader can change tempos, loop the exercises, transpose them, etc. $30.

Foundation Exercises for Bass

By Chuck Sher

A creative approach for any style of music, any level, acoustic or electric bass. Perfect for bass teachers!

Filled with hundreds of exercises to help you master scales, chords, rhythms, hand positions, ear training, reading music, sample bass grooves, creating bass lines on common chord progressions, and much more.

$24

Walking Bassics: The Fundamentals of Jazz Bass Playing

By swinging NY bassist Ed Fuqua

Includes transcriptions of every bass note on accompanying CD and step-by-step method for constructing solid walking bass lines. $22.

Endorsed by Eddie Gomez, Jimmy Haslip, John Goldsby, etc.

Concepts for Bass Soloing

By Chuck Sher and Marc Johnson, (bassist with Bill Evans, etc.) The only book ever published that is specifically designed to improve your soloing! $26

- Includes two CDs of Marc Johnson soloing on each exercise
- Transcriptions of bass solos by: Eddie Gomez, John Patitucci, Scott LaFaro, Jimmy Haslip, etc.

"It's a pleasure to encounter a Bass Method so well conceived and executed." – **Steve Swallow**

The Improvisor's Bass Method

By Chuck Sher. A complete method for electric or acoustic bass, plus transcribed solos and bass lines by Mingus, Jaco, Ron Carter, Scott LaFaro, Paul Jackson, Ray Brown, and more! Over 200 pages. $16

International Society of Bassists – "Undoubtedly the finest book of its kind."

Eddie Gomez – "Informative, readily comprehensible and highly imaginative"

Essential Grooves

FOR WRITING, PERFORMING AND PRODUCING CONTEMPORARY MUSIC

By 3 Berklee College professors: Dan Moretti, Matthew Nicholl and Oscar Stagnaro

- 41 different rhythm section grooves used in Soul, Rock, Motown, Funk, Hip-hop, Jazz, Afro-Cuban, Brazilian, music and more!
- Includes CD and multi-track DVD with audio files to create play-alongs, loops, original music, and more.

$24

The World's Greatest Fake Book

Jazz & Fusion Tunes by: **Coltrane, Mingus, Jaco, Chick Corea, Bird, Herbie Hancock, Bill Evans, McCoy, Beirach, Ornette, Wayne Shorter, Zawinul, AND MANY MORE!** $32

Chick Corea – "Great for any students of jazz.'

Dave Liebman – "The fake book of the 80's."

George Cables – "The most carefully conceived fake book I've ever seen."

SAXOPHONE OM

For E♭ Instruments • Transcribed Exactly from Artist Recorded Solos

Songs that were originally played on B♭ instruments have been transposed for E♭ instruments.
Some notes or phrases may be out of range, and may be played an octave higher.

ISBN 978-1-5400-9304-2

Visit Hal Leonard Online at
www.halleonard.com

World headquarters, contact:
Hal Leonard
7777 West Bluemound Road
Milwaukee, WI 53213
Email: info@halleonard.com

In Europe, contact:
Hal Leonard Europe Limited
1 Red Place
London, W1K 6PL
Email: info@halleonardeurope.com

In Australia, contact:
Hal Leonard Australia Pty. Ltd.
4 Lentara Court
Cheltenham, Victoria, 3192 Australia
Email: info@halleonard.com.au

CONTENTS

ARTIST INDEX

All the Things You Are

(Booker Ervin's solo)
from *Booker Ervin: The Songbook*
Lyrics by Oscar Hammerstein II
Music by Jerome Kern

*Originally performed on Tenor Saxophone.

C7
Fmaj7
B♭maj7
B♭m9
E♭9
Am7
A♭dim7
Gm7
C9
Fmaj9
N.C.
D
Sax Solo
Dm7
Gm7
C7
Fmaj7
B♭maj7
Bm7♭5
E7
3
Amaj7
Am7
Dm7
G7
Cmaj7
C7
Fmaj7
F♯m7♭5
B7
Emaj7
A6
G♯m7
G9
E
F♯m7
B7♭9
Emaj7
D♯m7
G♯9
C♯maj9

A7♯5(♯9)
F
Dm7
Gm7
C7
Fmaj7
B♭maj7
B♭m9
E♭9
Am7
A♭dim7
Gm7
C9
Fmaj9
Em7♭5
A7
G
Dm7
Gm7
C7
Fmaj7
B♭maj7
Bm7♭5
E7
Amaj7
Am7
Dm7
G7
Cmaj7
C7
Fmaj7
F♯m7♭5
B7
Emaj7
A6
G♯m7
G9
H
F♯m7
B7♭9
Emaj7

D♯m7 G♯9 C♯maj9
A7♯5(♯9)
I
Dm7 Gm7
C7 Fmaj7 B♭maj7
B♭m9 E♭9 Am7 A♭dim7
Gm7 C9 Fmaj9
Em7♭5 A7
J
Dm7 Gm7 C7
Fmaj7 B♭maj7 Bm7♭5 E7
Amaj7 Am7
Dm7 G7 Cmaj7 C7 Fmaj7

K
F♯m7♭5
B7
Emaj7
3
A6
G♯m7
G9
F♯m7
B7♭9
Emaj7
D♯m7
G♯9
C♯maj9
A7♯5(♯9)
L
Dm7
Gm7
C7
Fmaj7
B♭maj7
B♭m9
E♭9
Am7
A♭dim7
Gm7
C9
Fmaj9
M
Piano Solo
Em7♭5
A7
Dm7
Gm7
34
N
36
O
36
P
Head
Dm7
Gm7
C7
Fmaj7

B♭maj7
Bm7♭5
E7
3
Amaj7
Am7
Dm7
G7
Cmaj7
C7
Fmaj7
F♯m7♭5
B7
3
Emaj7
A6
G♯m7
G9
Q
F♯m7
B7♭9
Emaj7
D♯m7
G♯9
C♯maj9
A7♯5(♯9)
R
Dm7
Gm7
C7
Fmaj7
B♭maj7
B♭m9
E♭9
Am7
A♭dim7
S Piano Solo
Gm7
3
C9
3
Dm6
E♭9
Dm6
E♭9
12
12
Fadeout...

Alone Together

(Joe Lovano's solo)

from *Joe Lovano: Joyous Encounter*

Lyrics by Howard Dietz

Music by Arthur Schwartz

*Originally performed on Tenor Saxophone.

G♯m7
C♯7
G7
Em7
A7♭9
D
G♯9♯11
G
F♯7♭9
Bmaj7
D
F♯m7♭5
B7
Em
Fm7
B♭7
Em7
A7
Dmaj7
G♯9♯11
E
G7
F♯7♭9
Bm
G♯7♯9
C♯m7♭5
F♯7♭9
Bm
G♯m7♭5
C♯7♯9
F♯7♭9
Bm
E7

G7
F♯7♭13
Bm11
C7
F
Piano solo
Bm
G♯7♯9
25
Bmaj7
G
Fills (Bridge)
F♯m7♭5
B7
Em
Fm7
B♭7
Em7
A7
Dmaj7
G♯9♯11
H
Head (last 8)
G7
F♯7♭13
Bm
G♯7♯9
C♯7♯9(♭13)
F♯7♭13
Bm
G♯m7♭5
C♯m9
F♯7♭13
Bm
E7
rit.
Freely
G7
F♯7♭9
Bm11

Angel Eyes

(Sonny Criss' solo)

from *Sonny Criss: Saturday Morning*

Words by Earl Brent

Music by Matt Dennis

C♯m7♭5
F♯7♭13
Bm
G7
Bm
G♯m7♭5
G7
F♯7♭13
E
Solo
Bm
Bm
G♯m7♭5
C♯m7♭5
F♯7♭13
Bm
G♯m7♭5
G7
F♯7♭13
F
Bm
F♯7♭13
Bm
G♯m7♭5
C♯m7♭5
F♯7♭13
Bm
G♯m7♭5
G7
F♯7♭13
G
Bm
F♯7♭13
Am7
D7♭13
Gmaj7
Bm7
E7
Am7
D7♭13
Gmaj7
G♯m7
C♯7
F♯maj7
Cm7
F7

H
C♯m7
F♯7
Bm
G♯m7♭5
C♯m7♭5
F♯7♭13
Bm
G♯m7♭5
G7
F♯7♭13
I
Piano Solo
Bm
F♯7♭13
Bm
31
J
Head (last half)
Am7
D7♭13
Gmaj7
Bm7 E7
Am7
D7♭13
Gmaj7
G♯m7
C♯7
F♯maj7
K
Cm7
F7
C♯m7
F♯7♭13
Bm
G7
Bm
E13♯11
Bm
G♯m7♭5
C♯m7♭5
F♯7♭13
Bm
G7
Bm
G♯m7♭5
Slowly, freely
G7
F♯7♯9(♭13)
N.C.
E13♯11

Anthropology

(Charlie Parker's solo)
from *Charlie Parker: Fragments*
By Charlie Parker and Dizzy Gillespie

G7 C7 G7 E7 Am D7
G Am D7 Bm E7 Am D7
G7 C G
E B7 E7
A7 D7
F G Am D7 G E7
Am D7 G7 C7 G E7
Am D7 G G Am D7 Bm E7

Am D7 G7 C G
Am D7 G Am D7 Bm E7
Am D7 G7 C Cm G
H
B7 E7
A7 D7
I G Am D7 Bm E7
Am D7 G7 C7 C♯dim G7
Am D7 J G Am D7 G

Am
D7
Dm
G7
C
G7
3
Am
D7
G
Am
D7
G
E7
Am
D7
G7
C
G
K
B7
3
E7
3
3
A7
3
D7
3
L
G
Am
D7
3
G
Am
D7
3
G
G7
C
C♯dim
G
Am
D7
M
G
Am
D7
Trumpet Solo
30
N
32
O
32
P
Piano Solo
32
Q
32
D.S. al Fine
(with repeat)

Bags' Groove

(Chris Potter's solo)

from *Chris Potter: Live performance* (Intenet Video)

By Milt Jackson

*Alto Saxophone

*Originally performed on Tenor Saxophone.

G Bm7 E7
Am7 D7 G Am7 D7
D
G C7 G
C7
G Bm7 E7 Am7
D7 G Am7 D7
E
G C7 G
C7 G
Bm7 E7 Am7
D7 G

F
Am7
D7
G
C7
G
C7
G
Bm7
E7
Am7
D7
G
Am7
D7
G
G
C7
G
C7
G
Bm7
E7
Am7
D7
G
Am7
D7

H
G
C7
G
8va
C7
(8va)
G
Bm7
E7
Am7
D7
G
Am7
D7
I
G
C7
G
C7
G
Bm7
E7
Am7

D7
G
Am7
D7
J
G
3
3
C7
G
3
C7
G
Bm7
E7
Am7
3
5
3
D7
G
3
Am7
D7
K
G
8va
7

C7
(8va)
G
5
3
(8va)
C7
3
G
Bm7
E7
3
Am7
D7
G
Am7
D7
L
G
C7
G
C7
G
Bm7
E7
Am7
D7
G
Am7
D7
M
G
C7
G
C7

8va
G
Bm7
E7
Am7
(8va)
D7
3
G
3
3
Am7
D7
N
G
C7
G
3
C7
G
Bm7
E7
Am7
D7
3
G
Am7
D7
O
Head
G
3
C7
3
G
C7
3
3
G
Bm7
E7
Am7
3
D7
3
G
1.
Am7
D7
2.

Cotton Tail

(Ben Webster's solo)

from *Ben Webster: King of the Tenors*

By Duke Ellington

*Originally performed on Tenor Saxophone.

D
Sax Solo
G
Em7
A7
D7
G
Em7
A7
D7
G
G7/B
C
C♯dim7
G/D
tr
Am7
D7
G
Em7
A7
D7
G
3
Em7
A7
D7
G
G7/B
C
C♯dim7
G/D
D7
G
E
B7
E7
A7
D7
F
G
Em7
A7
D7
G
Em7
A7
D7
G
G7/B
C
C♯dim7
G/D
D7
G
Gdim7
Growl
3
3
G
Em7
A7
D7
G

A7 D7 G G7/B C C♯dim7 G/D
D7 G
H
B7 E7
A7 D7
I
G Em7 A7 D7 G Em7
3
A7 D7 G G7/B C C♯dim7 G/D
3
D7
J
G Em7 A7 D7 G Em7
A7 D7 G G7/B C C♯dim7 G/D
Am7 D7 G Em7 A7 D7 G Em7
A7 D7 G G7/B C C♯dim7
G/D D7 G
K
B7
3

E7
A7
D7
L
G
Em7
A7
D7
G
Em7
A7
D7
G
G7/B
C
C♯dim7
G/D
D7
M
G
Em7
A7
D7
G
Em7
A7
D7
G
G7/B
C
C♯dim7
G/D
Am7
D7
G
Em7
A7
D7
G
Em7
A7
D7
G
G7/B
C
C♯dim7
G/D
D7
G
N
B7
E7
A7
D7
O
G
Em7
A7
D7

G Em7 A7 D7 G G7/B C C♯dim7
G/D D7
P
G Em7 A7 D7
G Em7 A7 D7 G G7/B C C♯dim7
G/D Am7 D7 G Em7 A7 D7
G Em7 A7 D7 G G7/B
3
C C♯dim7 G/D D7 G
Q
B7
3
E7
A7 D7
R
Head (last 8 bars)
A7 E7♯5(♭9) A7 D7
G G7/B C C♯dim G/D D9 G6 N.C./G

Bernie's Tune

(Scott Hamilton's solo)

from *Scott Hamilton: East of the Sun*

Music by Bernie Miller

*Originally performed on Tenor Saxophone.

E
Bass Solo
Bm
30
C♯m7♭5
F♯7♭9
F
Sax Solo
Bm
G9
C♯m7♭5
F♯7♭9
Bm
C♯m7♭5
F♯7
G
Bm
G9
C♯m7♭5
F♯7♭9
Bm
Am7
D7
H
G
G♯dim
Am7
A♯dim
Bm7
E7
Am7
D7
G
Em7
Am7
D7
G
C♯m7♭5
F♯7♭9
I
Bm
G9
C♯m7♭5
F♯7♭9
Bm
C♯m7♭5
F♯7♭9
J
Bm
G9

C♯m7♭5
F♯7♭9
Bm
C♯m7♭5
F♯7
K
Bm
G9
C♯m7♭5
F♯7♭9
Bm
Am7
D7
L
G
Em7
Am7
A♯dim
Bm7
E7
Am7
D7
G
Em7
Am7
D7
G
C♯m7♭5
F♯7♭9
M
Bm
G9
C♯m7♭5
F♯7♭9
Bm
C♯m7♭5
F♯7♭9
N
Bm
sfzp
sfzp
G9
C♯m7♭5
F♯7♭9
Bm
C♯m7♭5
F♯7

O
Bm
G9
C♯m7♭5
F♯7♭9
Bm
Am7
D7
P
G
Em7
Am7
D7
Bm7
E7
Am7
D7
G
Em7
Am7
D7
G
C♯m7♭5
F♯7♭9
Q
Bm
G9
C♯m7♭5
F♯7♭9
Bm
C♯m7♭5
F♯7♭9
R
Piano Solo
Bm
30
S
Trade 8's (Sax)
Bm
G9
C♯m7♭5
F♯7♭9
Bm
C♯m7♭5
F♯7

T
(Drums)
Bm
7
U
(Sax)
G
Em7
Am7
D7
Bm7
E7
Am7
D7
G
Em7
Am7
D7
G
3
C♯m7♭5
F♯7♭9
V
(Drums)
Bm
6
W
Trade 4's
(Sax)
C♯m7♭5
F♯7♭9
Bm
G9
(Drums)
4
X
(Sax)
Bm
G9
(Drums)
C♯m7♭5
2
Am7
D7
Y
(Sax)
G
Em7
Am7
D7
Bm7
E7
Am7
D7
3
(Drums)
G
Em7
2
C♯m7♭5
F♯7♭9
Z
(Sax)
Bm

(Drums)
G9
C♯m7♭5
3
AA
Head
Bm
G9
C♯m7♭5
F♯7♭9
Bm
C♯m7♭5
F♯7
BB
Bm
G9
C♯m7♭5
F♯7♭9
Bm
Am7
D7
CC
G
Em7
Am7
D7
Bm7
E7
Am7
D7
G
Em7
Am7
D7
G
C♯m7♭5
F♯7♭9
DD
Bm
G9
C♯m7♭5
F♯7♭9
Bm
E13♯11

Body and Soul

(Coleman Hawkins' solo)

from *Coleman Hawkins: Body and Soul*

Words by Edward Heyman, Robert Sour and Frank Eyton

Music by John Green

*Originally performed on Tenor Saxophone.

Am7♭5
D7
Gm7
Cm7
F7
B♭
F♯7
C
B
C♯m7
D♯m7
Em7
A7
D♯m7
G♯7
C♯m7
F♯7
B
Bm7
E7
C♯m7
Cdim7
Bm7
E7
6
A7
A♭7
G7
D
Cm
G7
Cm7
B7
B♭
E♭
Dm7
D♭dim7
Cm7
Am7♭5
D7
Gm7
B

E Solo
B♭ G7 Cm G7
Cm7 B7 B♭ E♭
Dm7 D♭dim7 Cm7
Am7♭5 D7 Gm7 Cm7 F7
F
B♭ Cm G7
Cm7 F7 B♭ E♭
Dm7 D♭dim7 Cm7
Am7♭5 D7 Gm7 Cm7 F7
G
B♭ F♯7 B C♯m7

D♯m7
Em7
A7
D♯m7
G♯7
C♯m7
F♯7
B
Bm7
E7
C♯m7
Cdim7
Bm7
E7
3
A7
A♭7
G7
H
Cm
G7
8va
Cm7
B7
B♭
E♭
(8va)
Dm7
D♭dim7
Cm7
Cadenza
Rubato
Am7♭5
D7
Gm7
3
N.C.
B♭

Cherokee

(Indian Love Song)
(Eddie "Lockjaw" Davis' solo)
from *The Best of Johnny Griffin*
Words and Music by Ray Noble

*Originally performed on Tenor Saxophone.

D
A7
Am7
D7
G
G7
Cmaj7
F7♯11
G
A7
Am7
D7
G
E
Sax Solo
G7
Cmaj7
3
F7♯11
G
3
A7
Am7
D7
Am7
D7♯5
F
G
3
G7
Cmaj7
F7♯11
3
3
G
A7

Am7
D7
G
G
A♯m7
D♯7
G♯maj7
G♯m7
3
C♯7
F♯
3
F♯m7
B7
Emaj7
Em7
A7
Am7
3
D7
3
H
G
G7
Cmaj7
F7♯11
G
3
A7
3
Am7
D7
G
I
G7

Cmaj7
F7♯11
G
A7
Am7
D7
Am7
D7♯5
J
G
G7
Cmaj7
F7♯11
G
A7
Am7
D7
G
K
A♯m7
D♯7
G♯maj7
G♯m7
C♯7
F♯

F♯m7
B7
Emaj7
Em7
A7
Am7
D7
3
L
G
3
G7
Cmaj7
F7♯11
G
A7
Am7
D7
G
M
G7
Cmaj7
F7♯11
G
A7
3
3

Am7
D7
Am7
D7♯5
N
G
G7
Cmaj7
F7♯11
G
A7
Am7
D7
G
O
A♯m7
D♯7
G♯maj7
G♯m7
C♯7
F♯
F♯m7
B7
Emaj7
Em7
A7
Am7
D7

P
G
G7
Cmaj7
F7♯11
G
A7
Am7
D7
G
Q
G7
Cmaj7
F7♯11
G
A7
Am7
D7
Am7
D7♯5
R
G
G7

Cmaj7
F7♯11
G
A7
Am7
D7
G
S
A♯m7
D♯7
G♯maj7
G♯m7
C♯7
F♯
F♯m7
B7
Emaj7
Em7
A7
Am7
D7
T
G
G7
Cmaj7
F7♯11
G
A7

Am7
D7
G
3
U
Piano Solo
127
V
Drum Solo
64
W
Sax Solo
G
G7
Cmaj7
F7♯11
G
A7
Am7
D7
Am7
D7♯5
X
G
G7
Cmaj7
F7♯11
G
A7
Am7

Y
D7
G
A♯m7
D♯7
G♯maj7
G♯m7
C♯7
F♯
F♯m7
B7
3
Emaj7
Em7
A7
Am7
D7
Z
Head (last 16)
G
G7
Cmaj7
F7♯11
G
A7
Am7
D7
Freely
G
3
3
3
3

Donna Lee

from *Joe Lovano: Bird Songs*

By Charlie Parker

***Alto Saxophone**

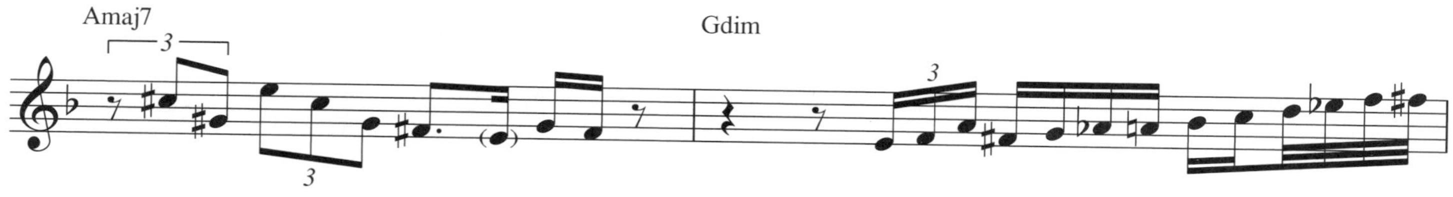

*Originally performed on Tenor Saxophone.

C♯m7
F♯7♭9
Bm7
E7♭9
Amaj7
Gdim
Am7
D7♭9
A
Solo
Gm7
C7♭9
Fmaj7
D7
G7
Gm7
C7
B
Fmaj7
Cm7
F7
B♭maj7
E♭7
Fmaj7
D7
G7

Gm7
C7
C
Fmaj7
D7
G7
A7
Dm7
Em7♭5
A7
D
Dm7
A7♭9
Dm7
G♯dim
Am7
D7♭9
Gm7
C7♭9
Fmaj7

Gm7
C7
E
Fmaj7
3
3
D7
G7
Gm7
C7
Fmaj7
3
F
Cm7
F7
B♭maj7
E♭7
Fmaj7
D7
G7
3
Gm7
6

C7
3
3
G
Fmaj7
D7
G7
3
A7
3
Dm7
Em7♭5
A7
H
Dm7
A7♭9
3
Dm7
3
G♯dim
Am7
D7♭9
Gm7
C7♭9
3
6
rit.
Freely
F♯maj7
6
3
Fmaj7
6

Emily

(Frank Morgan's solo)

from *Frank Morgan and the McCoy Tyner Trio: Major Changes*

Music by Johnny Mandel

Words by Johnny Mercer

E
Dmaj7
G7
C♯m7♭5
F♯7
Bm7
E7
Amaj7
Bm7♭5
E7♭9
F
Piano Solo
Amaj7
39
G
Sax Solo
Amaj7
F♯m7
Bm7
E7
Em7
A7
Dmaj7
G7

H
F♯maj7
D♯m7
G♯m7
C♯7
F♯m7
B7
Bm7
E7
I
Amaj7
F♯m7
Bm7
E7
Em7
A7
Dmaj7
J
G♯m7♭5
C♯7♯9
F♯m
D♯m7♭5
G♯7

C♯m7
F♯7
Bm7
E7
C♯m7♭5
F♯7
K
Dmaj7
G7
C♯m7♭5
F♯7
Bm7
E7
Amaj7
L
Head
Bm7♭5
E7♭9
Amaj7
F♯m7
Bm7
E7
Em7
A7
Dmaj7
G7
M
F♯maj7

D♯m7 G♯m7 C♯7
F♯m7 B7 Bm7 E7
N
Amaj7 F♯m7 Bm7 E7
Em7 A7 Dmaj7 G♯m7♭5 C♯7♯9
O
F♯m D♯m7♭5 G♯7 C♯m7 F♯7
Bm7 E7 C♯m7♭5
P
F♯7 Dmaj7 G7 C♯m7♭5
F♯7 Bm7 E7 Freely
rit.
Amaj7

Everything Happens to Me

(Eric Alexander's solo)

from *Eric Alexander: Second Impression*

Words by Johnny Mercer

Music by Hoagy Carmichael

*Originally performed on Tenor Saxophone.

Cmaj7
A7♭9
Dm7
G7♭9(♭13)
Cmaj7
C♯m7♭5
F♯7♯9
Bmaj7
Em
Em(maj7)
A7sus
A7
A7♯5
D7
D
C♯m7♭5
Cm7
Bm7
B♭dim
Am7
D7
Cm7
F7
Bm7
E7
G♯dim
Am7♭5
Bm7
B♭dim
Am7
D7
E
Twice as fast
Sax Solo
G
E7♭9
Am7
D7♭9
Bm7
B♭dim
Am7
D7
F7
E7
G♯dim

Am7♭5
Bm7
B♭dim
Am7
D7
Bm7
E7♭9
F
Am7
3
3
D7♭9
Bm7
B♭dim
3
Am7
3
D7
F7
E7
G♯dim
Am7♭5
Bm7
3
3
B♭dim
Am7
D7
3
3
G
G
Dm7
3
G7
Cmaj7
A7
3
Dm7
G7
3
Cmaj7
3

C♯m7♭5
F♯7♭13
Bmaj7
Em
A7sus
A7
E♭7
D7
H
C♯m7♭5
Cm7
Bm7
B♭dim
Am7
D7
F7
E7
G♯dim
Am7♭5
Bm7
B♭dim
Am7
D7
G
E7
I
Piano Solo
30
Em7
E♭7
J
Head (2nd half)
Dm7
G7♯9
Cmaj7

A7♭9
Dm7
G7♭9
Cmaj7
5
C♯m7♭5
F♯7♭13
Bmaj7
Em
Em(maj7)
A7sus
A7
E♭7
D7
K
Tempo I
C♯m7♭5
Cm
Bm7
B♭dim
Am7
D7
F7sus
F7
E7sus
E7
G♯dim
Am7♭5
Bm7
B♭dim
Slowly, freely
Am7
rit.
D13♭9
G13
F♯13♭9
F13
E13♯9
E♭13
A♭maj7/D
3
Gmaj13♯11
3

A Foggy Day

(In London Town)
(Lester Young's solo)
from *Lester Young: Intégrale Jazz Vol. 5*
Music and Lyrics by George Gershwin and Ira Gershwin

*Originally performed on Tenor Saxophone.

C
Sax Solo
C6/9
A7#5(b9)
D9
G7#5(b9)
C6/9
Eb9
D9
G7#5(#9)
Gm7/C
Gm9
C13
Fmaj13
Bb9
Em7
A7sus
A7
D9
G7b9
3
3
D
C6/9
A7#5(b9)
D9
G7#5(b9)
C6/9
Eb9
D9
G7#5(b9)
3
Gm7/C
Gm9
C13
Fmaj13
Bb9
Cmaj7
Dm7
Cmaj7
Dm7
Cmaj7
A7#5(b9)
Dm7
G13b9
C6
N.C./G
G7#5(#9)
E
C6/9
A7#5(b9)
3

D9
G7♯5(♭9)
C6/9
Growl
E♭9
D9
G7♯5(♯9)
Gm7/C
Gm9
C13
Fmaj13
B♭9
Em7
A7sus
A7
D9
G7♭9
F
C6/9
A7♯5(♭9)
D9
G7♯5(♭9)
C6/9
E♭9
D9
G7♯5(♭9)
Gm7/C
Gm9
C13
Fmaj13
B♭9
Cmaj7
Dm7
Cmaj7
Dm7
Cmaj7
A7♯5(♭9)
Dm7
G13♭9
C6
N.C./G
G7♯5(♯9)
G
Trumpet Solo
C6/9
33
H
34
I
Piano Solo
34
J
Bass Solo
34

K
Sax Solo
C6/9
A7#5(b9)
D9
G7#5(b9)
C6/9
Eb9
D9
G7#5(#9)
Gm7/C
Gm9
C13
Fmaj13
Bb9
Em7
A7sus
A7
D9
G7b9
C6/9
A7#5(b9)
D9
Lay back
G7#5(b9)
L
C6/9
Eb9
D9
G7#5(b9)
Gm7/C
Gm9
C13
Fmaj13
Bb9
Cmaj7
Dm7
Cmaj7
Dm7
Cmaj7
A7#5(b9)
Dm7
G13b9
C6 N.C./G
G7#5(#9)

M Trading 4's
C6/9
3
C6/9
E♭9
D9
G7♯5(♯9)
Gm7/C
3
Em7
A7sus
A7
D9
G7♭9
N
C6/9
3
C6/9
E♭9
D9
G7♯5(♭9)
Gm7/C
Gm9
C13
Fmaj13
B♭9
Cmaj7
Dm7
O Tag (Latin feel)
Cmaj7
Dm7
Cmaj7
A7♯5(♭9)
Dm7
G13♭9
C6/9
Dm7
Dm7/G
C6/9
Dm7
Dm7/G
C6/9
Dm7
Dm7/G
C

Flying Home

(Illinois Jacquet's solo)

from *Illinois Jacquet: Flying Home – The Best of the Verve Years*

Music by Benny Goodman and Lionel Hampton

*Originally performed on Tenor Saxophone.

D
Sax Solo
F
F7/A
B♭
Bdim
F/C
Dm7
G7
C7
F
F/E♭
B♭/D
Bdim
F/C
D7
G7
C7
E
F
F7/A
B♭
Bdim
F/C
Dm7
G7
C7
F
F7/A
B♭
Bdim
F/C
C7
3
F
F
F7
B♭
G7
C7
G
F
F7/A
B♭
Bdim
F/C
Dm7
G7
C7
3
F
F7/A
B♭
Bdim

F/C Dm7 G7 C7
H
F F7/A B♭ Bdim
F/C Dm7 G7 C7 F F/E♭ B♭/D Bdim
F/C D7 G7 C7
I
F F7/A B♭ Bdim
F/C Dm7 G7 C7 F F7/A B♭ Bdim
F/C C7 F
J
F7
B♭ G7
C7♭9
K
F F7/A B♭ Bdim
F/C Dm7 G7 C7 F F7/A B♭ Bdim
(Solo break)
F/C Cdim C7sus F
3

L
Bb
Bb/D
Eb
Edim
Bb/F
Gm7
Cm7
F7sus
Bb
Bb/D
Eb
Edim
1.
Bb/F
Gm7
Cm7
F7sus
2.
Bb/F
Gm7
Cm7
F7sus
M
Bb7
Eb7
C7
unison
3
3
3
N
Bb
Bb/Ab
Eb/G
Edim
Bb/F
Gm7
Cm7
F7sus
Bb
Bb7/D
Eb
Edim
unison
B9#11
Bb6/9

Footprints

from *Wayne Shorter: Adam's Apple*

By Wayne Shorter

B13
E9
C♯m7♭5
To Coda
F♯7
Am7
C
Tenor Solo
Am7
Dm7
Am7
B13
E9
C♯m7♭5
F♯7
Am7
D
Am7

Dm7
Am7
tr
2
B13
E9
C♯m7♭5
F♯7
Am7
E
Am7
Dm7
Am7
B13
E9

C♯m7♭5
F♯7
Am7
tr
tr
F
Am7
Dm7
Am7
B13
E9
3
C♯m7♭5
F♯7
Am7
Piano Solo
71
(3 Choruses)
Bass Solo
48
D.S. al Coda
(2 Choruses)
CODA
Am7

Frenesi

(Benny Carter's solo)

from *Cosmopolite: The Oscar Peterson Verve Sessions*

Words and Music by Alberto Dominguez

N.C.
G13 G♯13 A13
D
Bm7
Em7
A7
D
N.C.
E
Sax Solo
Em7
A7
Em7
A7
D
G
D
F♯m7
B7
F
Em7
A7
Em7
A7
D
G
D
G♯m7
C♯7
G
F♯
G♯m7
C♯7
F♯
G♯m7
C♯7
F♯
Bm7
Em7
A7
H
Em7
A7

Em7
A7
D
G
D
F♯m7
B7
I
Em7
A7
Em7
A7
D
G
D
F♯m7
B7
J
Em7
A7
Em7
A7
D
G
D
G♯m7
C♯7
K
F♯
G♯m7
C♯7
F♯
G♯m7
C♯7
F♯
Bm7
Em7
A7
L
Em7
A7
Em7

A7
D
G
D
F♯m7
B7
M
Em7
A7
Em7
A7
D
G
3
F♯m7
B7
N
Em7
A7
Em7
A7
D
G
D
G♯m7
C♯7
O
F♯
G♯m7
C♯7
F♯
G♯m7
C♯7
F♯
Bm7
Em7
A7
P
Em7
A7
Em7
A7
D
G
D
F♯m7
B7

Q
Piano Solo
Em7
A7
31
R
31
S
Sax Solo
Em7
A7
Em7
A7
D
3
G
D
F♯m7
B7
T
Em7
A7
Em7
A7
D
G
3
D
G♯m7
C♯7
U
F♯
G♯m7
C♯7
F♯
G♯m7
C♯7
F♯
Bm7
Em7
A7
V
Em7
A7
Em7
A7
D
3
G
3
D
F♯m7
B7
3
W
Em7
3

A7
Em7
A7
D
F♯dim
G
G♯dim
D
F♯m7
B7
X
Em7
A7
Em7
A7
D
F♯dim
G
G♯dim
D
G♯m7
C♯7
Y
F♯
G♯m7
C♯7
F♯
Bm7
Em7
A7
Z
Head (Last 8)
G13
G♯13
A13
N.C.
G13
G♯13
A13
N.C.
D
F♯dim
G
G♯dim
Em7
A7
D

Georgia on My Mind

(Gene Ammons' solo)

from *Gene Ammons & Dodo Marmarosa: Jug & Dodo*

Words by Stuart Gorrell

Music by Hoagy Carmichael

*Alto Saxophone

*Originally performed on Tenor Saxophone.

C
Gm7
Gm7/C
C7♭9
Fmaj7
Em7
A7♭9
Dm
Dm7
G7
B♭m7/A♭
B♭m6/A♭
Am7
D9
Gm9
C13
Fmaj7
B♭maj9
Fmaj7
D Sax Solo
Fmaj7
Double-time feel
Em7
A7♭9
Dm
Dm7
G9
G♯dim7
Am7
D7
Gm7
C7
Am7
D7♭9
Gm7
C7♭9
Fmaj7
Em7
A7♭9
Dm
Dm7
G9
G♯dim7
Am7
D7

Gm7
C7
Fmaj7
B♭maj7
Fmaj7
A7♭9
E
Dm7
B♭9
Dm7
B♭9
Dm7
B♭9
Dm7
G9
Dm7
G♯dim7
Am7
G♯m9
Gm9
C13
F
Fmaj7
Em7
A7♭9
Dm
Dm7

G9
G♯dim7
Am7
D7
Gm7
C7
Fmaj7
Lay back
B♭6/9
Fmaj7
G Piano Solo
Dm
6
H Head (last section)
Fmaj7
Em7
A7♭9
Dm
Dm7
G7
B♭m7/A♭
B♭m6/A♭
Am7
D9
Gm9
C13
Freely
N.C.
accel.
rit.
Freely
Fmaj7

Giant Steps

(John Coltrane's solo)

from *John Coltrane: Giant Steps*

By John Coltrane

*Alto Saxophone

*Originally performed on Tenor Saxophone.

Dm7
G7
C
F♯m7
B7
E
B♭m7
E♭7
A♭
D
E
* Fingered as A, overtone sounds as E

E Bbm7 Eb7 Ab Dm7 G7
RUSH
C Bbm7 Eb7 F Ab B7 E G7
C F#m7 B7 E G7 C Eb7
Ab Dm7 G7 C F#m7 B7
E Bbm7 Eb7 Ab
3
Dm7 G7 C Bbm7 Eb7
G Ab B7 E G7 C F#7 B7
E G7 C Eb7 Ab Dm7 G7
C F#m7 B7 E
Bbm7 Eb7 Ab Dm7 G7
3
C Bbm7 Eb7 H Ab B7 E G7

C F♯m7 B7 E G7 C E♭7
A♭ Dm7 G7 C
F♯m7 B7 E B♭m7 E♭7
A♭ Dm7 G7 C B♭m7 E♭7
A♭ B7 E G7 C F♯m7 B7
E G7 C E♭7 A♭ Dm7 G7
C F♯m7 B7 E B♭m7 E♭7
A♭ Dm7 G7 C B♭m7 E♭7
A♭ B7 E G7 C F♯m7 B7
E G7 C E♭7 A♭ Dm7 G7
C F♯m7 B7 E B♭m7 E♭7

A♭
Dm7
G7
C
B♭m7
E♭7
K
A♭
B7
E
G7
C
F♯m7
B7
E
G7
C
E♭7
A♭
Dm7
G7
C
F♯m7
B7
E
B♭m7
E♭7
A♭
Dm7
G7
C
B♭m7
E♭7
L
A♭
B7
E
G7
C
F♯m7
B7
E
G7
C
E♭7
A♭
RUSH
Dm7
G7
C
F♯m7
B7
E
B♭m7
E♭7
A♭
Dm7
G7
C
B♭7
E♭7
M
A♭
B7
E
G7
C
F♯m7
B7
E
G7
C
E♭7

A♭ Dm7 G7 C
F♯m7 B7 E B♭m7 E♭7
A♭ Dm7 G7 C B♭m7 E♭7
N A♭ B7 E G7 C 13 O 16
P 16 Q 16 R A♭ B7 E G7
C F♯m7 B7 E G7
C E♭7 A♭ Dm7 G7
C F♯m7 B7 E B♭m7 E♭7
A♭ Dm7 G7 C B♭m7 E♭7
S A♭ B7 E G7 C F♯m7 B7
E G7 C E♭7 A♭ Dm7 G7

C
F♯m7
B7
E
B♭m7
E♭7
A♭
Dm7
G7
C
B♭m7
E♭7
T
Head
A♭
B7
E
G7
C
F♯m7
B7
E
G7
C
E♭7
A♭
Dm7
G7
C
F♯m7
B7
E
B♭m7
E♭7
A♭
Dm7
G7
C
B♭m7
E♭7
U
A♭
B7
E
G7
C
F♯m7
B7
E
G7
C
E♭7
A♭
Dm7
G7
C
F♯m7
B7
E
B♭m7
E♭7
A♭
Dm7
G7
C (Hold on C)

I Can't Give You Anything but Love

(James Carter's solo)

from *Amazing Keystone Big Band au Festival Django Reinhardt 2015* (Internet Video)

Words and Music by Jimmy McHugh and Dorothy Fields

*Originally performed on Tenor Saxophone.

E7
A
F♯7
Bm7
E7
E
Guitar Solo
A
15
F
Trumpet Solo
16
G
Sax Solo
A
D7
C♯m7
F♯7
Bm7
E7
A
D7
C♯m7
F♯7
Bm7
E7
H
Em7
A7
D
B7
8va
E7sus
I
A
D7
C♯m7
F♯7
Bm7
E7

Em7
6
6
6
A7
5
3
D
J
D♯dim
A/E
F♯7
8va
Bm7
E7
A
F♯7
Bm7
E7
(8va)
K
A
D7
C♯m7
F♯7
Bm7
E7
(8va)
A
D7
C♯m7
F♯7
Bm7
E7
(8va)
3
3
L
Em7
A7
3
3
D
B7
6

E7sus
M
A
D7
C♯m7
F♯7
Bm7
E7
Em7
A7
D
N
D♯dim
A/E
F♯7
8va
Bm7
(8va)
E7
A
F♯7
Bm7
E7
O
Head 2nd time
A
D7
C♯m7
F♯7
Bm7
E7
A
D7
C♯m7
F♯7
Bm7
E7

P
Em7
A7
D
3
B7
E7sus
15ma
Q
A
D7
C♯m7
F♯7
Bm7
E7
Em7
R
D♯dim
A/E
Outro
Bm7
C♯m7♭5
E13sus
8va
E7♯5
(8va)
A13
Slowly, freely

Ginger Bread Boy

(Jimmy Heath's solo)

from *Jimmy Heath Quintet: On the Trail*

By Jimmy Heath

*Alto Saxophone

Medium Bop (♩ = 212)

Ⓐ Head N.C./G /D /A /D /G G7♯9

N.C./C /D♭ /C /D /G G7♯9

G7♯5(♯9) E7♯5(♭9) A7♭5(♭9) D7♯5(♯9)

G7♯9 1.

2. Ⓑ Guitar Solo 12 12 12 12 12

Ⓒ Sax Solo G7 C7

G7 3 E7 Am7

D13 G D7

*Originally performed on Tenor Saxophone.

D
G7
C7
3
G7
E7
Am7
D13
G
3
D7
E
G7
C7
G7
E7
Am7
3
D13
G
D7
F
G7
3
C7
G7
E7

Am7
D13
G
D7
G
G7
C7
G7
E7
Am7
D13
G
D7
H
G7
C7
G7
E7
Am7
D13
G
D7
I
G7
3

C7
G7
E7
Am7
D13
G
D7
J
G7
Piano Solo
8
12
12
12
12
12
12
11
K Head
N.C./G
/D
/A
/D
/G
G7♯9
N.C./C
/D♭
/C
/D
/G
G7♯9
G7♯5(♯9)
E7♯5(♭9)
A7♭5(♭9)
D7♯5(♯9)
1.
G7♯9
2.
Vamp ad lib. and Fade
G7♯9

Groovin' High

(Art Pepper's solo)
from *Art Pepper + Eleven*
By John "Dizzy" Gillespie

Alto Saxophone

Moderately fast (♩ = 208)

Intro

C ped   A♭/G   G   G♭/G

(cues)

G9sus   G7♭9(♭13)   (A) Head   C

F♯m7   B9sus   B9   C

Em7   A9sus   A9   (B)   D

Dm7   G13sus   G7♭9(♭13)   Em7   E♭m7

Dm7   G7♭9   (C)   𝄋   C

F♯m7   B9sus   B9   C

Em7   A9sus   A9   (D)   D

To Coda
Dm7
G7
Dm7
Dm7♭5
E
A♭maj7
D♭maj7
G♭maj7
C♭maj7
Cmaj7
G7sus
F
Sax Soli
C
F♯m7
B9sus
B9
C
Em7
A9sus
A9
G
D
Dm7
G13sus
G7♭9(♭13)
Em7
E♭m7
Dm7
G7♭9
H
Trumpet Solo
C
13
C
Dm7
G7
I
Sax Solo
C
F♯m7
B7
C

J
Em7
A7
D
Dm7
G7
Em7
D♯m7
3
Dm7
G7
K
C
F♯m7
B7
C
Em7
L
A7
D
Dm7
G7
Dm7
G7
C
M
Dm7
G7
C
F♯m7
B7
C
3
Em7
N
A7
D
Dm7

G7
Em7
D♯m7
Dm7
O
G7
C
F♯m7
B7
C
Em7
P
A7
D
Dm7
G7
Dm7
G7
Q
C
Dm7
G7
C
B7
C
Em7
A7
R
D
Dm7
G7
G7
D.S. al Coda
CODA
A♭maj7
D♭maj7
G13♯11
C7♯9(♭13)
F13♯11
B♭7♯9(♭13)
E♭13♯11
A♭7♯9(♭13)
D♭13♯11
Cmaj13

Hot House

(Ernie Watts' solo)

from *Ernie Watts: To the Point*

By Tadd Dameron

*Originally performed on Tenor Saxophone.

8va
(8va)

8va
8va
Fast Swing (♩ = 296)
Intro

A
Head
Em7♭5
A7♯5
Dm7♭5
G7♯5
Bm7♭5
3
E7♯5
Amaj7
B
Emb5
A7♯5
Dm7♭5
G7♯5
Bm7♭5
E7♯5
Amaj7
3
3
C
Am7
D7
3
Gmaj7
F7
E7

D
Em7♭5
A7♯5
Dm7♭5
G7♯5
Bm7♭5
3
E7♯5
Amaj7
Fine
E Sax Solo
Em7♭5
A7♯5
Dm7♭5
G7♯5
Bm7♭5
E7♯5
Amaj7
3
F
Em♭5
A7♯5
Dm7♭5
G7♯5
3
Bm7♭5
E7♯5
Amaj7
3
G
Am7
D7
Gmaj7
3
F7
E7
H
Em7♭5
A7♯5
Dm7♭5
G7♯5
Bm7♭5
E7♯5
Amaj7

I
Em7♭5
A7♯5
Dm7♭5
G7♯5
Bm7♭5
E7♯5
Amaj7
8va
J
Em♭5
(8va)
A7♯5
Dm7♭5
G7♯5
Bm7♭5
E7♯5
Amaj7
K
Am7
D7
Gmaj7
F7
E7
L
Em7♭5
A7♯5
Dm7♭5
G7♯5
Bm7♭5
E7♯5
Amaj7
M
Em7♭5
A7♯5
Dm7♭5
G7♯5
Bm7♭5
E7♯5

Amaj7
N
Em♭5
A7♯5
Dm7♭5
G7♯5
Bm7♭5
E7♯5
Amaj7
O
Am7
D7
Gmaj7
F7
E7
P
Em7♭5
A7♯5
Dm7♭5
G7♯5
Bm7♭5
E7♯5
Amaj7
Q
Em7♭5
A7♯5
Dm7♭5
G7♯5
Bm7♭5
E7♯5
Amaj7
R
Em♭5
A7♯5
Dm7♭5
G7♯5

Bm7♭5
E7♯5
8va
Amaj7
S
Am7
(8va)
D7
Gmaj7
F7
E7
T
Em7♭5
A7♯5
Dm7♭5
G7♯5
Bm7♭5
E7♯5
Amaj7
U
Em7♭5
A7♯5
Dm7♭5
G7♯5
Bm7♭5
E7♯5
Amaj7
V
Em♭5
A7♯5
Dm7♭5
G7♯5
Bm7♭5
E7♯5
Amaj7
W
Am7
D7
Gmaj7

F7
E7
X
Em7♭5
A7♯5
Dm7♭5
G7♯5
Bm7♭5
E7♯5
Amaj7
Y
Em7♭5
A7♯5
Dm7♭5
G7♯5
Bm7♭5
E7♯5
Amaj7
Z
8va
Em♭5
A7♯5
Dm7♭5
G7♯5
Bm7♭5
E7♯5
Amaj7
AA
Am7
D7
Gmaj7
F7

BB
E7
Em7♭5
A7♯5
Dm7♭5
G7♯5
Bm7♭5
E7♯5
CC
Amaj7
Piano Solo
96
DD
Trade 8's
Em7♭5
A7♯5
Dm7♭5
G7♯5
Bm7♭5
E7♯5
Amaj7
Drums 8
Piano 8
Drums 8
Em7♭5
A7♯5
Dm7♭5
G7♯5
Bm7♭5
E7♯5
Amaj7
Drums 8
Piano 15
Drums
D.S. al Fine

I Hadn't Anyone Till You

(Houston Person's solo)
from *Houston Person: Blue Velvet*
Words and Music by Ray Noble

*Alto Saxophone

Moderately (♩ = 82)
Intro
3

A
Head
Em Em(maj7) Em7 A7

D6 Em7 E♯dim D/F♯ G♯m7♭5 C♯7 F♯m7 B7

E13

B
Em Em(maj7) Em7 A7 C♯m7♭5 F♯7

Bm7 Bm/A G♯m7♭5 C♯7♭9 F♯maj7 D♯m7 G♯13 C♯7

F♯13 B9 Em7 A7 D♯dim

C
Em Em(maj7) Em7 A13

D6 Em7 E♯dim D/F♯ G♯m7♭5 C♯7 F♯m7 B7

E13

D
G G♯dim

*Originally performed on Tenor Saxophone.

D7
C♯7
F♯m7♭5
B7♯9(♭13)
Em7
F♯m7 B7♭9
Em7
G♯dim A7♭9
D
F♯m7
B7
E
Piano Solo
16
F
Sax Solo
Em7
A7
D6
Em7
E♯dim
D/F♯
G♯m7♭5
C♯7
F♯m7
B7
E13
G
G
G♯dim
D7
C♯7
F♯m7♭5
B7♯9(♭13)
Em7
F♯m7 B7♭9
Em7
A7♭9
D
F♯m7
B7
H
Em7
A7
D6
Em7
E♯dim
D/F♯
G♯m7♭5
C♯7

F♯m7
B7
E13
Ⓘ
Em
5
6
A7
C♯m7♭5
F♯7
Bm7
3
Bm/A
G♯m7♭5
C♯7♭9
F♯maj7
D♯m7
G♯13
C♯7
Ⓙ
Head (2nd half)
F♯13
B9
Em7
A7
D♯dim
Em7
A7
D6
Em7
E♯dim
D/F♯
G♯m7♭5
C♯7
F♯m7
B7
E13
Ⓚ
G
G♯dim
D7
C♯7
F♯m7♭5
B7♯9(♭13)
Em7
F♯m7
B7♭9
Em7
A7♭9
Gm7
C9
Fm9
B♭9
Em9
A9
E♭7
Dmaj9

I Love Paris

(Buddy Collette's solo)

from *Buddy Collette: Jazz Loves Paris*

Words and Music by Cole Porter

*Originally performed on Tenor Saxophone.

D
E
Sax Solo
Bm7♭5
E7♭9
F
E7
Am7
G
A
F♯m7
B7
Bm7
E7

H
Dmaj7
Bm7
C♯m7
F♯7♭9
Bm7
E7♭9
3
Am
Bm7♭5
E7
I
Trombone Solo
Am
15
J
Guitar Solo
A
Bm7
E7
9
K
Head (last eight)
Dmaj7
D/C♯
Bm7
Amaj9
C♯m7♭5/F♯
F♯7♭9
Bm7
A♯dim
Bm7 E7sus
E7
A
Tresillo
L
Outro
Am7
4
3
B♭ locrian
A5
Am9

I Remember Clifford

(Bud Shank's solo)

from *By Request: Bud Shank Meets the Rhythm Section*

By Benny Golson

Am
Am/G
F♯m7♭5
B7♭9
D
Em7
A7
Dm7
G7
Cmaj7
E7♭13
Fmaj7
F♯dim
G7
G♯dim
Am
Am/G
F♯m7♭5
B7♭9
Em7♭5
A7♭9
Dm7
G7♭9(♭13)
E
Sax Solo
Cmaj7
G13♭9
Cmaj7
E7♭13
Fmaj7
F♯dim
G7
G♯dim
Am
Am/G
F♯m7♭5
B7
Em
Em/D
C♯m7♭5
F♯7
F
Dm7
G7♭9
Cmaj7
E7♭13
Fmaj7
F♯dim
G7
G♯dim

Am
Am/G
F♯m7♭5
B7♭9
Em7♭5
A7♭9
Dm7
G7♭13
Em7
Fmaj7
G
F♯m7♭5
B7♭9
Em7
A7
Dm7
G7♭13
Cmaj7
Bm7♭5
E7♭9
Am
Am/G
F♯m7♭5
B7♭9
Em7 A7♭9
Dm7 G7
H
Cmaj7
E7♭13
Fmaj7
F♯dim
G7
G♯dim
Am
Am/G
F♯m7♭5
B7♭9
Em7♭5
A7♭9
Dm7
G7♭13
Cmaj7
G13♭9

I
Bass Solo
Cmaj7
tr
14
Em7
Fmaj7
5
6
J
Head (2nd half)
F♯m7♭5
B7♭9
Em7
A7♭9
Dm7
G7♯5
Cmaj7
3
3
Bm7♭5
E7♯11
E7
Am
Am/G
6
3
6
F♯m7♭5
B7♭9
Em7
A7
Dm7
G7
3
K
Cmaj7
E7♭13
Fmaj7
F♯dim
G7
G♯dim
Am
Am/G
F♯m7♭5
B7♭9
Em7♭5
A7♭9
Dm7
G7♭9(♭13)
Slowly, freely
C
rit.
L
Outro
Fmaj7
E7♭13
G7♭9
3
E7♭9
Am7
Gm9
Fm9
E♭m9
Dm9
G13sus
G7♭9
C

I Remember You

(Spike Robinson's solo)

from *Spike Robinson: A Real Corker*

Words by Johnny Mercer
Music by Victor Schertzinger

*Originally performed on Tenor Saxophone.

Dmaj7
G♯m7♭5
Gm
F♯m7
Bdim
Em7
A7
E
Sax Solo
D
Dmaj7
G♯m7
C♯7
Dmaj7
Am7
D7
Gmaj7
Gm7
C7
F
F♯m7
B7
Em7
A7
Dmaj7
G♯m7
C♯7
Dmaj7
Am7
D7
Gmaj7
Gm7
C7
G
Dmaj7
Am7
D7
Gmaj7
C♯m7
F♯7
Bmaj7
C♯m7
F♯7
Bmaj7
Bm7
E7
H
Em7
A7
Dmaj7
G♯m7
C♯7
Dmaj7
Am7
D7
G
Gm7
C7

Dmaj7 G♯m7♭5 Gm F♯m7 Bdim Em7 A7
D B7 Em7 A7
I
Dmaj7 G♯m7 C♯7
Dmaj7 Am7 D7 Gmaj7 Gm7 C7
F♯m7 B7 Em7 A7
J
Dmaj7 G♯m7 C♯7
Dmaj7 Am7 D7 Gmaj7 Gm7 C7
Dmaj7 Am7 D7
K
Gmaj7 C♯m7 F♯7
Bmaj7 C♯m7 F♯7 Bmaj7 Bm7 E7
Em7 A7
L
Dmaj7 G♯m7 C♯7
Dmaj7 Am7 D7 G Gm7 C7

Dmaj7
G♯m7♭5
Gm
F♯m7
Bdim
Em7
A7
D
B7
Em7
A7
M
Guitar Solo
Dmaj7
35
N
36
O
Bass Solo
36
P
36
Q
Trade 8's
Dmaj7
G♯m7
C♯7
Dmaj7
3
Am7
D7
Gmaj7
Gm7
C7
F♯m7
B7
Em7
A7
R
Drums
Dmaj7
7
S
Guitar
8
T
Drums
12
U
Dmaj7
3
G♯m7
C♯7
Dmaj7
Am7
D7
Gmaj7
Gm7
C7
F♯m7
B7
Em7
A7
V
Drums
Dmaj7
7
W
Guitar
8

X
Drums
11
Y
Head
Dmaj7
G♯m7
C♯7
Dmaj7
Am7
D7
Gmaj7
Gm7
C7
F♯m7
B7
3
Em7
A7
Z
Dmaj7
3
G♯m7
C♯7
Dmaj7
Am7
D7
3
Gmaj7
Gm7
C7
Dmaj7
Am7
D7
AA
Gmaj7
3
C♯m7
F♯7
Bmaj7
C♯m7
F♯7
Bmaj7
Bm7
E7
Em7
3
A7
BB
Dmaj7
G♯m7
C♯7
Dmaj7
Am7
D7
G
C7
3
D
G♯m7♭5
Gm
F♯m
B7
Em7
A7
Tag
Am
G♯7
Gm7
C7
F♯m
B7
Em7
A7
D

Line for Lyons

(Gerry Mulligan's solo)

from *Gerry Mulligan with Chet Baker and Friends*

By Gerry Mulligan

G♯m7 C♯7 F♯m7♭5 B7 E C♯7♭9 F♯m7 B7
E C♯7♭9 F♯m7 B7 Emaj7 Am7 D7
G♯m7 C♯7 F♯m7 B7♭9 E C♯7♭9 3 F♯m7 B7♭9
E6 E (Background w/tpt.) Amaj7 D♯7♭9
G♯m(maj7) G♯m7 C♯7sus♭9 C♯7♭9 F♯m(maj7) F♯m7 B7sus B7
Emaj7 Fdim7 F♯m7 B7 F E Am7 D7
G♯m7 C7 F♯m7 B7 Emaj7 C♯7♭9 F♯m7 B7♯9
Emaj7 Fdim7 F♯m7 B7 G E Am7 D7

G♯m7 C♯7 F♯m7 B7 E C♯m7 F♯m7 B7
Emaj7 C♯7♯11 F♯m7 B7 E Am7 D7
G♯m7 C♯7♭9 F♯m7 B7 Emaj7 C♯7♭9 F♯m7 B7
Emaj7 E7♯11
H
Amaj7♭5 D♯7♭9
G♯m(maj7) G♯m7 C♯7♭9 F♯m(maj7) F♯m7 B7 Emaj9 C♯7♯5(♭9)
F♯m B7
I Head
E E7♭9 Am7 D7 G♯m7 C♯7
F♯m7 B7 Emaj7 C♯7♭9 F♯m7 B7♭9 E Fdim7
F♯m7 B7 Emaj7 Fdim7 F♯m7 B7sus B7sus♭9 Emaj7

I'm Old Fashioned

(Ravi Coltrane's solo)

from *Glenn Zaleski: My Ideal*

Lyrics by Johnny Mercer

Music by Jerome Kern

*Originally performed on Tenor Saxophone.

Gm11
A♭maj13♯11
D
B♭6/9
A♭maj7♯5
D7add4
B♭6/9
E♭maj13♯11
Fmaj9
E♭maj13♯11
D7sus
Fm7♭5
B♭7
Em7
A7♭9♯11
Dm
A♭maj13
E
Moderately fast, steadily (♩ = 132)
F
Piano Solo
G
12
36
35
H
Sax Solo
B♭6/9

I
E♭maj13♯5
B♭6/9
D♭maj7♭5
Am11
D13♭9
J
C13sus
A/C
G/C
E/D
D/C
E/F♯
D♯m9
B/A
Am11
Gm11
A♭maj13♯11
K
B♭6/9

A♭maj7♯5
D7add4
B♭6/9
E♭maj13♯11
Fmaj9
E♭maj13♯11
D7sus
Fm7♭5
B♭7
Em7
A7♭9♯11
Dm
A♭maj13
B♭6/9
L
B♭6/9
M
E♭maj13♯5

Bb6/9
Dbmaj7b5
Am11
D13b9
N
C13sus
3
A/C
G/C
E/D
D/C
E/F#
D#m9
B/A
Am11
Gm11
Abmaj13#11
O
Head (last 12)
Bb6/9
Abmaj7#5
D7add4
Bb6/9
Ebmaj13#11
Fmaj9
Ebmaj13#11
D7sus
Fm7b5
Bb7
Em7
A7b9#11
Dm
Abmaj13

Outro (fills)
B♭6/9
P
Q
4

Idaho

(Al Cohn's solo)

from *Al Cohn: Cohn on the Saxophone*

Words and Music by Jesse Stone

*Originally performed on Tenor Saxophone.

Em7
A7
F♯m7
B7♭9
Em7
A7
Dmaj7
F♯m7
B7♭9
Em7
Em7/A
A7
Dmaj7
G
Gm7
C7
Fmaj7
F♯m7
B7♭9
E7
A7
Dmaj7
F♯m7
B7♭9
Em7
Em7/A
A7
Dmaj7
B7♭9
Em7
A7
H
Dmaj7

F♯m7
B7♭9
Em7
A7
F♯m7
B7♭9
Em7
A7
Dmaj7
3
F♯m7
B7♭9
Em7
Em7/A
A7
Dmaj7
I
Gm7
3
C7
Fmaj7
F♯m7
B7♭9
E7
A7
3
Dmaj7
F♯m7
B7♭9
Em7
Em7/A
A7
Dmaj7
B7♭9
Em7
A7
J Trading 4's
Dmaj7
Trombone:
3
Drums:
4
Sax:
Dmaj7

Drums:
Trombone:
F♯m7
B7♭9
Em7
3
4
Drums:
Sax:
Dmaj7
4
3
F♯m7
B7♭9
Drums:
Em7
2
Piano:
K
Head
D
D+
D6
D7
A7/E
G/A
A7
D
D
D+
D6
D7
A7/E
G/A
A7
D
Drums:
L
Sax:
D
8
D+
D6
D7
A7/E
G/A
A7
Em7
E♯dim7
F♯m7
B7
Em7
A7
D

Inner Urge

(Joe Henderson's solo)

from *Joe Henderson: Inner Urge*

By Joe Henderson

*Originally performed on Tenor Saxophone.

D
Bass Solo
72
E
Sax Solo
D♯ locrian
3
Dmaj7♭5
3
3
3
3
3
3
F
Cmaj7♭5
3
3
3
B♭maj7♭5
G
C♯maj7
3
B♭maj7
Bmaj7
A♭maj7
3
Amaj7
F♯maj7
G13♯11
3
Emaj7
H
D♯ locrian
Dmaj7♭5
3
3
3
I
Cmaj7♭5
3

B♭maj7♭5
J
C♯maj7
B♭maj7
Bmaj7
A♭maj7
Amaj7
F♯maj7
G13♯11
Emaj7
K
D♯ locrian
Dmaj7♭5
L
Cmaj7♭5
B♭maj7♭5
M
C♯maj7
B♭maj7
Bmaj7

A♭maj7
Amaj7
F♯maj7
G13♯11
Emaj7
N
D♯ locrian
Dmaj7♭5
O
Cmaj7♭5
B♭maj7♭5
P
C♯maj7
B♭maj7
Bmaj7
A♭maj7
Amaj7
F♯maj7
G13♯11
Emaj7
Q
D♯ locrian
8va
Dmaj7♭5

R
Cmaj7♭5
B♭maj7♭5
S
C♯maj7
B♭maj7
Bmaj7
A♭maj7
Amaj7
F♯maj7
G13♯11
Emaj7
T
D♯ locrian
8va
Dmaj7♭5
(8va)
U
Cmaj7♭5
(8va)
B♭maj7♭5
V
C♯maj7
B♭maj7
Bmaj7
A♭maj7

Amaj7
F♯maj7
G13♯11
Emaj7
W
D♯ locrian
Dmaj7♭5
X
Cmaj7♭5
B♭maj7♭5
Y
C♯maj7
B♭maj7
Bmaj7
A♭maj7
Amaj7
F♯maj7
G13♯11
Emaj7
Z
D♯ locrian
Dmaj7♭5

AA
Cmaj7♭5
B♭maj7♭5
BB
C♯maj7
B♭maj7
Bmaj7
A♭maj7
Amaj7
F♯maj7
G13♯11
CC
Piano Solo
Emaj7
D♯ locrian
DD
Drum solo
Dmaj7♭5
139
88
EE
Sax Solo
D♯ locrian
Dmaj7♭5

FF
Cmaj7♭5
B♭maj7♭5
GG
C♯maj7
B♭maj7
Bmaj7
A♭maj7
Amaj7
F♯maj7
G13♯11
Emaj7
HH
D♯ locrian
Dmaj7♭5
II
Cmaj7♭5
B♭maj7♭5
JJ
C♯maj7
B♭maj7

Bmaj7
A♭maj7
Amaj7
F♯maj7
KK
G13♯11
Emaj7
D♯ locrian
Dmaj7♭5
LL
Cmaj7♭5
B♭maj7♭5
MM
C♯maj7
B♭maj7
Bmaj7
A♭maj7
Amaj7
F♯maj7
G13♯11
Emaj7

NN
Head
D♯m7♭5
Dmaj7♯11
OO
Cmaj7♯11
Bmaj7♯11 Cmaj7♯11
B♭sus Bsus4 Fsus2/E B♭maj7♯11
3
A/B♭
PP
D♭maj7♭5
B♭maj9
1.
Bmaj9
A♭maj9
Amaj13♯11
3
F♯maj9
Dm(maj7)
Emaj9
2.
Bmaj9
A♭maj9
Amaj13♯11
F♯maj9
G13♯11
Emaj9 Bmaj13 G♯ A F♯ A6/G Emaj7

Jam for Bobbie

(Benny Golson's solo)

from *Benny Golson: Gone with Golson*

By Benny Golson

*Originally performed on Tenor Saxophone.

G6
N.C./D
C
G7
C7
G/D
E7♭9
Am7
D7♯5(♭9)
G6
N.C./D
D
G7
C7
G/D
E7♭9
Am7
D7♯5(♭9)
G6
N.C./D
E
G7

C7
G/D
E7♭9
Am7
D7♯5(♭9)
G6
N.C./D
F
G7
C7
G/D
E7♭9
Am7
D7♯5(♭9)
G6
N.C./D
G
G7
C7
G/D
E7♭9
Am7

D7♯5(♭9)
G6
N.C./D
H
G7
3
3
C7
3
G/D
E7♭9
Am7
3
D7♯5(♭9)
3
3
3
G6
3
3
N.C./D
I
G7
3
C7
G/D
E7♭9
Am7
D7♯5(♭9)
G6
N.C./D

J
G7
C7
G/D
E7♭9
Am7
D7♯5(♭9)
G6
N.C./D
K
G7
C7
G/D
E7♭9
Am7
D7♯5(♭9)
G6
N.C./D
L
G7
C7

G/D
E7♭9
Am7
D7♯5(♭9)
G6
N.C./D
M
G7
C7
G/D
E7♭9
Am7
D7♯5(♭9)
3
G6
N.C./D
N
G7
C7
G/D
E7♭9
8va
Am7
D7♯5(♭9)
3

G6
N.C./D
O
G7
C7
G/D
E7♭9
Am7
D7♯5(♭9)
G6
N.C./D
P
G7
C7
G/D
E7♭9
Am7
D7♯5(♭9)
G6
N.C./D
Q
G
R Trombone Solo
8
12

12
12
12
12
12
12
12
12
12
12
S Trading 4's with Trombone
G7
3
C7
3
Am7
D7♯5(♭9)
G6
N.C./D
T G7
2
C7
G/D
E7♭9
3
4
U G7
3
C7
3
Am7
D7♯5(♭9)

G6
N.C./D
V
G7
3
C7
G/D
E7♭9
Am7
3
W
G7
8va
3
3
3
C7
3
Am7
3
3
D7♯5(♭9)
3
3
3
3
G6
3
3
3
3
N.C./D
3
3
X
G7
3
C7
G/D
E7♭9
Am7
Y Bass Solo
3
12
12
12
12

Z
Trading 4's (Trombone/ Drums/ Sax/ Drums)
7
3
Am7
3
D7♯5(♭9)
3
G6
N.C./D
AA
G7
11
G7
C7
7
BB
4
C7
G/D
E7♭9
Am7
CC
Head
3
G7
C6
C♯dim7
G/D
G7
C7
C♯dim7
G/D
G/C
Bm7♭5
E7♭9
Am7
Am7/D
F♯
G6
1.
N.C./D
2.
G6
G7♯9

Just One of Those Things

(Hank Mobley's solo)

from *The Jazz Messengers at the Cafe Bohemia*

Words and Music by Cole Porter

*Originally performed on Tenor Saxophone.

D
Bm7
C♯m7♭5
F♯7
Bm7
B♭m7
Am7
D7
G
C7
F♯m7
B7
Em7
A7
E
Trumpet Solo
F
Sax Solo
D
4
192
Bm7
C♯m7♭5
F♯7
Bm7
B♭m7
Am7
D7
G
C7
F♯m7
B7
Em7
A7
D
C♯m7♭5
F♯7
G
Bm7
C♯m7♭5
F♯7
Bm7
B♭m7
Am7
D7
G
C7
3
F♯m7
B7
Em7
A7
D
3
Dm7
G7

H
Cmaj7 Dm7 G7
C Bm7 E7
A F♯7 D♯m7♭5 G♯7 Dm7 G7
C♯m7 F♯7 Bm7 E7 A C♯m7♭5 F♯7
I
Bm7 C♯m7♭5 F♯7
Bm7 B♭m7 Am7 D7 G C7
F♯m7 B7 Em7 A7
D Em7 E♯dim D C♯m7♭5 F♯7
J
Bm7 C♯m7♭5 F♯7
Bm7 B♭m7 Am7 D7 G C7

F♯m7
B7
Em7
A7
D
C♯m7♭5
F♯7
K
Bm7
C♯m7♭5
F♯7
Bm7
B♭m7
Am7
D7
G
C7
F♯m7
B7
Em7
A7
D
Dm7
G7
L
Cmaj7
Dm7
G7
C
Bm7
E7
A
F♯7
D♯m7♭5
G♯7
Dm7
G7
C♯m7
F♯7
Bm7
E7
A
C♯m7♭5
F♯7

M
Bm7
C♯m7♭5
F♯7
Bm7
B♭m7
Am7
D7
G
C7
F♯m7
B7
Em7
A7
D
Em7
E♯dim
D
C♯m7♭5
F♯7
N
Bm7
C♯m7♭5
F♯7
Bm7
B♭m7
Am7
D7
G
C7
F♯m7
B7
Em7
A7
D
C♯m7♭5
F♯7
O
Bm7
C♯m7♭5
F♯7
Bm7
B♭m7
Am7
D7
G
C7

F♯m7
B7
Em7
3
A7
D
3
Dm7
G7
P
Cmaj7
Dm7
G7
C
Bm7
E7
A
3
F♯7
D♯m7♭5
G♯7
Dm7
G7
C♯m7
F♯7
Bm7
E7
3
A
C♯m7♭5
F♯7
Q
Bm7
C♯m7♭5
F♯7
Bm7
B♭m7
3
3
Am7
D7
G
3
3
C7
F♯m7
B7
Em7
A7
D
Em7
E♯dim
D
C♯m7♭5
F♯7

R
Bm7
C♯m7♭5
F♯7
Bm7
B♭m7
Am7
D7
G
C7
F♯m7
B7
Em7
3
A7
D
C♯m7♭5
F♯7
S
Bm7
C♯m7♭5
F♯7
3
3
3
Bm7
B♭m7
Am7
D7
G
C7
F♯m7
B7
Em7
A7
D
Dm7
G7
T
Cmaj7
Dm7
G7
3
3
3
3
C
Bm7
E7

A
F♯7
D♯m7♭5
G♯7
Dm7
G7
C♯m7
F♯7
Bm7
E7
A
C♯m7♭5
F♯7
U
Bm7
C♯m7♭5
F♯7
Bm7
B♭m7
Am7
D7
G
C7
F♯m7
B7
Em7
A7
D
Em7
E♯dim
D
C♯m7♭5
F♯7
V
Bm7
C♯m7♭5
F♯7
Bm7
B♭m7
Am7
D7
G
C7
F♯m7
B7
Em7
A7
D
C♯m7♭5
F♯7
W
Bm7

C♯m7♭5
F♯7
Bm7
B♭m7
Am7
D7
G
C7
F♯m7
B7
Em7
A7
D
Dm7
G7
X
Cmaj7
Dm7
G7
C
Bm7
E7
A
F♯7
D♯m7♭5
G♯7
Dm7
G7
C♯m7
F♯7
Bm7
E7
A
C♯m7♭5
F♯7
Y
Bm7
C♯m7♭5
F♯7
Bm7
B♭m7
Am7
D7
G
C7
F♯m7
B7
Em7
A7

D
Em7
E♯dim
D
C♯m7♭5
F♯7
Z
Piano Solo
Bm7
127
AA
Trade phrases
(Trumpet)
8
(Drums)
8
BB
Bm7
(Alto)
C♯m7♭5
F♯7
Bm7
B♭m7
Am7
D7
G
Gm6
F♯m7
B7
Em7
A7
D
Dm7
G7
CC
(Drums)
Cmaj7
7
(Trumpet)
8
DD
(Alto)
Bm7
C♯m7♭5
F♯7
Bm7
B♭m7
Am7
D7
G
Gm6
F♯m7
B7
Em7
A7
D
rit.

Lester Leaps In

(Lester Young's solo)

from *Count Basie: The Essential Count Basie Vol. II*

By Lester Young

*Originally performed on Tenor Saxophone.

Am7 D7♯5 G6 G7/B C C♯dim7 G D7
G E B7 E7 3
A7♭9 D7
F G13 G7♯5/B C6 C♯dim7 G/D B♭dim7
Am7 D7♯5 G G7♯5/B C6 C♯dim7 G/D D7♭9
Stop-time
G Sax Solo
G G/B B♭dim7 Am7 G6
G7/B C Cm G
D7 G
3 3

H
B7
E7
A7
D7
I
G
G6
G
J
3
Am7
D7♯5
G
G7/B
C
C♯dim7
G/D
(Lip down)
G
D7
3
Am7
D7
G
G7/B
C
C♯dim7
G/D
D7
G
K
4
A7
D7♯5
L
G

3
G
G7/B
C
C♯dim7
G6
M
2
G/D
B♭m
Am
D7
D7♯5
G
Em7
C
D9
G
G7♯5/B
7
N
8
O
G
G7/B
C
C♯dim7
G/D
G/B
B♭dim7
Am7
D7
G
D7
P
G
G7/B
C
C♯dim7
G/D
5
8
Q
G
G7/B
C
C♯dim7
G/D
B♭dim7
Am7
D7♯5
G
D7♯5
G6

Lover Man

(Oh, Where Can You Be?)

(Jackie McLean's solo)

from *Presenting...Jackie McLean*

Words and Music by Jimmy Davis, Roger Ramirez and Jimmy Sherman

C
D
F♯m7
B7
F♯m7
B7
Emaj7
F♯m7
G♯m7
F♯m7Emaj7
Em7
A7
Em7
A7
Dmaj7
C♯m7♭5
F♯7
D
Bm7
E7
Bm7
E7
Em7
A7
Em7
A7
Dm6
G7
Fm7
B♭7
Em7
A7
D
C♯m7♭5
F♯7
E
Sax Solo
Bm7
E7

Bm7
E7
3
Em7
A7
3
Em7
A7
12
Dm6
3
12
G7
3
Fm7
B♭7
Em7
A7
D
C♯m7♭5
F♯7
F
Bm7
E7
Bm7
E7
Em7
A7
Em7
A7
Dm6
G7
3
Fm7
B♭7
Em7
A7
D
3
G
F♯m7
B7
F♯m7
3
B7

Emaj7
Amaj7
G♯m7
F♯m7
Emaj7
Em7
A7
Em7
A7
Dmaj7
11
C♯m7♭5
F♯7
H
Bm7
E7
Bm7
E7
Em7
A7
Em7
A7
Dm6
G7
Fm7
B♭7
Em7
A7
D
I
Piano Solo
7
J
8
K
Head (2nd half)
F♯m7
B7
F♯m7
B7
Emaj7
F♯m7
G♯m7
F♯m7
Emaj7
Em7
A7

Em7
A7
Dmaj7
C♯m7♭5
F♯7
L
Bm7
E7
Bm7
E7
Em7
A7
Em7
A7
Dm6
G7
Freely
Fm7
B♭7
Em7
(Cadenza)
A7♭9
Dmaj7♯11

Lulu's Back in Town

(Branford Marsalis' solo)

from *Ellis & Branford Marsalis: Loved Ones*

Words by Al Dubin

Music by Harry Warren

*Alto Saxophone

Moderate Swing (♩ = 152)

Intro

Piano:

N.C./D D5

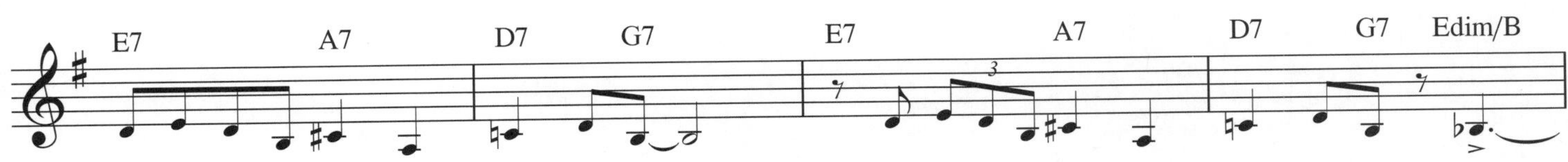

*Originally performed on Tenor Saxophone.

C♯7♭5(♯9) F♯7♯5 Bm7 E7 A9 N.C./D
C
E7 A7 D7 G7 E7 A7 D7 G7 Edim/B
C C♯dim G/D E7 A7 D7sus A♭maj9
8va
D Sax Solo
E7 A7 D7 G7 E7 A7
D7 G7 C7 C♯dim7 G/D E7
A7 D7sus G E7 A7
D7 G7 E7 A7 D7 G
C C♯dim G/D E7 A7 D7sus G
E
C C♯dim7 G/D

C
C♯dim7
G/D
C♯m7
F♯7♯5
Bm7
E7
A9
D7
F
E7
A7
D7
G7
E7
A7
D7
G
C
C♯dim7
G/D
E7
A7
D7sus
A♭maj9
G
E7
A7
D7
G7
E7
A7
D7
G7
C7
C♯dim7
G/D
E7
A7
D7sus
G
E7
A7

D7 G7 E7 A7 D7 G7
C C♯dim G/D E7 A7 D7
G
H
C C♯dim7
G/D C C♯dim7 G/D
C♯m7 F♯7♯5 Bm7 E7 A9
D7
I
E7 A7 D7 G7 E7 A7
D7 G7 Edim/B C C♯dim7 G/D E7
A7 D7sus A♭maj9
J
Piano Solo
E7 A7
32

K Head
Piano:
E7 A7 D7 G7 E7 A7 D7 G7 Edim/B
C C♯dim G/D E7 A7 D7sus G
E7 A7 D7 G7 E7 A7 D7 G7
C C♯dim G/D E7 A7 D7sus G
L
C Gmaj7 C Gmaj7
C♯7♭5(♯9) F♯7♯5(♯9) Bm7 E7 A9 G/D Cm(maj7) C♯dim D7
M
E7 A7 D7 G7 E7 A7 D7 G7
C C♯dim G/D E7 A7 C/D G6 E7♭5(♯9)
Sax:
A7 C/D G6 E13♭5(♯9) A7 C/D N.C. G7

Luck Be a Lady

(Ken Peplowski's solo)

from *Ken Peplowski: A Good Reed*

By Frank Loesser

*Originally performed on Tenor Saxophone.

B
A
Dm7/A
B♭maj7
Amaj7♯5/G♯
B♭maj7
B13
B♭maj7
Amaj7♯5/G♯
B♭maj7
B13
B♭maj7
A♭13
3
G7♭13
Cm7♭5
F7♭9
B♭maj7
Amaj7♯5/G♯
B♭maj7
C♯m7
F♯7
C
Swing
Bmaj7
C♯m7
D♯m7
E13
3
A9
G♯m7
C♯7
B7
A7
G7
F♯m
F♯m(maj7)
F♯m7
D♯m7♭5
G♯7♯9
C♯m7
Cdim
D
Latin
Bm7
E7♭13
Amaj7
Dm7/A
Amaj7
Dm7/A
Amaj7
Dm7/A
Amaj7
Dm7/A
Amaj7
Bm7
3

C♯m7
Dm
A/C♯
Amaj7
Dm7/A
E
Sax Solo
A
B♭7
A
B♭7
A
B♭7
A
B♭7
A
B♭7
A
B♭7
A
B♭7
A
B♭7
A
B♭7
A
F
B♭maj7
B13
B♭maj7
Amaj7♯5/G♯
B♭maj7
B13
B♭maj7
Amaj7♯5/G♯
B♭maj7
A♭7
G7♭13
F♯7
F7
B♭maj7
Amaj7♯5/G♯
B♭maj7

G
Swing
C♯m7 F♯7 Bmaj7 C♯m7
D♯m7 E13 A9 G♯m7
C♯7 B7 A7 G7 F♯m
F♯m(maj7) F♯m7 D♯m7♭5 G♯7♯9
C♯m7 Cdim Bm7 E7♭13
H
Amaj7 Dm7/A Amaj7 Dm7/A Amaj7 Dm7/A
Amaj7 Dm7/A Amaj7
Bm7 C♯m7 Dm
C♯m7 C7 Bm7 B♭7 A
I
Latin
E7 A B♭7 A

B♭7
A
B♭7
A
B♭7
A
B♭7
A
B♭7
A
B♭7
A
B♭7
A
J
B♭maj7
B13
B♭maj7
Amaj7♯5/G♯
B♭maj7
B13
B♭maj7
Amaj7♯5/G♯
B♭maj7
A♭13
G7♭13
F♯7
F7
B♭maj7
Amaj7♯5/G♯
B♭maj7
C♯m7
F♯7
K
Swing
Bmaj7
C♯m7
D♯m7
E13
A9

G♯m7
C♯7
B7
A7
G7
F♯m
F♯m(maj7)
F♯m7
D♯m7♭5
G♯7♯9
C♯m7
Cdim
Bm7
E7♭13
L
Amaj7
Dm7/A
Amaj7
Dm7/A
Amaj7
Dm7/A
Amaj7
Dm7/A
Amaj7
Bm7
C♯m7
Dm
C♯m7
C7
Bm7
B♭7
A
E7
M
Latin
Piano Solo
A
63

N
Drum Solo
7
B♭7
(fills)
A
B♭7
A
B♭7
A
2
B♭7
A
O
B♭maj7
B13
B♭maj7
Amaj7♯5/G♯
B♭maj7
2
Amaj7♯5/G♯
B♭maj7
A♭13
G7♭13
F♯7
F7
B♭maj7
Amaj7♯5/G♯
B♭maj7
C♯m7
F♯7
P
Bmaj7
7
F♯m
F♯m(maj7)
F♯m7
D♯m7♭5
G♯7♯9
C♯m7
Cdim
Bm7
E7♭13
Q
Amaj7
14

R
Interlude
E7
N.C.
A
Bb/A
A
Bb/A
4
S
Head
A
3
Bb/A
A
Bb/A
A
Bb/A
A
Dm7/A
A
3
Dm7/A
A
Dm7/A
A
Dm7/A
A
Dm7/A
3
T
Bbmaj7
Amaj7#5/G#
Bbmaj7
B13
Bbmaj7
Amaj7#5/G#
Bbmaj7
B13
Bbmaj7
Ab13
3
G7b13
3
Cm7b5
F7b9
Bbmaj7
Amaj7#5/G#

U
Swing
B♭maj7
C♯m7
F♯7
Bmaj7
C♯m7
D♯m7
E13
A9
G♯m7
C♯7
B7
A7
G7
F♯m
F♯m(maj7)
F♯m7
D♯m7♭5
G♯7♯9
C♯m7
Cdim
Bm7
E7♭13
V
Swing
Amaj7
Dm7/A
Amaj7
Dm7/A
Amaj7
Dm7/A
Amaj7
Dm7/A
Amaj7
Dm7/A
Amaj7
Bm7
C♯m7
Dm
A/C♯
W
Outro
Amaj7
B♭maj7
Amaj7
B♭maj7
Amaj7
B♭maj7
Amaj7

B♭maj7
Amaj7
B♭maj7
Amaj7
B♭maj7
Amaj7
B♭maj7
Amaj7
B♭maj7
X
Amaj7
B♭maj7
Amaj7
B♭maj7
Amaj7
B♭maj7
tr
Amaj7
B♭maj7
(tr)
Amaj7
B♭maj7
Amaj7
B♭maj7
Amaj7
B♭maj7
Amaj7
B♭maj7
Y
N.C.
A13
Freely
tr
tr
tr
tr
tr

Mood Indigo

(Johnny Hodges' solo)

from *Jazz 'Round Midnight: The Duke Ellington/Billy Strayhorn Songbook*

Words and Music by Duke Ellington, Irving Mills and Albany Bigard

E♭7
D7
6
3
D
G7
6
5
C
3
F7
G
A7
D7
G
E
Trumpet Solo
16
F
Trombone Solo
16
G
Piano Solo
11
F7
Sax Solo (Last 4)
G
A7
D7
G
D.S. al Coda
CODA
Dm
D+
G

My Melancholy Baby

(Lee Konitz's solo)
from *The Real Lee Konitz*
Words by George Norton
Music by Ernie Burnett

Alto Saxophone

E
Sax Solo
G
F7
E7
Am7
E7♯5
Am7
F
D7
F♯m7
B7
Em7
A7
Am7
D7
G
G
F7
E7
Am7
E7♯5
Am7
H
B♭dim
G/B
E7
Am7
D7
G
E7
Am7
D7
I
G
F7
E7
Am7
E7♯5
Am7

J
D7
F♯m7
B7
Em7
A7
Am7
D7
K
G
F7
E7
Am7
E7♯5
Am7
L
B♭dim
G/B
E7
Am7
D7
G
E7
Am7
D7
M
G
F7
E7
Am7
E7♯5
Am7
N
D7
F♯m7
B7
Em7
A7
Am7
D7

O
G
3
F7
E7
Am7
E7♯5
Am7
P
B♭dim
G/B
E7
Am7
D7
G
E7
Am7
D7
Q
G
F7
E7
Am7
E7♯5
Am7
R
D7
F♯m7
B7
3
3
Em7
A7
Am7
D7
S
G
F7
E7
Am7
E7♯5
Am7

T
B♭dim
G/B
E7
Am7
D7
G
E7
Am7
D7
U
G
F7
E7
3
Am7
E7♯5
Am7
V
D7
F♯m7
B7
Em7
A7
Am7
D7
W
G
F7
E7
3
Am7
E7♯5
Am7
3
X
(Fadeout begins)
B♭dim
G/B
E7
(Fadeout complete)
Am7
D7
G
E7
Am7
D7

Oleo

(Sonny Rollins' solo)
from *Miles Davis: Bag's Groove*
By Sonny Rollins

*Originally performed on Tenor Saxophone.

D Sax Solo
G
E7
Am7
B♭dim7
Bm7
E7
Am7
D7
G
C7
3
C
C♯dim7
G/D
E7
Am7
D7
G7
3
C
Cm7
G
D7
G
E
B7
E7
A7
2
D7♯9
G
Am7
D7
G
E7
Am7
D7
G7
G7/F
3
C/E
C7
G
F
G
3
C7
D7
Bm7
E7
Am7
D7
G7

C
C♯dim7
G/D
E7
Am7
D7
G
E7
Am7
D7
Bm7
E7
Am7
D7
G
C
D7
G
G
B9
B7♯9
E7sus
E7
A7
Am7/D
D13♯9
G
Am7
D7
Bm7
E7
Am7
D7
3
G
G7
C
C♯dim7
G/D
E7
Am7
D7
H
G
Piano Solo
63
I
Trumpet Solo
32
D.C. al Fine

My One and Only Love

(Michael Brecker's solo)

from *Michael Brecker*

Words by Robert Mellin

Music by Guy Wood

*Alto Saxophone

*Originally performed on Tenor Saxophone.

Slowly, freely
A
Head (alone)
B

C

D

Moderately slow, steadily (𝅗𝅥 = 60)
E
Head (with ensemble)
C
Am7
Dm7
G7
G♯dim
Am7
Gm7
Fmaj7
Em7
A7
Dm7
Bm7♭5
E7♯9(♭13)
Am7
D7
Dm7
G7
Em7
A7
Dm7
G7
F
C
Am7
Dm7
G7
G♯dim
Am7
Gm7
Fmaj7
Em7
A7
Dm7
Bm7♭5
E7♯9(♭13)
Am7

D7
Dm7
G7
C
F♯m7♭5
B7
G
Em
F♯m7♭5
B7♯9(♭13)
Em
G7
F♯m7♭5
B7♯9(♭13)
Em
Em(maj7)
Em7
A7
Dm7
A7
Dm7
G♯m7
C♯7
H
C
Am7
Dm7
G7
G♯dim
Am7
Gm7
Fmaj7
Em7

A7
Dm7
Bm7♭5
E7♯9(♭13)
Am7
D7
Dm7
G7
C
Dm7
G7
I
Guitar Solo
C
62
F♯m7♭5
B7
J
Head (2nd half)
Em
F♯m7♭5
B7♯9(♭13)
Em
G7
F♯m7♭5
B7♯9(♭13)
Em
Em(maj7)
Em7
A7
Dm7
A7
Dm7
G♯m7
C♯7

K
C
Am7
Dm7
G7
G♯dim
Am7
Gm7
Fmaj7
Em7
A7
Dm7
Bm7♭5
E7♯9(♭13)
Am7
D7
Freely
Dm7
C♯13
Cmaj9

Oh, Lady Be Good!

(Zoot Sims' solo)

from *Zoot Sims and the Gershwin Brothers*

Music and Lyrics by George Gershwin and Ira Gershwin

*Originally performed on Tenor Saxophone.

E7
G♯m7
C♯7
F♯7
B7
E7
C♯7
F♯7
B7
G
E7
A7
E7
G♯m7
C♯7
F♯7
B7
E7
C♯7
F♯7
B7
H
E7
A7
E7
G♯m7
C♯7
F♯7
B7
E
E7
I
A
A♯dim
E/B
E
F♯7
B7
J
E7
A7
E7
G♯m7
C♯7
F♯7
B7
E7
C♯7
F♯7
B7

K
E7 A7 E7 G♯m7 C♯7
F♯7 B7 E7 C♯7 F♯7 B7
L
E7 A7 E7 G♯m7 C♯7
F♯7 B7 E E7
M
A A♯dim E/B E
F♯7 B7
N
E7 A7 E7 G♯m7 C♯7
F♯7 B7 E7 C♯7 F♯7 B7
O
E7 A7 E7 G♯m7 C♯7
F♯7 B7 E7 C♯7 F♯7 B7

P
E7
A7
E7
G♯m7
C♯7
3
F♯7
B7
E
E7
Q
A
A♯dim
E/B
3
E
F♯7
5
5
B7
R
E7
A7
E7
G♯m7
C♯7
F♯7
B7
S
Outro (Fadeout)
E7
C♯7
F♯7
B7
E7
C♯7
F♯7
B7
E7
C♯7
F♯7
B7
E7
C♯7
F♯7
B7
E7
C♯7
F♯7
B7
E7
C♯7
F♯7
B7
(Fadeout complete)
E7
C♯7
F♯7
B7
3
E7
C♯7
F♯7
B7

On a Slow Boat to China

(Sonny Stitt's solo)

from *Sonny Stitt: A Little Bit of Stitt*

By Frank Loesser

*Originally performed on Tenor Saxophone.

E Sax Solo
G Am7 D7 G Em7
Am7 A♯dim G F♯m7 B7
F
C Bdim Am7 A♯dim
G F7 E7 A7
Am7 D7
G
G Bm7 E7 Am A♯dim
G F♯m7 B7 C Bdim Am7
H
C F7 F♯dim G Bm7♭5 E7♭9
Am7 D7 G Am7 D7
I
Piano Solo
G 30 Am7 D7

J
Head
G
Em7
Am7
A♯dim
G
F♯m7
B7
C
Bdim
Am7
K
3
A♯dim
G
F7
E7
A7
Am7
3
3
D7
L
G
3
Bm7
E7
Am
A♯dim
G
F♯m7
B7
C
Bdim
Am7
M
C
F7
F♯dim
G
Bm7♭5
E7♭9
Tag
Am7
D7
Bm7♭5
E7
Am7
D9sus
D13♭9
G
G13♭9

Quiet Nights of Quiet Stars
(Corcovado)
(Stan Getz's solo)
from *Stan Getz with Laurindo Almeida*
English Words by Gene Lees
Original Words and Music by Antonio Carlos Jobim

*Originally performed on Tenor Saxophone.

C Chorus-Guitar Solo
Amaj6/9
B9
35
D Sax Solo
B13
Fdim7
Delay
Em7
A7sus♭9
E♭maj7
A7
Dmaj6/9
Dm7
G7
Amaj6/9
F♯7♯5(♭9)
B13
Dm6
Bm7
F♯m F♯m/C♯
E
B13
Fdim7
Em7
A7♭9
Dmaj7
Dm7
C♯m7
F♯m7
Bm7
E13♭9
C♯m7♭5/E
C♯m7♭5/G
F♯7♭9(♯11)
Bm7
E13♭9

Amaj6/9
F
B13
Piano Solo
35
G Head
B9
Fdim7
Em7
A7sus
E♭
Dmaj7
Dm7
Amaj7
F♯7♯5(♭9)
B9
Dm6
Ddim7
F♯m7
H
B13
Fdim7
Em7
A7sus
Dmaj7
Dm
C♯m7
F♯m7
Bm7
E13♭9
Em6
Em6/G
F♯7♯9(♯11)
Bm7
E7sus♭9
E7♭9
Amaj6/9

Ramblin'

(Ornette Coleman's solo)

from *Ornette Coleman: Change of the Century*

By Ornette Coleman

B
E
B
F♯
D
B
3
3
E
B
E
F♯
B
E
E
B
E
B
F♯
B
F

E
B
F♯
B
G
E
B
E
B
F♯
B
H
E
B
F♯
B
I
E

B
E
B
F♯
B
J
E
B
F♯
B
K
Trumpet Solo
52
Bass Solo
47
L
Head
3
3
M
Head 2nd time

3
3
N
Fills
3
3
5
O
Ending

St. Thomas

(Sonny Rollins' solo)

from *Sonny Rollins: Saxophone Colossus*

By Sonny Rollins

*Alto Saxophone

*Originally performed on Tenor Saxophone.

C Sax Solo
A9 C♯m7♭5 F♯13♯11 Bm11 E7♯11 A B♭7
A C♯m7♭5 F♯7 Bm7 E13 A6 E9♯5
C♯m7♭5 F♯7♭9 Bm7 F7♯5 E7 E13 E7♭9♯5
A9 A13/C♯ D D♯dim7 A/E E7♭9♯11 A
D
A6/9 Cm7♭5 F♯7♭9 Bm7 E13 Amaj9 E7
A6/9 C♯m11♭5 F♯13♭9♯11 Bm11 E13♭9
3
A C♯m7♭5 F♯7
3
Bm7 F13♭9 E13♭9 A A7/C♯
3 3
D D♯dim7 A/E E13 A6/9 E9♯5

E
A6/9 F♯9 Bm7 E13♭9 A6/9 E13♭9
A6 F♯7♭9♯11 Bm7 E13♭9 A6/9
C♯m7♭5 F♯7 Bm7♭5 E7 E13 E7♭9♯5
A7 D D♯dim7 A6/9/E E7♭9♯11
A
F
A6/9 C♯m7 F♯7♭9
Bm7 E9♯5 A6/9 E13♭9 A6/9 F♯7♯11
Bm11 E7 Amaj9 C♯m7♭5 F♯7♯9
Bm7♭5 E7♯9♯5 A9 A7/C♯ D D♯dim7
A/E A E9♯5
G
A6/9 F♯7♭9

Bm7
E7
A6
E13♭9
A6/9
F♯7♭9
Bm7
E13♭9
A6/9
E7♭9
A9
F♯7♭9♯11
Bm7♭5
E7♭9♯11
A7
A7/C♯
D
D♯dim7
A/E
E7sus♭9
A
E7♭9♯11
H
A
Drum Solo
79
I Sax Solo
A
Bm7
C♯m7
F♯7♯11
Bm7
E7♭9♯5
A6/9
E13♭9
A6/9
C♯m7
F♯7
Bm7
E7♭9♯11
A6/9
C♯m7♭5
F♯7♭9♯5

Bm7
E7♭9♯5
A9
D6
D♯dim7
A/E
E7♭9♯11
A6/9
J
A6/9
F♯13♭9
Bm7
E13♭9♯11
Amaj9
A6/9
F♯dim7
Bm11
E9♯5
A6/9
C♯m11♭5
F♯7♯9♯5
Bm11♭5
E7♭9♯11
E13♭9
A6
D6
D♯dim7
A/E
E7♯5
A6/9
E7♯9
K
A6/9
F♯7♭9♯5
Bm9
E13
E7♭9♯5
A6/9
F♯13♭9
Bm7
E7♯9♯5
A6/9

C♯m7♭5
F♯7♭9♯5
Bm7♭5
E7♯9♯5
A6
A7/C♯
D
D♯dim7
E13sus
E7♭9♯11
E13♭9
A6/9
E9♯5
L
A9/E
G/D
C♯m7♭5
F♯7♭9♯5
Bm7
E13♭9
A6/9
E13♭9
A6/9
F♯7♭9♯5
Bm7
E7♭9♯11
A6/9
E9♯5
C♯m7♭5
F♯13♭9
Growl
Bm7♭5
E7♯9♯5
A6
A7♯11/C♯
D
D♯dim7
A6/E
E7
E9♯5
M
A9
Piano Solo
63

N
Head
A6/9
E7♭9♯11 A6
E13
Amaj9
C♯m7
F♯7♯5
Bm9
E7♯11
A
E9♯5
C♯m7♭5
F♯7♯9♯5
Bm7♭5
E7♯9♯5
A9
A7/C♯
D
D♯dim7
A/E
E9♯5
A6/9
E13♭9
Half-tongue
O
A6/9
F♯7♭9
E13
A6/9
E13
A6/9
C♯m7
F♯7♭9
Bm11
E13♭9
A6/9
C♯m7♭5
G7
F♯7
Bm7
Fmaj7♯5
E9sus
A7
A7/C♯
D
D♯dim7
A/E
E7♯5
A6/9

Recorda Me

(Joe Henderson's solo)

from *Joe Henderson: Page One*

By Joe Henderson

*Originally performed on Tenor Saxophone.

G
Gm7
C7
F
Fm7
B♭7
E♭
Em7
A7
D
C♯7♯9(♭13)
C
F♯m13
Am13
D7
G
Gm7
C7
F
3
Fm7
B♭7
E♭
Em7
3
A7
D
C♯7♯9(♭13)
D
F♯m13

Am13
D7
G
Gm7
C7
F
Fm7
B♭7
E♭
Em7
A7
D
C♯7♯9(♭13)
E
F♯m13
Am13
D7
G
Gm7
C7
F
Fm7
B♭7
E♭
Em7
A7
D
C♯7♯9(♭13)

F
Trumpet Solo
F♯m13
78
G
Piano Solo
31
C♯7♯9(♭13)
H
(Piano solo continues)
F♯m13
Am13
D7
7
1.
2.
I
Head
F♯m13
Am13
D7
G
Gm7
C7
F
Fm7
B♭7
E♭
Em7
A7
1.
D
C♯7♯9(♭13)
2.
D
C♯7♯9(♭13)

Seven Come Eleven

(Dexter Gordon's solo)

from *Lionel Hampton Presents Dexter Gordon*

By Benny Goodman and Charles Christian

*Alto Saxophone

1.

2.

B

B7

E7

A7

D7

G7

*Originally performed on Soprano Saxophone.

C
C
D
Sax Solo
C Edim F F♯dim Em7 A7 Dm7 G7
C Edim F F♯dim Em7 A7 Dm7 G7
E
C Edim F F♯dim Em7 A7 Dm7 G7
C Edim F F♯dim Dm7 G7 C
F
B7 E7
A7 D7 G7

G
C Edim F F♯dim Em7 A7 Dm7 G7
C Edim F F♯dim Em7 A7 Dm7 G7
H
C Edim F F♯dim Em7 A7 Dm7 G7
C Edim F F♯dim Em7 A7 Dm7 G7
3
I
C Edim F F♯dim Em7 A7 Dm7 G7
C Edim F F♯dim Dm7 G7 C
J
B7 E7
A7 D7 G7
K
C Edim F F♯dim Em7 A7 Dm7 G7
C Edim F F♯dim Em7 A7

L
Dm7 G7 C Edim F F♯dim Em7 A7
Dm7 G7 C Edim F F♯dim
M
Em7 A7 Dm7 G7 C Edim
3
F F♯dim Em7 A7 Dm7 G7 C Edim
N
F F♯dim Dm7 G7 C B7
E7 A7
O
D7 G7 C Edim
F F♯dim Em7 A7 Dm7 G7
C Edim F F♯dim Em7 A7 Dm7 G7
P
Vibraphone Solo
C
Q
31
32

R
Guitar Solo
32
S
Piano Solo
32
T
Trade 4's with Vibes
4
C
Edim
F
F♯dim
Em7
A7
Dm7
G7
C
Edim
2
Dm7
G7
C
Edim
F
F♯dim
Dm7
G7
C
4
A7
3
D7
G7
3
G7
C
Edim
F
F♯dim
Em7
A7
Dm7
G7
U
4
C
Edim
F
F♯dim
Em7
A7
Dm7
G7
C
Edim
2
Dm7
G7
C
Edim
F
F♯dim
Dm7
G7
C
4
A7

D7
G7
4
C
Edim
F
F♯dim
Em7
A7
Dm7
G7
V
Head (1st half)
(Fadeout begins)
C
(cues: rhythm section in unison)
W
(Fadeout complete)

Take Five

(Paul Desmond's solo)

from *Dave Brubeck Quartet: Time Out*

By Paul Desmond

Cm Gm7 Cm Gm7
3
D
Solo
Cm Gm7
Cm Gm7 Cm Gm7 Cm Gm7
Cm Gm7 Cm Gm7 Cm Gm7
E
Cm Gm7 Cm Gm7 Cm Gm7
Cm Gm7 Cm Gm7 Cm Gm7
Cm Gm7 Cm Gm7 Cm Gm7
F
Cm Gm7 Cm Gm7 Cm Gm7
Cm Gm7 Cm Gm7 Cm Gm7
G
Drum Solo
Cm Gm7 Cm Gm7 Cm Gm7
Cm Gm7
87
Cm Gm7

H
Head
Cm
Gm7
Cm
Gm7
Cm
Gm7
3
3
Cm
Gm7
Cm
Gm7
Cm
Gm7
3
Cm
Gm7
3
Cm
Gm7
I
A♭
D7♭5/A♭
Gm
Cm/G
Fm
B♭7/F
E♭
Gm
A♭
D7♭5/A♭
Gm
Cm/G
Fm
B♭7/F
J
D7♭5
G7
Cm
Gm7
Cm
Gm7
3
Cm
Gm7
3
Cm
Gm7
Cm
Gm7
K
Outro
Cm
Gm7
3
Cm
Gm7
3
Cm
Gm7
Cm
Gm7
3
Cm
Gm7
Cm
Gm7
3
Cm
Gm7
Cm
Gm7
3
Cm
Gm7
Cm
Gm7
Cm
Gm7
Cm

What a Little Moonlight Can Do

(Lew Tabackin's solo)

from *Lew Tabackin: What a Little Moonlight Can Do*

Words and Music by Harry Woods

*Alto Saxophone

Fast (𝅗𝅥 = 154)

Intro

G C7

D B7

Em7 A7

D N.C. 3 (A) Head D

F♯m7 B7 Em

Em7

A7 D

(B) Am7 3 D7 Gmaj7

*Originally performed on Tenor Saxophone.

Gm7
D
F♯m7
B7
E7
Em
3
B7
Em7
A7
C
D
F♯m7
B7
Em
3
F♯m7♭5
B7
Em
C♯m7♭5
F♯7
Bm
D
Am7
D7
Gmaj7
Gm
D
F♯m7
B7
Em7

A7
D
3
E
Sax Solo
Em7
A7
D
F♯m7
B7
Em
3
Em7
3
A7
D
F
Am7
D7
Gmaj7
3
Gm7
D
F♯m7
B7
E7
3
3
3
3
3
3
3
Em
B7
G
Em7
A7
D
3

F♯m7
B7
Em
F♯m7♭5
3
B7
Em
C♯m7♭5
F♯7
Bm
3
H
Am7
D7
Gmaj7
Gm
D
F♯m7
B7
Em7
A7
D
Em7
I
A7
D
F♯m7
B7
Em
3
Em7

A7
D
J
Am7
D7
Gmaj7
Gm7
D
F♯m7
B7
E7
Em
K
B7
Em7
A7
D
F♯m7
B7
Em
F♯m7♭5
B7
Em
C♯m7♭5
F♯7
Bm
Am7
D7

L
Gmaj7
Gm
D
F♯m7
B7
Em7
A7
D
Em7
A7
M
Piano Solo
D
63
N
Bass Solo
64
O
Sax Solo
D
F♯m7
B7
Em
Em7
A7
D
P
Am7
D7
Gmaj7

Gm7
D
F♯m7
B7
E7
Em
B7
Q
Head (2nd half)
Em7
A7
D
F♯m7
B7
Em
F♯m7♭5
B7
Em
C♯m7♭5
F♯7
Bm
Am7
D7
R
Gmaj7
Gm
D
F♯m7
B7
Em7
A7
D
Amaj7♯5/D

Turnaround

(Joshua Redman's solo)
from *Joshua Redman: Wish*
By Ornette Coleman

*Originally performed on Tenor Saxophone.

A7
D7
A7
F♯7
B7
E7
A
F♯m7
Bm7
E7
D
A7
D7
A7
D7
A7
F♯7
B7
E7
A
F♯m7
Bm7
E7
E
A7
D7
A7
D7
A7
F♯7
B7
E7

A
F♯m7
Bm7
E7
F
A7
D7
A7
D7
A7
8va
F♯7
B7
E7
A
F♯m7
Bm7
E7
G
A7
D7
A7
D7
A7
F♯7
B7
E7
A
F♯m7
Bm7
E7
H
A7
D7
A7

D7
A7
F♯7
B7
E7
A
F♯m7
Bm7
E7
I
A7
D7
A7
D7
A7
F♯7
B7
E7
A
F♯m7
Bm7
E7
J
Guitar Solo
A7
59
K
Bass Solo
47
D.S. al Coda
CODA
A/E
E7
A/E
E7
A/E
E7
G♯5
A5

Undecided

(Lucky Thompson's solo)

from *Lucky Thompson: Complete Parisian Small Group Sessions 1956-1959*

Words by Sid Robin

Music by Charles Shavers

*Alto Saxophone

Moderately fast Swing (♩ = 218)

Intro 8

(A) Head

G

C7 Am7 D7

1. G G♯dim Am7 D7 2. G

(B) G7 C

A7 D7

(C) G C7

Am7 D7 G Am7 D7

(D) Sax Solo

G C7

*Originally performed on Tenor Saxophone.

Am7
D7
G
G♯dim
Am7
D7
E
G
C7
Am7
D7
G
F
G7
C
A7
D7
G
G
C7
Am7
D7
G
G♯dim
Am7
D7
H
G
C7
Am7
D7
G
G♯dim
Am7
D7
I
G
C7

Am7
D7
G
J
G7
C
A7
D7
K
G
C7
Am7
D7
G
G♯dim
Am7
D7
L
Guitar Solo
G
15
M
Vibes Solo
16
N
Piano Solo
32
31
Am7
D7
O
Sax Solo
G
C7
Am7
D7

P
G
G♯dim
Am7
D7
G
C7
Am7
D7
G
Q
G7
C
A7
R
Head (last 8)
D7
D7+
G
C7
Am7
D7
Tag
G/D
G7/D
Outro
G7

Walk On By

(Stanley Turrentine's solo)
from *Blue Note Plays Bacharach*
Lyric by Hal David
Music by Burt Bacharach

*Alto Saxophone

*Originally performed on Tenor Saxophone.

Em
A
Dm7
Em7
Dm7
Em7
Am
Em
Fmaj7
G7
D
Cmaj7
Fmaj7
Cmaj7
Fmaj7
Cmaj7
Fmaj7
Cmaj7
E
Sax Solo
Em
A
Em
A
Em
A
Dm7
3
3
Em7
3
Dm7
Em7
Am
Em
3
Fmaj7
F
G7
Cmaj7

Fmaj7
Cmaj7
Fmaj7
Cmaj7
Fmaj7
3
Cmaj7
G
Em
A
3
Em
A
Em
A
Dm7
6
3
Em7
3
Dm7
3
Em7
Am
Em
3
Fmaj7
H
G7
Cmaj7
Fmaj7

Cmaj7
Fmaj7
Cmaj7
Fmaj7
Cmaj7
3
I
Trumpet Solo
Em
19
J
Head
Em
A
Em
A
Em
A
Dm7
Em7
Dm7
Em7
Am
Em
Fmaj7
3
3
G7
3
3
K
Fadeout begins
Cmaj7
Fmaj7
Cmaj7
Fmaj7
Cmaj7
Fmaj7
Cmaj7
Fmaj7
3
Cmaj7
Fadeout ends

Work Song

(Cannonball Adderley's solo)

from *The Cannonball Adderley Quintet - Paris 1960*

By Nat Adderley

A ped
C
Dm7
lay back
Tutti
A7
Dm7
B♭7
A7♭9
Dm7
D7
G7
A7
D
Dm7
A7
Dm7
B♭7
A7
Dm7
lay back
Tutti
D7
B♭7
A7+
Dm7
A7
E
Dm7

B♭7
A7♭9
F
D6/9
3
3
E7
A7♯9
D7
G7
A7
Dm7
A7
G
Dm6
A7
Dm7
A7
Dm(maj7)
3
3
3
B♭7
3
H
Dm7
3
3
3
3
D7
G7

Em7
A7
Dm7
A7
I
Dm7
6
tr
3
Fm7
B♭7
Em7
A7
J
Dm7
Em7
A7♭9
Dm7
Em7♭5
A7
D7
G7
B♭7
A7
Dm7
Trumpet Solo (1.–7.)
Piano Solo (8.–13.)
15
1.–12.
13.
D.S. al Coda
Bass cues
CODA
N.C.
Sax a cappella
Rim shot
Cornet cues

HAL•LEONARD®
SAXOPHONE PLAY-ALONG

The Saxophone Play-Along Series will help you play your favorite songs quickly and e ily. Just follow the music, listen to the audio to hear how the saxophone should sou and then play along using the separate backing tracks. Each song is printed twice the book: once for alto and once for tenor saxes. The online audio is available streaming or download using the unique code printed inside the book, and it inclu ***PLAYBACK+*** *options such as looping and tempo adjustments.*

1. ROCK 'N' ROLL
Bony Moronie • Charlie Brown • Hand Clappin' • Honky Tonk (Parts 1 & 2) • I'm Walkin' • Lucille (You Won't Do Your Daddy's Will) • See You Later, Alligator • Shake, Rattle and Roll.
00113137 Book/Online Audio $19.99

2. R&B
Cleo's Mood • I Got a Woman • Pick up the Pieces • Respect • Shot Gun • Soul Finger • Soul Serenade • Unchain My Heart.
00113177 Book/Online Audio $19.99

3. CLASSIC ROCK
Baker Street • Deacon Blues • The Heart of Rock and Roll • Jazzman • Smooth Operator • Turn the Page • Who Can It Be Now? • Young Americans.
00113429 Book/Online Audio $19.99

4. SAX CLASSICS
Boulevard of Broken Dreams • Harlem Nocturne • Night Train • Peter Gunn • The Pink Panther • St. Thomas • Tequila • Yakety Sax.
00114393 Book/Online Audio. $19.99

5. CHARLIE PARKER
Billie's Bounce (Bill's Bounce) • Confirmation • Dewey Square • Donna Lee • Now's the Time • Ornithology • Scrapple from the Apple • Yardbird Suite.
00118286 Book/Online Audio $16.99

6. DAVE KOZ
All I See Is You • Can't Let You Go (The Sha La Song) • Emily • Honey-Dipped • Know You by Heart • Put the Top Down • Together Again • You Make Me Smile.
00118292 Book/Online Audio $19.99

7. GROVER WASHINGTON, JR.
East River Drive • Just the Two of Us • Let It Flow • Make Me a Memory (Sad Samba) • Mr. Magic • Take Five • Take Me There • Winelight.
00118293 Book/Online Audio $19.99

8. DAVID SANBORN
Anything You Want • Bang Bang • Chicago Song • Comin' Home Baby • The Dream • Hideaway • Slam • Straight to the Heart.
00125694 Book/Online Audio $19.99

9. CHRISTMAS
The Christmas Song (Chestnuts Roasting on an Open Fire) • Christmas Time Is Here • Count Your Blessings Instead of Sheep • Do You Hear What I Hear • Have Yourself a Merry Little Christmas • The Little Drummer Boy • White Christmas • Winter Wonderland.
00148170 Book/Online Audio $16.99

10. JOHN COLTRANE
Blue Train (Blue Trane) • Body and Sou Central Park West • Cousin Mary • Giant St • Like Sonny (Simple Like) • My Favorite Thi • Naima (Niema).
00193333 Book/Online Audio $16

11. JAZZ ICONS
Body and Soul • Con Alma • Oleo • Speak Evil • Take Five • There Will Never Be Anot You • Tune Up • Work Song.
00199296 Book/Online Audio $16

12. SMOOTH JAZZ
Bermuda Nights • Blue Water • Europa • F • Love Is on the Way • Maputo • Songbir Winelight.
00248670 Book/Online Audio $19

13. BONEY JAMES
Butter • Let It Go • Stone Groove • Stop, Lo Listen (To Your Heart) • Sweet Thing • T Tock • Total Experience • Vinyl.
00257186 Book/Online Audio $16

Prices, contents, and availability subject to change without notice.

Visit Hal Leonard online at **www.halleonard.com**

The Best-Selling Jazz Book of All Time Is Now Legal!

The Real Books are the most popular jazz books of all time. Since the 1970s, musicians have trusted these volumes to get them through every gig, night after night. The problem is that the books were illegally produced and distributed, without any regard to copyright law, or royalties paid to the composers who created these musical masterpieces.

Hal Leonard is very proud to present the first legitimate and legal editions of these books ever produced. You won't even notice the difference, other than all the notorious errors being fixed: the covers and typeface look the same, the song lists are nearly identical, and the price for our edition is even cheaper than the originals!

Every conscientious musician will appreciate that these books are now produced accurately and ethically, benefitting the songwriters that we owe for some of the greatest tunes of all time!

VOLUME 1

00240221 C Edition $49.99
00240224 B♭ Edition $49.99
00240225 E♭ Edition $49.99
00240226 Bass Clef Edition $49.99
00286389 F Edition $39.99
00240292 C Edition 6 x 9 .... $39.99
00240339 B♭ Edition 6 x 9 .... $44.99
00147792 Bass Clef Edition 6 x 9 .... $39.99
00200984 Online Backing Tracks: Selections $45.00
00110604 Book/USB Flash Drive Backing Tracks Pack $85.00
00110599 USB Flash Drive Only $50.00

VOLUME 2

00240222 C Edition $49.99
00240227 B♭ Edition $49.99
00240228 E♭ Edition $49.99
00240229 Bass Clef Edition $49.99
00240293 C Edition 6 x 9 .... $39.99
00125900 B♭ Edition 6 x 9 .... $39.99
00125900 The Real Book – Mini Edition $39.99
00204126 Backing Tracks on USB Flash Drive $55.00
00204131 C Edition – USB Flash Drive Pack $85.00

VOLUME 3

00240233 C Edition $49.99
00240284 B♭ Edition $49.99
00240285 E♭ Edition $49.99
00240286 Bass Clef Edition $49.99
00240338 C Edition 6 x 9 .... $39.99

VOLUME 4

00240296 C Edition $49.99
00103348 B♭ Edition $49.99
00103349 E♭ Edition $49.99
00103350 Bass Clef Edition $49.99

VOLUME 5

00240349 C Edition $49.99
00175278 B♭ Edition $49.99
00175279 E♭ Edition $49.99

VOLUME 6

00240534 C Edition $49.99
00223637 E♭ Edition $49.99

Also available:

00154230 The Real Bebop Book C Edition $34.99
00295069 The Real Bebop Book E♭ Edition $34.99
00295068 The Real Bebop Book B♭ Edition $34.99
00240264 The Real Blues Book $39.99
00310910 The Real Bluegrass Book $39.99
00240223 The Real Broadway Book $39.99
00240440 The Trane Book $25.00
00125426 The Real Country Book $45.00
00269721 The Real Miles Davis Book C Edition $29.99
00269723 The Real Miles Davis Book B♭ Edition $29.99
00240355 The Real Dixieland Book C Edition $39.99
00294853 The Real Dixieland Book E♭ Edition $39.99
00122335 The Real Dixieland Book B♭ Edition $39.99
00240235 The Duke Ellington Real Book $29.99
00240268 The Real Jazz Solos Book $44.99
00240348 The Real Latin Book C Edition $39.99
00127107 The Real Latin Book B♭ Edition $39.99
00120809 The Pat Metheny Real Book C Edition $34.99
00252119 The Pat Metheny Real Book B♭ Edition $29.99
00240358 The Charlie Parker Real Book C Edition $25.00
00275997 The Charlie Parker Real Book E♭ Edition $25.00
00118324 The Real Pop Book C Edition – Vol. 1 .... $45.00
00295066 The Real Pop Book B♭ Edition – Vol. 1 .... $39.99
00286451 The Real Pop Book C Edition – Vol. 2 .... $45.00
00240331 The Bud Powell Real Book $25.00
00240437 The Real R&B Book C Edition $45.00
00276590 The Real R&B Book B♭ Edition $45.00
00240313 The Real Rock Book $39.99
00240323 The Real Rock Book – Vol. 2 .... $39.99
00240359 The Real Tab Book $39.99
00240317 The Real Worship Book $35.00

THE REAL CHRISTMAS BOOK

00240306 C Edition $39.99
00240345 B♭ Edition $35.00
00240346 E♭ Edition $35.00
00240347 Bass Clef Edition $35.00

THE REAL VOCAL BOOK

00240230 Volume 1 High Voice $40.00
00240307 Volume 1 Low Voice $40.00
00240231 Volume 2 High Voice $39.99
00240308 Volume 2 Low Voice $39.99
00240391 Volume 3 High Voice $39.99
00240392 Volume 3 Low Voice $39.99
00118318 Volume 4 High Voice $39.99
00118319 Volume 4 Low Voice $39.99

Complete song lists online at www.halleonard.com

Prices, content, and availability subject to change without notice.

0223
318